OXFORD WORLD'S CLASSICS

THE OXFORD SHAKESPEARE

General Editor · Stanley Wells

The Oxford Shakespeare offers new and authoritative editions of
Shakespeare's plays in which the early printings have been
scrupulously re-examined and interpreted. An introductory
essay provides all relevant background information together
with an appraisal of critical views and of the play's effects
in performance. The detailed commentaries pay particular
attention to language and staging. Reprints of sources, music
for songs, genealogical tables, maps included where
necessary; many of the volumes are illustrated all contain
an index.

ROGER WAR ona in the
Oxford Shake nd *Henry
VI, Part Two*, a ells for the
series.

THE OXFORD SHAKESPEARE

OXFORD WORLD'S CLASSICS

WILLIAM SHAKESPEARE

The Two Gentlemen of Verona

Edited by
ROGER WARREN

OXFORD
UNIVERSITY PRESS

OXFORD

UNIVERSITY PRESS

Great Clarendon Street, Oxford ox2 6DP

Oxford University Press is a department of the University of Oxford.
It furthers the University's objective of excellence in research, scholarship,
and education by publishing worldwide in

Oxford New York

Auckland Cape Town Dar es Salaam Hong Kong Karachi
Kuala Lumpur Madrid Melbourne Mexico City Nairobi
New Delhi Shanghai Taipei Toronto

With offices in

Argentina Austria Brazil Chile Czech Republic France Greece
Guatemala Hungary Italy Japan Poland Portugal Singapore
South Korea Switzerland Thailand Turkey Ukraine Vietnam

Oxford is a registered trade mark of Oxford University Press
in the UK and in certain other countries

Published in the United States
by Oxford University Press Inc., New York

British Library Cataloguing in Publication Data

Data available

Library of Congress Cataloging-in-Publication Data

Data available

Typeset by RefineCatch Limited, Bungay, Suffolk
Printed in Great Britain
on acid-free paper by
Clays Ltd, Elcograf S.p.A.

ISBN 978–0–19–812367–5 (hbk.)
ISBN 978–0–19–283142–2 (pbk.)

8

PREFACE

IN preparing this edition, I have benefited from research undertaken by Dr Anthony Telford Moore, acknowledged in the commentary.

I have also exploited the expertise of friends: Gordon Campbell, Duncan Cloud, John Gough, Edward Hall, Peter Hall, Barbara Jefford, Finbar Lynch, Michael Pavelka, Frances Whistler, and everyone at the libraries of the Shakespeare Institute and the Shakespeare Centre, Stratford-upon-Avon. I am very grateful to them all.

My special thanks go to Guy Woolfenden for researching and arranging the music; to the General Editor for his customary help and advice; to Christine Buckley who copy-edited with her usual skill; and above all to Angie Kendall for her help at every stage.

ROGER WARREN

CONTENTS

CONTENTS

LIST OF ILLUSTRATIONS

INTRODUCTION

Theatrical Issues

IN her programme note for *The Two Gentlemen of Verona* at
Stratford-upon-Avon in 1970, Hilary Spurling described the
play's world as one of

knights errant, distracted lovers, and as preposterous a band of brigands
as ever strode a stage. This is an Italy of true romance, where Milan is
reached from Verona by sea. Proteus abandons Julia, betrays Valentine,
abducts Silvia, and when his career of complicated treachery is finally
unmasked, apologises as casually as though he had just sneezed. Where-
upon our hero, Valentine, is so overcome that he promptly offers to hand
over his beloved to the man who, not three minutes before, had meant to
rape her.

There in a nutshell Hilary Spurling pins down the crucial issue
of this play. A 'romance' world, generally dramatized with lyrical
grace and wit, in which the extravagances of the young lovers are
placed in perspective by their more down-to-earth comic servants
(and a dog) is suddenly invaded by an attempted rape and its
aftermath. The main challenge facing any production is to find
a way of accommodating these extremes without underplaying
them.

Perhaps for this reason, major productions have been infrequent, at least by comparison, not only with popular favourites
such as *A Midsummer Night's Dream* and *Twelfth Night*, but also
with plays like *The Comedy of Errors* and *Love's Labour's Lost*,
which were once as neglected as *The Two Gentlemen*, but which
have been triumphantly re-established in the modern theatre. The
play must have been staged in Shakespeare's own time, because it
is included in the list of Shakespeare's works given by Francis
Meres in his *Palladis Tamia* (1598), and it was not available in print
until the First Folio of Shakespeare's plays appeared in 1623.
The earliest recorded performance, however, was at Drury
Lane, London, as late as 1762. This was a re-written version, by
Benjamin Victor; he established a tradition of bringing all the
Verona scenes together, avoiding Shakespeare's own alternation

between Verona and Milan; he greatly expanded the clowns' scenes, with new lines; and in the final scene he omitted Valentine's controversial handing over of Silvia to her potential rapist. His lead was followed by subsequent directors in the late eighteenth and early nineteenth centuries, and was still influential as late as 1895, as Bernard Shaw's devastating review of Augustin Daly's production makes entertainingly clear:

In preparing the text of his version, Mr Daly has proceeded on the usual principles, altering, transposing, omitting, improving, correcting, and transferring speeches from one character to another. . . . Everybody who pays to see what is, after all, advertised as a performance of Shakespear's play . . . does care more or less about the art of Shakespear. Why not give them what they ask for, instead of going to great trouble and expense to give them something else?[1]

It seems clear that these eighteenth- and nineteenth-century versions need not detain us if we are looking for theatrical illumination of Shakespeare's play, as distinct from adaptations of it.[2] So instead, I shall try to focus what the few significant modern stagings have had to offer, and it will be useful to begin with a brief survey of these.

Opposed to Augustin Daly, and to nineteenth-century spectacle in general (and the textual cuts and re-writes which it necessitated) was William Poel, who pursued what became known as 'Elizabethan Methodism', that is, an attempt to recover what Poel considered Elizabethan traditions: an un-scenic platform stage and swift, musical speech—what he called his 'tunes', which he drilled into the amateur actors of his first production of *The Two Gentlemen* in 1892. But in 1910, Herbert Beerbohm Tree, in some ways the high priest of scenic Shakespeare, invited Poel to direct *The Two Gentlemen* at Tree's own London theatre, His Majesty's. It was, says Robert Speaight, like asking 'the wolf to step into the sheepfold'. For this, an apron stage was built out over the theatre's

---

[1] *The Saturday Review*, 6 July 1895, reprinted in Stanley Wells's anthology *Shakespeare in the Theatre* (Oxford, 1997), 132–8; pp. 133–4.

[2] Details of them may be found in Carol J. Carlisle and Patty S. Derrick, *'The Two Gentlemen of Verona* on Stage', in *Shakespeare's Sweet Thunder: Essays on the Early Comedies*, ed. M. J. Collins (Newark, Delaware, 1997), 126–54, and in Michael D. Friedman, *'The World Must be Peopled': Shakespeare's Comedies of Forgiveness* (Madison, New Jersey, 2002).

orchestra pit, an early attempt at a pseudo-Elizabethan stage; but this should be set against curious eccentricities, like casting actresses in male roles and then accusing them of lacking 'virility'. As Speaight, admirer and chronicler of Poel, puts it: 'When people dismissed Poel as a visionary crank, it was not always easy to gainsay them. Most of his productions had a lunatic fringe, and some of them a lunatic foreground.'[1]

In one respect, however, Poel anticipated later developments. His production at His Majesty's was given only a single performance, so foreshadowing the play's subsequent infrequent appearances. Some of these, moreover, have only been made possible by a particular theatre's attempt to present a group of plays, or even the entire Shakespeare canon, as when the Old Vic theatre, London, performed all the plays in the First Folio between 1953 and 1958. They staged *The Two Gentlemen* in January 1957; and in so far as one can judge from reading about a production rather than actually seeing it,[2] this seems to have been the first time in its history that the play achieved a major success (unless the fact that Francis Meres had heard of it by 1598 indicates greater popularity in its own time than the lack of any other contemporary allusion would suggest).

There is no doubt that a major factor in the appeal of the 1957 production was visual. The 1950s were the heyday of lavishly pictorial Shakespeare at both of the major centres at the time, the Old Vic and Stratford-upon-Avon, and *The Two Gentlemen* was the work of one of the most distinguished designers of the day, Tanya Moiseiwitsch. The director, Michael Langham, set the play in early nineteenth-century Italy, and Moiseiwitsch provided a series of extremely beautiful landscapes of Verona, Milan, and the forest. The idea was to locate the romantic world of the play in a context which the audience could easily recognize as romantic—indeed, Romantic—and, as Mary Clarke points out, this helped the actors to catch the extravagance and the 'self-conscious romanticism' of their characters. Proteus, for example, with his

---

[1] Robert Speaight, *Shakespeare on the Stage* (1973), pp. 132–8.

[2] My account of this production is based on the very detailed description, fully illustrated, by Mary Clarke, *Shakespeare at the Old Vic*, 5 vols. (1954–8), iv (1957); there are no page numbers. My descriptions of all subsequent productions draw on my own experience, supported by the reviews cited.

dark curls and purple suit, became a Byronic hero, and this helped Keith Michell to bring out both the passion and the Byronic irony, even cynicism, of the character's behaviour. Barbara Jefford's love-sick Julia was also aware of the heroine's absurdities. Mary Clarke reports that in 1.2, 'when Julia was finally left alone to collect the scraps of her torn letter, she sank down on her knees in a flutter of taffeta to croon over every word. She was still in this position when Lucetta returned and was hard put to it to carry off the situation with a desperately prosaic "Well, let us go"' (fig. 1). And the production was able to use its change of period to offer an ingenious solution to Valentine's offering Silvia to Proteus at the end. The rape was not compromised: Proteus even threatened

1. Barbara Jefford as Julia, Old Vic, London, 1957.

Silvia with a pistol; but when Valentine intervened, Proteus swung to the other extreme, to another Romantic attitude, and threatened to shoot himself. Valentine got the pistol away from him, and in the heat of the moment made the offer to distract his potentially suicidal best friend.

The next major production was at Stratford-upon-Avon in 1960, when Peter Hall became the Director of what was then called the Shakespeare Memorial Theatre, and began the process of creating what became the Royal Shakespeare Company. His opening season comprised a sequence of six plays designed to trace 'the range, development, and paradox of Shakespearian Comedy', beginning with *The Two Gentlemen*. Reviewing the opening productions, A. Alvarez thought Hall's 'great virtue' was 'his prime concern for Shakespeare's poetry. This means that the verse-speaking is neither hammed into rant and ripe elocutionism nor is it ironed out into prose; it is, instead, a medium for the feeling intelligence and demands nothing less from the actors' (*New Statesman*, 28 May 1960). Visually, however, *The Two Gentlemen* evoked a rather murky late medieval/early Renaissance, at odds, felt John Russell Brown, with Hall's 'attitude to speaking Shakespeare's verse and prose: he [seeks] liveliness, humour, and point—in a word, vitality'.[1] Hall emphasized the potential humour in the lovers' excesses, notably in the case of Julia (Frances Cuka) who, as Barbara Jefford had done at the Old Vic, made much of the letter-tearing scene. But by general consent the outstanding achievement of the production was Patrick Wymark's Lance (fig. 2) who, said Brown:

animated his speeches by a variety of timing and emphasis, based . . . on a sympathetic understanding of the large-minded, stubborn character. . . . He made the audience wait for words, . . . and so invited them to enter his view of the world of the play: correcting Speed for counting 'slow in words' among his maid's vices, he then looked in blank wonder at the audience so that the following line, 'To be slow in words is a woman's only virtue', was the necessary statement they had been waiting for . . . Such acting is well served by Peter Hall's quest for vitality.

---

[1] 'Three Directors: A Review of Recent Productions', *SS 14* (Cambridge, 1961), 129–37. Forty-six years later, at the time of writing, Peter Hall's priorities remain the same. His Shakespeare productions are still based on a rigorous insistence upon the precise speaking of Shakespeare's verse and prose.

2. Speed (Jack MacGowran) and Lance (Patrick Wymark) with Crab, Shakespeare Memorial Theatre, Stratford-upon-Avon, 1960.

The play was not given another major production in Stratford's main house until 1970,[1] when it was directed by Robin Phillips. His emphasis was on the youth of the principal characters: 'It's about the awful problems of adolescence—and they are

---

[1] Theatregoround, the RSC's small-scale touring group at that time, had staged it the previous year.

awful. I set it in a finishing school because I wanted to show these young people emerging into adults—they had left school in every sense. Valentine has obviously matured by the end: after all, he has just seen his best friend try to rape his girl friend.'[1] Phillips's finishing school was clearly within reach of the Venetian Lido: Daphne Dare's set consisted of three huge golden panels which could carry magnified silhouettes (and, with the help of ropes, suggest a sinister forest), and a swimming-pool with, above it, a diving platform which doubled as Silvia's balcony (fig. 3). Harold Hobson thought the production 'no less than a transfiguration' (*Sunday Times*, 26 July 1970); but while he took on board Phillips's emphasis on youth, he did not accept the frequently encountered sentimental view that their youth necessarily excuses their behaviour. The production, he said, 'reaches the heart of Shakespeare's play—the rapture of youth and the *darkness of its treachery*' (my italics). Phillips has never been a director to avoid any opportunity for darkness, in this case obviously the attempted rape, but more surprisingly the characterization of Lance, as Hobson pointed out: 'Who would have thought that this servant . . . could so certainly be the play's sad dark angel, harsh and sinister, yet with such depth of feeling, . . . gravely contemplating the apparent happiness of his employers?' In this interpretation, the perspective that Lance's scenes provide on the lovers' behaviour was given quite a new twist.

The next RSC production, by John Barton in 1981, was at the furthest remove from Phillips's modern dress: it was given (in abbreviated form) as the second half of a double bill with an abbreviated *Titus Andronicus*, both presented as if by a band of Elizabethan travelling players, with much emphasis on artifice: actors sat and watched scenes they were not in, and props and costumes were paraded without apology, as when all the principal characters used hobby-horses (a horse's head and body suspended from the actor's shoulders, with a surcoat concealing the actor's own legs) in their flight to the forest. But, as often happens in such circumstances, the emphasis on artifice in both the staging and the language supported, rather than detracting from, truth of character, particularly in the case of Peter Chelsom's warm, attractive Valentine: when Proteus said he would not flatter Silvia

---

[1] *Directors' Theatre*, ed. Judith Cook (1974), pp. 129–30.

3. The opening tableau, Royal Shakespeare Theatre, Stratford-upon-Avon, 1970: Julia (Helen Mirren), Lance (Patrick Stewart, back to camera), Proteus (Ian Richardson), Valentine (Peter Egan), Silvia (Estelle Kohler, above).

(2.4.145–6), this Valentine replied 'O flatter *me*' with a giggle, one intimate friend to another. Both friends grew up before our eyes: Peter Land used Proteus' speech about the (potentially deceitful) power of poetry to make 'huge leviathans | Forsake unsounded deeps to dance on sands' (3.2.79–80) to express how far he had developed from the callow youth of the opening scenes; and his awkwardly sagging lip at the start was transformed into something like a snarl in the rape scene, where Valentine played 'All that was mine in Silvia I give thee' (5.4.83) as the kind of gesture he thought expected of him. To Barton's handling of the outlaws I will return in a later section.

When Robin Phillips became Director of the Canadian Shakespeare Festival at Stratford, Ontario, in 1975, he began with a re-staging of his RSC *The Two Gentlemen*. In 1984, Leon Rubin directed the play with the Young Company there. Like Phillips, he chose a contemporary image, this time the sexually ambiguous one of some then fashionable pop singers. The outlaws, always a tricky problem in modern-dress versions, were an aggressively ambidextrous rock group, choosing Valentine as their leader because he was 'beautified | With goodly shape' (4.1.53–4). The modern fashions helped to suggest the emotional confusions of the lovers. Most productions stress their youth, but often the cast have to *act* youth; here, they were genuinely young, and persuasive. Julia and Proteus played their farewell scene in bed: their affair had gone much further than is usual, so even more seemed at stake when he betrayed her. Valentine's speech of forgiveness at the end was altered from 'All that was mine in Silvia I give thee' to 'All my love to Silvia I also give to thee', making it clear that Valentine was not simply handing Silvia over to the man who had just attempted to rape her. The two friends embraced, watched distrustfully by the two girls, a sexual division that has been adopted in several subsequent productions.

The two most probing, and most successful, productions in my experience, by David Thacker in 1991 and Edward Hall in 1998, were both given at the Swan Theatre, Stratford-upon-Avon, whose intimacy suits this play. David Thacker set it in an elegant 1930s world. Its most prominent—and permanent—feature was an on-stage dance band, with a singer preceding and punctuating the action with hits from the period by Cole Porter, George Gershwin, and others. The obvious danger, that the music would overwhelm the play, was successfully avoided. The songs punctuating the action did not disrupt the play's own rhythm, because they were kept short, and nicely chosen to reflect mood: 'Love is the Sweetest Thing', or 'In the Still of the Night' for the serenade and forest scenes. At first I thought that Thacker might simply be using lightweight music to reflect lightweight writing, and perhaps even to evade the play's problems by distracting from them; but not at all. Robert Smallwood spoke for most reviewers when he said that 'the production took the play on board and faced its problems honestly, never mocking it'.[1] The two gentlemen were more

---

[1] 'Shakespeare Performed', *SQ* 43 (1992), 351–3. Smallwood's review of this production and of Edward Hall's ('Shakespeare Performances in England, 1998', *SS* 52 (Cambridge, 1999), 229–53; pp. 230–1) offer full and reliable accounts of these two productions.

contrasted than usual. Valentine was tall, hearty, perhaps a bit dim-witted, Proteus slight, dark, more secretive and perhaps a little sinister (fig. 4). Their relationship was at once convincing—the attraction of opposites—and contained the seeds of its future collapse. It was no surprise that Proteus should fall for Clare Holman's enchanting Julia, who caught the full range of the part, from the conspiratorial lightness with Lucetta to the mixture of heartbreak and resourceful wit later on. Their final reunion—'I have my wish for ever. | And I mine' (5.4.118–19)—was unusually convincing; but that was partly because it followed a staging of the rape scene that was, by general consent, especially successful. I shall discuss it in detail, together with Edward Hall's and other solutions, later in this introduction.

While Thacker's production was in early twentieth-century costume, Hall's was in genuine modern dress. Saluting a 'searching, challenging production', Robert Smallwood pointed out that 'the journey of the play was marked by two single-gender, non-sexual embraces: at the end of the first scene by a valedictory hug of separation, expected all through the scene, between the leading men . . . ; at the end of the last scene, by an embrace of welcome and union, expected all through the scene, between the leading women. . . . The embraces framed the intervening account of the awkwardnesses and inadequacies of the play's heterosexual relationships'.[1] Their journey took place in a vulgar materialist society where the Duke wants Thurio as a son-in-law 'Only for his possessions are so huge' (2.4.173), and where even Lance wants to marry his milkmaid for her wealth. The outlaws were the dark underbelly of that society, literally, emerging from a manhole in the floor of Michael Pavelka's otherwise elegant, shuttered set (fig. 5). But the success of the production was founded on something very simple. It was exceptionally well spoken, the two gentlemen handling their elaborate verse, and the servants their prose, with great ease. It was from this above all that Hall's production derived its sense of emotional truth.[2]

Finally, two productions that stand somewhat outside what might be regarded as the theatrical mainstream. As part of its

---

[1] See preceding note; p. 230.
[2] RSC videos of both Thacker's and Hall's productions can be viewed at the Shakespeare Centre, Stratford-upon-Avon.

4. Finbar Lynch as Proteus, Richard Bonneville as Valentine, Swan Theatre, Stratford-upon-Avon, 1991.

filming of Shakespeare's Complete Works, BBC television produced *The Two Gentlemen* in 1983.[1] Don Taylor's production is set in a beautiful, romantic context of vine-covered pillars, fountains, and cypress-lined avenues. Silvia presides over a medieval 'Court of Love', a fragile, pastel-coloured world into which Proteus brings

[1] Available as a BBC DVD: DD. 21433.

5. Michael Pavelka's set design for Edward Hall's production, Swan Theatre, Stratford-upon-Avon, 1998.

a more realistic darkness, underlined by a clap of thunder and a sudden wind dashing the blossom from the trees. This version provides interesting comparisons and contrasts with several of those so far mentioned. The real youth of the actors in Leon Rubin's version is matched here. All four lovers are played by actors who, at the time, were virtually unknown. The image of the two gentlemen, with their flowing locks and shirts open almost to the waist, is one of sensuousness, if not exactly sexuality—though that suggestion is also present. Unlike Edward Hall's version, they do not embrace at the end of their first scene, though, as in Hall's, that is expected throughout the scene. Instead, they exchange friendly punches. The passionate embrace is reserved for the end, as Valentine forgives Proteus, and they fall into each other's arms. The centre of the production is Tyler Butterworth's excellent Proteus. Young, attractive, he charts all the character's developments—first love, new love, betrayal, treachery, attempted rape, remorse—with unerring skill; and in the process he suggests the range of interpretation possible in this part, since he is at the furthest extreme from Keith Michell's more mature, Byronic Proteus at the Old Vic in 1957.[1] It is, therefore, a great shame that he is partnered by a Julia who has all the faults and none of the advantages of inexperience. She overstresses both the giggly youth of the start and the weepiness later, where she draws out the pace of 4.4, especially, beyond endurance. It is unfortunate that an otherwise enjoyable production which can be repeatedly viewed should be endangered like this, but it also emphasizes the hard way how crucial Julia is to the play as a whole. The other problem is that, unlike Edward Hall's production, the BBC one is in general vilely spoken. This is partly because of the naturalism that the television studio encourages, but chiefly because few of the actors know how to speak verse—the main fault is to stress personal pronouns when the text doesn't—which is the other side of inexperience.

That inexperience, however, was as nothing compared to Nós do Morro, a young professional company from Brazil, who in August 2006 gave a single performance—shades of William Poel in 1910!—as part of the Royal Shakespeare Company's presentation of the Complete Works at Stratford-upon-Avon in 2006–7. The actors spoke in Portuguese, while Shakespeare's text was projected as 'surtitles' above the stage. Allowing for the fact that such circumstances inevitably preclude direct, moment-to-moment communication between actors and audience, it was a great success. The youth of Leon Rubin's and the BBC's casts was here carried to the extreme: Valentine, for example, was only 17—and he was the rule rather than the exception. The mutual affection, separation, and reunion of the two heroes was wholly convincing:

---

[1] For an interesting interpretation of the conversation between the Duke and Proteus (3.1.4–50), see the commentary.

the attempted rape was followed by a striking physical encounter typical of the company's style: it was half violent fight, half dance. But the most interesting feature of this staging was that Crab was not played by a dog but by one of the actors, something that I, at least, had not seen before. It had one very interesting consequence. Crab instinctively mistrusted Proteus—as animals sometimes do—and menaced him with growls; so at 3.1.260–1, Lance's 'I am but a fool, look you, and yet I have the wit to think my master is a kind of a knave', where commentators have felt that the text as it stands gives Lance no grounds for thinking this, arose here from his trust in his dog's instinctive dislike. This fascinating detail was a reminder that illumination of Shakespeare's text can sometimes arise from what might appear to be unpromising circumstances.

Origins

In the programme note to her husband's 1981 production, Anne Barton defines the central topic of *The Two Gentlemen* as 'how to bring love and friendship into a constructive and mutually enhancing relationship'. In dramatizing this, Shakespeare interweaves two principal narratives. The first—the triangular story of Proteus, Julia, and Silvia—comes from a Spanish prose romance, the *Diana* of the Portuguese writer Jorge de Montemayor, first published in 1559. It is unlikely that Shakespeare could read Spanish; he may have used the French translation of Nicolas Collin (1578, 1587) or the English one by Bartholomew Young, not published until 1598 but completed, Young's preface tells us, sixteen years earlier, so that Shakespeare may have seen it in manuscript. But however he read the *Diana*, read it he certainly did, since the main lines of the plot are here: Felix (Proteus) woos and wins Felismena (Julia); but his father, 'telling him it was not meet that a young gentleman, and of so noble a house as he was, should spend his youth idly at home' (p. 233; compare 1.3.4–38) sends him to court, where he meets the princess Celia (Silvia) and falls in love with her.[1] Felismena follows him to court, disguised as

---

[1] Quotations from Montemayor, Sir Thomas Elyot, and Lyly's *Euphues* are taken from Geoffrey Bullough, *Narrative and Dramatic Sources of Shakespeare*, 8 vols., i (1957).

a page, and witnesses his courtship of Celia with a serenade
(compare 4.2). She is employed by Felix, who 'began to like so well
of [her] that he disclosed his whole love' for Celia to her (p. 240;
compare 4.4.39–40), and uses her to carry his messages of love
to Celia. When Felix takes her into his confidence, she criticizes
him, as Julia does Proteus: 'if the other lady, whom you served
before, did not deserve to be forgotten of you, you do her (under
correction, my lord) the greatest wrong in the world'; and, like
Proteus, Felix shuts her up and changes the subject: ' "Go to," said
Don Felix, "and speak no more of that" ' (pp. 240–1; compare
4.4.76–83). On her way to deliver Felix's message to Celia,
Felismena imagines 'the woeful estate whereunto my hapless love
had brought me' (p. 242), as Julia does more succinctly: 'How
many women would do such a message?' (4.4.88). When she and
Celia meet, Celia asks if she knows Felismena, as Silvia asks Julia;
but there are differences, too. Celia falls in love with the 'page',
whereas Silvia does not, and when her affection is not returned,
dies of love. And Felismena-as-page has adventures as an
Amazonian warrior before she rescues Felix from armed men
who outnumber him, and they are reunited. But when they are,
Felismena anticipates Julia's description of her male disguise as
'immodest raiment' (5.4.105) when she refers to her 'habit of a
base page' as something 'contrary to my rest and reputation'
(p. 251).[1]

To this plot, Shakespeare joins that of the intimate friends Titus
and Gisippus. Their story is told with his usual stylish mastery by
Boccaccio in *The Decameron* 10.8, but some verbal details make
it virtually certain that Shakespeare drew, not on Boccaccio's
version, but on that in Sir Thomas Elyot's *The Governor* (1531),
where it is presented as 'a right goodly example of friendship'.
Titus and Gisippus were so alike that they might have been twins:
'these two young gentlemen, as they seemed to be one in form and
personage, so . . . the same nature wrought in their hearts such
a mutual affection that their wills and appetites daily more and
more so confederated . . . that it seemed none other . . . but that
they had only changed their places, issuing (as I might say) out of
the one body, and entering into the other' (p. 212). The intensity
of this, and the sexual overtone of the phrasing, is far removed

---

[1] Other detailed resemblances to *Diana* are noted in the commentary.

from Boccaccio's suave elegance: 'Being regularly in one another's company, the two young men discovered that they shared many interests in common.'[1] A marriage is arranged for Gisippus, but he, 'having his heart already wedded to his friend Titus', initially refuses—until he meets the lady and falls in love with her, 'notwithstanding the fervent love that he had to his friend Titus'. He unwisely introduces her to Titus, who 'had the heart through pierced with the fiery dart of blind Cupid. Of the which wound the anguish was so exceeding and vehement, that neither the study of philosophy, neither the remembrance of his dear friend Gisippus who so much loved and trusted him, could anything withdraw him from that unkind appetite, but that of force he must love inordinately that lady whom his said friend had determined to marry' (p. 213). When Gisippus discovers this, he arranges for them to change places on the wedding night. Since they are near-identical in appearance, this gives the 'bed-trick' especial plausibility and provides an interesting variant on those which Shakespeare used later in *Measure for Measure* and *All's Well That Ends Well*, where it is the man, not the woman, who is deceived.

Perhaps because he was the father of twins, Shakespeare was fascinated by twins and what they feel for one another, to the extent, in *Twelfth Night*, of creating a play about twins from a story that was not about twins at all.[2] Of course, Proteus and Valentine are neither twins nor physically identical, but the play hinges on the closeness of their relationship, and the near-identity of Titus and Gisippus in Elyot's version may well have given Shakespeare the spur he needed to dramatize that closeness, a closeness which is summed up by Elyot in a passage preceding the Titus and Gisippus story: friendship 'is a blessed and stable connection of sundry wills, making of two persons one, in having and suffering. And therefore a friend is properly named of philosophers the other I'.[3] But what clinches Shakespeare's use of

---

[1] *The Decameron*, translated by G. H. McWilliam, Penguin Classics, 2nd edn. (1995), 745–64; p. 746.

[2] As Michael Dobson points out in his introduction to the revised Penguin Shakespeare edition (2005), p. lviii. The heroine of Montemayor's *Diana* was also a twin, but nothing is subsequently made of this.

[3] Book 2, Chapter 11. (The passage is not given in Bullough.) The phrase 'the Other I' derives from Cicero's *De Amicitia* 21.79–80, where the friend is said to be 'another self' (*alter idem*). Shakespeare also uses the idea at Sonnet 42.13: 'my friend and I are one'.

Elyot rather than Boccaccio is that, at the climactic moment of the play, the wording of Valentine's offer 'All that was mine in Silvia I give thee' is very close to Elyot's phrasing of Gisippus' to Titus: 'Here I renounce to you clearly all my title and interest that I now have or might have in that fair maiden' (p. 216). This may be contrasted with the characteristically cool, analytic tone of Boccaccio's version: 'since I can find another wife, but not another friend, with the greatest of ease, I prefer, rather than to lose you, not to lose her exactly, but as it were to transfer her. For I shan't lose her by giving her to you, but simply hand her over to my second self, at the same time changing her lot for the better' (pp. 751–2). Surely Shakespeare echoes Elyot's tone rather than Boccaccio's.

I said above that Shakespeare combines Montemayor's and Elyot's narratives; but there is another possibility. On 3 January 1585, the Queen's Men performed *Felix and Philiomena* at court.[1] It is usually assumed that this lost play was a dramatization of Montemayor's *Diana*, and that 'Philiomena' was a slip for 'Felismena'. But it is a strange coincidence that the narrator of the Titus and Gisippus story in Boccaccio is called Filomena. It is, therefore, just possible that 'Philiomena' is not a mistake, and that the play performed by the Queen's Men in 1585 had already conflated the *Diana* plot with Boccaccio's Titus and Gisippus story, renaming Felismena 'Filomena' ('Philiomena'); that this suggested the conflation of the plots to the young Shakespeare; and that he then consulted Montemayor and Elyot to flesh out the detail.

However that may be, by comparison with Montemayor and Elyot, other influences are of secondary importance. If *Felix and Philiomena* was a re-working for the stage of Montemayor, then it is an example of the 'romance' dramas of the 1580s, including Anthony Munday's *Fedele and Fortunio ... A Very Pleasant ... comedy of Two Italian Gentlemen* (1585, probably performed at court in 1584). This play has sometimes been connected with *The Two Gentlemen*—largely, I think, because of its sub-title, since the

---

[1] E. K. Chambers, *The Elizabethan Stage*, 4 vols. (Oxford, 1923), ii. 106, iv. 160. For further possible links between the young Shakespeare and the Queen's Men, see pp. 24–5 below.

plays have little in common.[1] Non-dramatic romance may be more relevant. Arthur Brooke's long narrative poem *Romeus and Juliet* (1562), obviously the source for *Romeo and Juliet*, may have given some hints for *The Two Gentlemen* as well: the name Friar Laurence, the corded ladder with which Valentine plans to abduct Silvia; but I am not persuaded by the arguments of Clifford Leech and others that Brooke's poem contributed much to the verbal detail of *The Two Gentlemen*: it seems absurd, for example, for Leech to suggest (p. xliii) that 'Brooke gives Shakespeare the cue' for 'as one nail by strength drives out another' (2.4.191), since this was a common proverb. Geoffrey Bullough's moderate summary seems fair: 'Obviously Shakespeare had been reading Brooke's poem before writing *The Two Gentlemen of Verona*; and maybe the Verona setting may be ascribed to this' (p. 209). To move from Brooke's laborious poem to Sidney's *Arcadia* (published 1590, 1593) is to enter a romance world on an altogether higher level of achievement. Here, Zelmane follows her beloved Pyrocles as his page. Pyrocles' half-recognition of her—'And still methought I had seen that face'—has something in common with Proteus' unconscious response to the disguised Julia (4.4.39–40, 65–7); and as Zelmane dies, she says that, in her disguise as a page, she has 'put off' both 'the apparel of a woman', and 'modesty', as Julia says that she has 'took upon me | Such an immodest raiment' (5.4.104–5).[2] Yet since both these details occur in Montemayor's *Diana*, the influence of the *Arcadia*, for all its widespread popularity, should not be overstated, either here or in the suggestion that Valentine's becoming the outlaws' leader derives from Pyrocles becoming captain of the Helots at *Arcadia* 1.6.

Shakespeare and Lyly

If Montemayor and Elyot were the main narrative influences on *The Two Gentlemen*, the chief stylistic influence was that of John Lyly. His hugely popular prose narrative, *Euphues* (1578), like

---

[1] A similar description in the list of characters ('two gentlemen of Greece') may have been the motive for citing Richard Edwards's *Damon and Pithias* (1571) as a source for *The Two Gentlemen*. I can perceive none of the 'remarkable connections' detected by Clifford Leech in his Arden edition of 1969, p. xxxviii.

[2] Quotations from the *Arcadia* are from Maurice Evans's Penguin Classics edition (Harmondsworth, 1977), pp. 359, 365.

Elyot's *The Governor*, presents two inseparable friends, Euphues and Philautus: 'they used not only one board but one bed. . . . Their friendship augmented every day, insomuch that the one could not refrain the company of the other one minute; all things went in common between them, which all men accounted commendable' (Bullough, p. 219). But a woman, Lucilla, comes between them. When Philautus introduces Euphues to her as his 'shadow', she tartly replies that 'in arguing of the shadow, we forgo the substance', a contrast frequent in *The Two Gentlemen* and in Shakespeare's later work. In this version, it is the woman, rather than one of the men, who transfers her affections; and the two friends at the end 'renewed their old friendship, both abandoning Lucilla as most abominable' (p. 225). But as Bullough says, 'Shakespeare's debt to Lyly was probably more one of technique than of matter' (p. 204), and it is with Lyly's plays, his court comedies written for the boy actors of St Paul's, that the greatest parallels with *The Two Gentlemen* exist.

The essential features of Lyly's style are symmetry and balance. In his comedy *Endymion*, for example, Endymion's friend Eumenides has to choose between rescuing Endymion from an enchanted sleep and winning his beloved Semele:

The love of men to women is a thing common, and of course; the friendship of man to man infinite and immortal.—Tush, Semele doth possess my love.—Ay, but Endymion hath deserved it. I will help Endymion; I found Endymion unspotted in his truth.—Ay, but I shall find Semele constant in her love. I will have Semele.—What shall I do? (3.4.121–7)

It is a short step from the style of this to that of Proteus, similarly caught between love and friendship:

> To leave my Julia shall I be forsworn;
> To love fair Silvia shall I be forsworn;
> To wrong my friend I shall be much forsworn.
> (2.6.1–3)

Lyly writes, as usual, in prose, Shakespeare (here) in verse; but the patterned formality is common to both, and such patterning is perhaps the principal stylistic feature of *The Two Gentlemen*, as will emerge later.

Nor is it confined to the aristocrats, or to verse, in the play. Lyly says that Euphues was 'of more wit than wealth, and yet of more

wealth than wisdom' (Bullough, p. 217); and when Speed is reading the catalogue of the virtues and vices of Lance's milkmaid, he
says: 'she hath more hair than wit, and more faults than hairs,
and more wealth than faults' (3.1.343–4). Clearly there are parallels in both rhythm and language. This discussion between Speed
and Lance has an even closer connection with one in Lyly's *Midas*,
where two pages, obvious relations of Speed, analyse a mistress's
qualities:

LICIO But sirrah, for thy better instructions I will unfold every
wrinkle of my mistress's disposition. . . .
PETULUS Proceed.
LICIO First, she hath a head as round as a tennis ball.
PETULUS I would my bed were a hazard.
LICIO Why?
PETULUS Nothing, but that I would have her head there among
other balls. . . .
LICIO Well, she hath the tongue of a parrot. . . .
PETULUS Then will I mutter 'A rope for a parrot, a rope!'
LICIO So mayst thou be hanged, not by the lips, but by the neck.
Then, sir, . . . she hath the ears of a want.
PETULUS Doth she want ears?
LICIO I say the ears of a want, a mole. Thou dost want wit to
understand me.

(1.2.20–57)

There is obviously a close family similarity between this dialogue
and that between Speed and Lance at 3.1.271–356. The word-play
about wanting ears is exactly what Speed means when he says
that Lance's 'old vice' is to 'mistake the word' (3.1.279), though
Speed himself is as guilty of that 'mistaking' at 1.1.73–119 and
2.1.30–66. Which came first? The evidence is not decisive; but the
name 'Licio' is adopted by Hortensio in his disguise as a music-
master in *The Taming of the Shrew*, where the proverbial slang
phrase '*Baccare*' ('Stand back!') also occurs, as it does earlier in the
Lyly scene; and Lyly's final line quoted above uses 'understand'
without the elaborate word-play at *The Two Gentlemen* 2.5.22–9;
so it seems likelier that Shakespeare drew upon Lyly's scene in
various places than that Lyly should have brought together
phrases from different Shakespeare plays (however close in date)
into one passage. To the question of priority I must return in

the next section; meanwhile, it is surely beyond doubt that Shakespeare is influenced by Lyly's style in important respects.

Shakespeare's Earliest Surviving Play?

In the excellent brief introduction to his Red Letter Shakespeare edition of 1905,[1] E. K. Chambers calls *The Two Gentlemen*

Shakespeare's first essay at originality, at fashioning for himself the out-lines of that romantic or tragicomic formula in which so many of his most characteristic dramas were afterwards to be cast. Something which is neither quite tragedy nor quite comedy, something which touches the heights and depths of sentiment and reveals the dark places of the human heart without lingering long enough there to crystallize the painful impression, a love story broken for a moment into passionate chords by absence and inconstancy and intrigue, and then reunited to the music of wedding-bells; such is the kind of dramatic scheme which floated before him, when he first set pen to paper in making a play of his very own. (pp. 5–6)

Chambers refers to 'Shakespeare's first essay at originality', rather than to 'Shakespeare's first play' because at that time he thought that the *Henry VI* plays were re-writings of existing texts; but the view that *The Two Gentlemen* might actually be Shakespeare's first play, originally suggested by Edmond Malone in 1821,[2] has been gaining ground in the last few decades. It is placed first in the Oxford *Complete Works* of 1986, where Stanley Wells contrasts the 'accomplished elegance' of its verse and the skill of its prose with the fact that some of its scenes, especially those involving more than four characters, 'betray an uncertainty of technique suggestive of inexperience' (p. 1).[3] This contrast between verbal accomplishment and underdeveloped theatrical technique seems to me exactly what might be expected from a young writer educated, presumably, at Stratford Grammar School with its largely classics-based curriculum, who, according to the most reliable tradition, had been 'in his younger years a schoolmaster

---

[1] Reprinted in *Shakespeare: A Survey* (1925), pp. 49–57.

[2] *Plays and Poems* (1821), iv. 7, where he dates the play 1591. This is a modification of the date of 1595 proposed in his edition of 1790, i. 297–300.

[3] Wells argues the case in more detail in 'The Failure of *The Two Gentlemen of Verona*', *Shakespeare Jahrbüch West* 99 (1963), 161–73.

in the country',[1] but who had so far lacked the practical experience of drama which only working in the professional theatre can provide.

In a famous passage, Dr Johnson also speaks of the 'strange mixture . . . of care and negligence' in the play. He considers some passages 'eminently beautiful' and the 'versification . . . often excellent', but goes on:

> The author conveys his heroes by sea from one inland town to another in the same country; he places the Emperor at Milan and sends his young men to attend him, but never mentions him more; he makes Proteus, after an interview with Silvia, say he has only seen her picture . . . The reason of all this confusion seems to be that he took his story from a novel which he sometimes followed and sometimes forsook, sometimes remembered and sometimes forgot.[2]

It might be truer to say that Shakespeare, perhaps writing in haste, 'sometimes remembered' what he himself had written in an earlier scene, and 'sometimes forgot'. The geographical confusions, for example, are plausibly explained by Jean E. Howard: 'Verona, Milan, Mantua, and Padua . . . often are used interchangeably and seem collectively to be Shakespeare's shorthand for "Italy" rather than distinct places.'[3] The confusion between the 'Emperor' and 'Duke' of Milan is also easily explained in terms of a writer not having yet made up his mind about the character's rank; it is significant that all but one of the references to the Emperor occur early in the play, before the Duke actually appears; for his own reference to 'an emperor', see the note to 2.4.74–5. As for Silvia's 'picture', presumably Proteus means only her outward appearance. Other inconsistencies which have worried editors seem to be compatible with an impatient young writer pressing on, getting his play down, without bothering too much about consistency—and surely also making discoveries as he goes along. For example, in the first scene Proteus has sent Valentine's servant Speed with a message to Julia. Why does he send Speed when he has a servant of his own, Lance? The obvious answer is that he

---

[1] John Aubrey, *Brief Lives*, ed. O. L. Dick (Harmondsworth, 1962), p. 335. Aubrey's informant was William Beeston, son of Christopher Beeston, an actor in Shakespeare's company.

[2] *Plays of William Shakespeare*, 8 vols. (1765), i .259.

[3] *The Norton Shakespeare Based on the Oxford Edition* (New York, 1997), p. 77.

hasn't thought of Lance yet. Some commentators have suggested that all the scenes involving Lance were added to the play at a later stage. It is true that they are detachable in the sense that they have no narrative function; but Lance and Speed surely have the dramatically important purpose of providing a mocking commentary on the love affairs of their masters. This effect could of course still be achieved in a revision; but the interweaving of the lovers' and servants' scenes does not suggest that.[1]

In a subsequent discussion, Stanley Wells highlights the strange paradox that the greatest dramatist in the language seems to have written nothing, or nothing that has survived, until the age of twenty six or more. It seems improbable.[2] As Wells says, 'In even his least mature works he shows himself already to be a highly accomplished writer, but so far as we know, nothing that he wrote in his youth or early manhood has survived. . . . He . . . may have written . . . plays for amateur performance before joining the professional theatre, but if so we have no record of them.'[3] But perhaps *The Two Gentlemen*, with its poetic accomplishment but arguably primitive dramatic technique, its brevity, and its small cast, might have been planned 'for amateur performance'. At 4.4.155–7 Julia in her boy's disguise says:

> at Pentecost,
> When all our pageants of delight were played,
> Our youth got me to play the woman's part.

In 1583, the Stratford corporation paid thirteen shillings and fourpence to 'Davy Jones and his company for his pastime at Whitsuntide [Pentecost]'.[4] Davy Jones, who later married into the Hathaway family, Shakespeare's in-laws, was clearly a local man; his 'company' was probably an amateur one. So it is possible that Shakespeare wrote *The Two Gentlemen* for such a company, and

---

[1] In his Arden edition, Leech proposes an elaborate four-stage revision of the play (p. xxx), based on what seem to me exaggerated views about the play's contradictions.

[2] So, in his 'early start' chronology, E. A. J. Honigmann dates *The Two Gentlemen* in 1587 (*Shakespeare's Impact on his Contemporaries* (1982), p. 88).

[3] *Shakespeare: A Dramatic Life* (1994), reissued as *Shakespeare: The Poet and his Plays* (1997), p. 39.

[4] S. Schoenbaum, *William Shakespeare: A Documentary Life* (Oxford, 1975), p. 89, drawing on research by Mark Eccles, *Shakespeare in Warwickshire* (Madison, Wisconsin, 1963), p. 83.

that 'Julia's words form a metatheatrical comment on the action'.[1]

But he might have written it for quite a different reason. We know that the Queen's Men visited Stratford in December 1587; what we do not know, annoyingly, is what they played. But this was the company that had performed *Felix and Philiomena* at court in January 1585 (see above, p. 17); so it is possible that this play was in their repertoire when they visited Stratford (or when they visited Coventry, only twenty miles away, in November 1585 and again, twice, in September 1587)[2] and that Shakespeare came to know it then. Of equal importance for *The Two Gentlemen*, however, the star of the Queen's Men was the most famous comic actor of the age, Richard Tarlton. In an interesting discussion about dogs on stage, Richard Beadle shows that the clown with a dog was 'a familiar image drawn from . . . popular entertainment, whose roots in medieval and antique comic tradition ran deep', and that Tarlton 'retained the popular entertainer's traditional affinity with dogs, and was remembered as working with one'.[3] In *Tarlton's Jests*, for example, a collection of anecdotes published after his death,[4] several involve a dog. One of them says that Tarlton 'had a dog of fine qualities' but that on one occasion the dog let him down and did not perform as expected, so that Tarlton 'would never trust to his dog's tricks more' (sig. E3–E3ᵛ), a phrase which Beadle says suggests 'that the sight of him working with a dog was likely to have been a familiar one'. This is supported by an anecdote in the State Papers, Domestic, in which Queen Elizabeth 'bade them take away the knave [Tarlton] for making her to laugh so excessively as he fought against her little dog Perrico de Faldas with his sword and long staff, and bade the Queen take off her mastie [mastiff]'.[5] So if Shakespeare saw the Queen's Men play

---

[1] Stanley Wells, *Shakespeare: For All Time* (2002), p. 17.

[2] This information is taken from the lists in Scott McMillin and Sally-Beth MacLean, *The Queen's Men and their Plays* (Cambridge, 1998), pp. 176–7.

[3] 'Crab's pedigree', in *English Comedy*, ed. M. Cordner, P. Holland, and J. Kerrigan (Cambridge, 1994), 12–35; pp. 12–13.

[4] There were editions in ?1590 and 1600, reprinted together in 1613, cited here.

[5] *Eliz.* ccxv, 89 (E. K. Chambers, *The Elizabethan Stage* (Oxford, 1923), ii. 342, and Beadle, p. 19. A version of this anecdote is used in the deservedly popular film *Shakespeare in Love* (1998), where Judi Dench as Queen Elizabeth I, after glowering in sour disapproval at Valentine's love-talk, bursts into raucous laughter at a diminutive, beruffed Crab literally running rings round a dismayed Lance.

Felix and Philiomena and/or Tarlton and his dog performing with the company, he may have written *The Two Gentlemen,* or added Lance and Crab to an existing version for amateur performance, in the hope of having it performed by the Queen's Men.[1] But if so, that would put the date of composition before 3 September 1588, when Tarlton died.[2]

The major obstacle to this early dating is the play's relationship with the comedies of John Lyly, referred to in the previous section and in the commentary. There is no problem with *Campaspe* or *Sappho and Phao* (both published in 1584). *Endymion* was not published until 1591, but its title-page says that it was played by the Children of Paul's before the Queen 'on Candlemas day [2 February] at night'. David Bevington in his Revels edition interprets this as 2 February 1588 because 'in no other year between 1580 and 1591 is there a Candlemas payment to Paul's boys' (p. 8); but as he also notes, some records of court performances in 1585–7 are lost, and R. W. Bond in the original Arden edition of *The Two Gentlemen* proposes 2 February 1586 (p. xxi). In either case, that would involve Shakespeare seeing, rather than merely reading, *Endymion.* But the real stumbling-block is *Midas,* which Bevington dates 1589 or early 1590, published 1592. In the previous section, I cited a passage from *Midas* that closely resembles *The Two Gentlemen* 3.1.271–356, and suggested that, while there is no decisive proof which came first, Shakespeare is the likelier borrower. If that is so, *The Two Gentlemen* cannot be earlier than 1589–90, and my argument that Shakespeare wrote it in Stratford and for Richard Tarlton collapses, unless we fall back on the theory that some passages were revised, which I have already considered unlikely. If *The Two Gentlemen* is later than

---

[1] It is not necessary for my argument that Shakespeare should have *joined* the Queen's Men, though he may have done so. Both M. Eccles and S. Schoenbaum (see p. 23 n. 4 above) suggest that he might have been recruited during the Queen's Men's visit to Stratford in 1587 in order to replace their actor William Knell, who had been killed in a duel that June. In a judicious survey of the evidence, Scott McMillin and Sally-Beth MacLean (see p. 24 n. 2) argue that 'the probability of an unknown from a country town replacing a leading serious actor of the day is not strong' (p. 161), though of course he could have been hired for minor parts while another actor was promoted to replace Knell, with the consequent adjustments familiar in any theatre company.

[2] If *The Two Gentlemen* was ever performed by the Chamberlain's Men, the company to which Shakespeare belonged from 1594, Lance was presumably played by their resident clown Will Kemp.

Tarltons Iefts.

Drawne into thefe three parts.

{ 1 *His Court-wittie Iefts*
2 *His found Cittie Iefts.*
3 *His Country prettie Iefts.* }

Full of Delight, Wit, and honeft Myrth.

LONDON,
Printed for *Iohn Budge*, and are to be fold at his fhop, at the
great South doore of Paules. 1613.

6. Richard Tarlton, for whom the part of Lance may have been designed (from the title-page of *Tarlton's Jests*, 1613).

Midas, then the date of 1590–1 proposed by the Oxford *Complete Works* is safest. If the reverse, then my belief that *The Two Gentlemen* was written before Shakespeare came to London, and before Tarlton's death on 3 September 1588, may be worth considering. Either way, the view that *The Two Gentlemen* is Shakespeare's earliest surviving play meets with no serious objection.

'Certain Outlaws' and Knights Errant

A very early play, perhaps designed for local performance in Stratford, might help to explain two of the most curious features of *The Two Gentlemen*, the presentation of the outlaws and of Sir Eglamour. In both cases, the uncertainty of tone which also affects other scenes is at its most blatant, especially in one speech by the Third Outlaw. The first two have admitted that they were banished for abduction and murder; the third then says:

> And I, for suchlike petty crimes as these.
> But to the purpose, for we cite our faults
> That they may hold excused our lawless lives;
> And partly seeing you are beautified
> With goodly shape, and by your own report
> A linguist, and a man of such perfection
> As we do in our quality much want.
>
> (4.1.50–6)

There is surely a wide range, or confusion, of tone in this speech. On the one hand, the Third Outlaw dismisses abduction and murder as 'petty crimes'; on the other, he attempts to recruit Valentine because he is beautiful and speaks foreign languages. This double view, or inconsistency, continues into the last scene. Despite their declared detestation of 'vile, base practices' (4.1.71), Valentine says that he has 'much to do / To keep them from uncivil outrages' (5.4.16–17); yet at the end he tells the Duke that

> They are reformèd, civil, full of good,
> And fit for great employment, worthy lord.
>
> (5.4.154–5)

Shakespeare seems to be mocking the tradition of romantic outlaws at the same time as using it for narrative purposes, and this makes interpretation difficult.

Perhaps this wobbling tone is just Shakespeare's inexperience; but the allusions to Robin Hood in these scenes, one specific, to Friar Tuck (4.1.35), the other implied (4.1.68–71), suggest that these outlaws derive from the legends of Robin Hood preserved in the popular tradition of outlaws who rob the rich to help the poor, a tradition summed up in a description of Robin Hood given in an account of Richard I's reign in Richard Grafton's *A Chronicle at Large*, a book Shakespeare used in writing his early histories:[1] 'one thing was much commended in him, that he would suffer no woman to be oppressed, violated, or otherwise abused. The poorer sort of people he favoured, and would in no wise suffer their goods to be touched or spoiled, but relieved and aided them with such goods as he got from the rich' (p. 84). This is the tradition behind the dialogue at 4.1.68–71; and it was a tradition sustained in popular celebrations: folk-plays, morris dances, May games. Noting that such folk customs were 'all firmly rooted in the Midlands', Stephen Greenblatt speculates that the young Shakespeare may have seen, or participated in, 'a coarse Robin Hood show, with a drunken Friar Tuck and a lascivious Maid Marion'.[2] So it may be, if *The Two Gentlemen* was originally intended for local performance, that the Robin Hood aspects of the outlaws were meant as a mocking comment on such popular pastimes, a theatrical in-joke almost, and that the uncertainty of tone arises from conflating this with the outlaws of romantic fiction.

A related inconsistency affects Sir Eglamour. He is apparently a chivalrous knight who, when his lady died, vowed 'pure chastity' on her grave (4.3.20–1), and who then escorts Silvia to join Valentine, only to abandon her at the first sign of danger (5.3.6). Was Shakespeare merely poking rather crude fun at the figure of the knight errant? An interesting solution to both the outlaws and Sir Eglamour was offered by John Barton in 1981, when he staged *The Two Gentlemen* in a double bill with *Titus Andronicus* (see p. 7 above). Doing two such dissimilar plays together encouraged Barton to push the contrasts to extremes, and after the bloodletting of *Titus*, he presented the most broadly funny outlaws' scenes I have ever encountered. The three outlaws of the Folio text became nine, with the speeches redistributed so that Sheila

---

[1] See my edition of *2 Henry VI* in this series, pp. 30–2.

[2] *Will in the World* (2004), pp. 38–40.

Hancock, who had played Tamora in *Titus*, could go to the other extreme and play a delightfully tongue-in-cheek leader of the outlaws. It was she who had stabbed a gentleman 'in my mood' (4.1.49), who admired Valentine's 'goodly shape' and praised him in rapt terms as 'a *linguist!*', and who later told Silvia in obvious disappointment that Valentine would 'not use a woman lawlessly' (5.3.13). And the production's context also enabled Patrick Stewart, who as Titus had used a quiet, gentlemanly manner as he perpetrated atrocious actions, to use that same gentlemanly tone to present Sir Eglamour as an ageing knight errant, a Don Quixote. This presentation at once suggested the origins of the character in an ironic view of the chivalric world, and, since he took on all nine outlaws at once, provided an answer to the textual difficulty of Silvia's chivalrous escort taking to his heels, since he was so hopelessly outnumbered. The production demonstrated that the inconsistencies of the text can be turned to dramatic advantage, and, still more important, that an ironic attitude to the romance world need not imperil the emotional impact of the final scene.

'The Two Gentlemen' and Shakespeare's Later Work

E. K. Chambers, like most commentators, suggests that *The Two Gentlemen* anticipates many of Shakespeare's later works (see p. 21 above). There is a danger in this approach, since it can imply that *The Two Gentlemen* is *only* of interest because it anticipates later successes. That danger was not entirely avoided at Stratford-upon-Avon in 1960, where the play was the first in a series designed to trace the range of Shakespearian comedy, particularly since the production of *The Two Gentlemen* was less successful in itself than those of *The Merchant of Venice* and (notably) *Twelfth Night* which followed it into the repertoire. As Geoffrey Bullough points out, 'there are interesting parallels to *The Merchant of Venice*' (p. 209), and these emerged strongly, especially when Julia's discussion of her suitors with Lucetta (1.2) was followed a week later by Portia's discussion of hers with Nerissa (also 1.2). But the differences were, and are, as interesting as the similarities: in *The Two Gentlemen* the mistress names the suitors and the maid evaluates them; in *The Merchant* it is the other way round. This is not a question of simple 'development' or 'improvement':

in performance each scene stood successfully on its own feet. Lance reappears as Lancelot Gobbo in *The Merchant*, 'hardly bettered' as E. K. Chambers puts it with sly shrewdness in his edition (p. 9), and as these performances confirmed. Bassanio's desperate declaration, in the trial scene of *The Merchant*, that he would sacrifice his wife to save his friend Antonio was a clear echo of Valentine's offer of Silvia to *his* friend, especially as both parts were played by the same actor. But again, the differences are as important as the similarities: Portia in her male disguise comments tartly 'Your wife would give you little thanks for that' (4.1.285), whereas Silvia says nothing at all, a point to which this introduction must return. The connections (and differences) between *The Two Gentlemen* and *Twelfth Night* were clearer still, and, provided that we avoid the trap of regarding the play as merely a prelude to better things, a comparison between *The Two Gentlemen* on the one hand and *Twelfth Night* and Shakespeare's Sonnets on the other may help to clarify its essential nature.

When at the climax, and crux, of *The Two Gentlemen* Valentine observes Proteus attempting to rape Silvia, he cries:

> The private wound is deepest. O time most accursed,
> 'Mongst all foes that a friend should be the worst!

Proteus, in his turn, repents:

> Forgive me, Valentine. If hearty sorrow
> Be a sufficient ransom for offence,
> I tender't here. I do as truly suffer
> As e'er I did commit.

To which Valentine replies:

> Then I am paid. . . .
> And that my love may appear plain and free,
> All that was mine in Silvia I give thee.
>
> (5.4.71–83)

In abbreviating this exchange, I may have exacerbated the problems of a scene already frequently attacked for its unseemly brevity; nevertheless, that is the essence of their dialogue. Expansion, and I think elucidation, may be provided by Shakespeare's Sonnets, which, says Colin Burrow in his edition for this series, 'meditate on the perverse effects and consequences of

sexual desire, on sacrifice and self-sacrifice, on the ways in which
a relationship of sexual passion might objectify or enslave both the
desirer and the desired, and they repeatedly complicate simple
binary distinctions between male and female'.[1] The linked Sonnets
33 and 34 express a crisis in the relationship of the poet and his
friend on which other sonnets cast light. The friend repents his
behaviour in tears, but the poet replies, treating his friend's and
his own tears metaphorically as well as literally:

> 'Tis not enough that through the cloud thou break
> To dry the rain on my storm-beaten face,
> For no man well of such a salve can speak
> That heals the wound and cures not the disgrace.
> Nor can thy shame give physic to my grief;
> Though thou repent, yet I have still the loss.
>
> (Sonnet 34.5–10)

These lines express, with great intensity and directness, the
difficulty of accepting even the repentance of someone whom you
love but who has caused you great pain: ''Tis not enough', 'I have
still the loss'. It still hurts. This is the tone of Valentine's 'The
private wound is deepest', though it surely goes beyond his perhaps too easy, half-line completion of Proteus' repentance: 'Then
I am paid', just as Sonnet 34's final couplet echoes but deepens
both Proteus' apology and Valentine's response:

> Ah, but those tears are pearl which thy love sheds,
> And they are rich, and ransom all ill deeds.
>
> (13–14)

Perhaps the final scene of *The Two Gentlemen* would have been
more satisfying if Valentine had been given something like this to
say.

What was it that the poet had to forgive? Other sonnets provide
the answer: the friend had an affair with the poet's mistress, and

---

[1] *Complete Sonnets and Poems*, The Oxford Shakespeare (Oxford, 2002), p. 5. I
follow Burrow in his use of 'the friend' as 'a short-hand way of referring to the
addressee of poems' before Sonnet 127, without attempting 'to reduce the manifest
erotic energy of these poems' (p. 123). It is also how I use 'friends' for Valentine
and Proteus. And like Burrow, I assume that Shakespeare writes about a single
friend, unlike, for example, Paul Edmondson and Stanley Wells, who argue that
Sonnets 1–126 may address 'more than one friend, more than one lover'
(*Shakespeare's Sonnets* (Oxford, 2004), p. 39).

the poet replies: 'Take all my loves, my love, yea, take them all' and continues:

> I do forgive thy robb'ry, gentle thief,
> Although thou steal thee all my poverty;
> And yet love knows it is a greater grief
> To bear love's wrong than hate's known injury.
>   Lascivious grace, in whom all ill well shows,
>   Kill me with spites, yet we must not be foes.
>   (Sonnet 40.1, 9–14)

The phrasing here corresponds to Valentine's forgiveness, although the oxymoron 'Lascivious grace'—someone who is at once endowed with 'grace' (beauty, maybe something more spiritual) and yet is sexually indulgent—is beyond the stylistic reach of *The Two Gentlemen*. But 'we must not be foes' is exactly in tune with Valentine's attitude to Proteus; and Sonnet 42 takes this further:

> That thou hast her, it is not all my grief,
> And yet it may be said I loved her dearly;
> That she hath thee is of my wailing chief,
> A loss in love that touches me more nearly.
>   (1–4)

Of course Proteus does not 'have' Silvia sexually, though he tries to; but the point is that the poet is more affected by his friend's betrayal than by the loss of his mistress to him. That is what lies behind those lines of Valentine's that have drawn such opprobrium:

> And that my love may appear plain and free,
> All that was mine in Silvia I give thee.

This is usually taken to mean that he is handing over his lady to her would-be rapist; and the words from Sir Thomas Elyot's *Governor* that I have suggested lie behind them seem to support that interpretation: 'Here I renounce to you clearly all my title and interest that I now have or might have in that fair maiden.' But it is possible to adopt another man's phrasing without necessarily taking over his exact meaning; and the lines from Sonnet 42 help to make it clear that Valentine means 'I give you all the love I feel for Silvia'—or even 'I love you as much as, or more than, Silvia'. This may not, for some members of the audience, make

Valentine's offer any easier to take; but that he places his love for
Proteus at least on the same level as, and probably more than,
that for Silvia seems to me beyond doubt. Is that why Silvia says
nothing thereafter—because there is nothing that she can usefully
say?[1]

The Sonnets further illuminate the use of specific words and
ideas as used in the play. The contrast between 'shadow' and
'substance' is much insisted on, particularly in the dialogue
between Proteus and Silvia at 4.2.120–8, where Silvia says that
she is 'very loath' to be Proteus' 'idol'; in the exchange between
Silvia and the disguised Julia at 4.4.117–18; and in Julia's
soliloquy at 4.4.194–8:

> Come, shadow, come, and take this shadow [Silvia's picture] up,
> For 'tis thy rival. O thou senseless form,
> Thou shalt be worshipped, kissed, loved, and adored;
> And were there sense in his idolatry
> My substance should be statue in thy stead.

In Sonnet 53, the poet asks his lover:

> What is your substance, whereof are you made,
> That millions of strange shadows on you tend?
>
> (1–2)

These 'shadows' are the celebrated archetypes of beauty from the
past—Adonis, Helen of Troy—but to the poet, his friend excels
them all because 'you [are] like none, none you, for constant
heart' (14). This stress on constancy, obviously challenged by the
friend's betrayal of the poet elsewhere in the sequence, recurs in
Sonnet 105, which the poet begins by saying 'Let not my love be
called idolatry, | Nor my belovèd as an idol show' (1–2) even in
the act of adoring him; compare the use of 'idol' at *The Two
Gentlemen* 2.4.142 and 4.2.125, and of 'idolatry' at 4.4.197. He
goes on:

---

[1] The final section of this introduction will describe some ways in which
directors have handled her silence. For a discussion of the play and Sonnet 42,
see Inga-Stina Ewbank, ' "Were man but constant, he were perfect": Constancy
and Consistency in "The Two Gentlemen of Verona" ', in *Shakespearian Comedy*,
Stratford-upon-Avon Studies 14 (1972), 31–57.

> Kind is my love today, tomorrow kind,
> Still constant in a wondrous excellence.
> Therefore my verse, to constancy confined,
> One thing expressing, leaves out difference.
> (5–8)

'Constant' and 'constancy' are also of central importance in *The Two Gentlemen*; and it is ironical that it should be the inconstant Proteus who uses the words in a variety of ways. In the course of the play he moves from his vow of 'constancy' to Julia (2.2.8) by way of a rationalization of his betrayal of Valentine —

> I cannot now prove constant to myself
> Without some treachery used to Valentine
> (2.6.31–2)

to his admission at the end: 'O heaven, were man | But constant, he were perfect' (5.4.109–10), and to his final re-statement of his initial commitment to Julia:

> What is in Silvia's face but I may spy
> More fresh in Julia's, with a constant eye?
> (5.4.113–14)

Proteus, like the friend of the Sonnets, alternates between constancy and inconstancy; and the verbal complexities, and implications, of those words are among the many things that connect *The Two Gentlemen* and *Twelfth Night*.

Both plays present a survey of lovers' behaviour—their extravagances, delusions, and eventually their recognition of the strength and limitations of their emotions. At the start of *The Two Gentlemen*, Valentine mocks Proteus' love for Julia; but when we next see him he is head-over-heels in love with Silvia. As he himself puts it to Proteus:

> I have done penance for contemning love,
> Whose high imperious thoughts have punished me
> With bitter fasts, with penitential groans,
> With nightly tears and daily heart-sore sighs.
> (2.4.127–30)

Valentine is going though the traditional torments of the courtly lover, and there is more than a hint in the language of the traditional lover's absurdity. Yet the play's view of lovers'

34

behaviour is not wholly ironic. When he is banished, Valentine's reaction (3.1.170–87) is heartfelt:

> Silvia is my self. Banished from her
> Is self from self. . . .
> She is my essence.

Like Valentine, Orsino in *Twelfth Night* follows traditional patterns of behaviour; and like Valentine, he has been criticized for it by influential critical opinion: 'in love with love', they say, rather than with an individual. There is some truth in this charge. Orsino has created his own image of Olivia, and prides himself on his constancy to it:

> such as I am, all true lovers are,
> Unstaid and skittish in all motions else
> Save in the constant image of the creature
> That is beloved.
>
> (2.4.16–19)

But the shrewd jester Feste, exploiting the licence of professional fools to say what others may not, openly criticizes Orsino for his *in*constancy: 'Now the melancholy god protect thee, and the tailor make thy doublet of changeable taffeta, for thy mind is a very opal. I would have men of such constancy put to sea' (2.4.72–5). Feste, in short, accuses Orsino of fashionable love-melancholy, as Speed does Valentine: 'you have learned, like Sir Proteus, to wreath your arms, like a malcontent' and so on (2.1.16–18). But again as with Valentine, Orsino's language complicates the situation. In the celebrated opening scene of *Twelfth Night*, Orsino asks for music to 'feed' his love; Feste's accusation of inconstancy is justified in that Orsino quickly tires of the music— 'Enough, no more, | 'Tis not so sweet now as it was before' (1.1.7–8); but when Orsino shifts (perhaps inconstantly) to a comparison of his love to the sea, the image has a vigorous life as well as extravagance. So, still more, has his comparison of his desires to the classical huntsman, Acteon, torn in pieces by his own hounds:

> my desires, like fell and cruel hounds,
> E'er since pursue me.
>
> (1.1.21–2)

Orsino's language is two-edged: if it is artificial in that it draws on convention, that impression is tempered by its immediacy and

7. A melancholy lover: an anonymous portrait of John Donne, *c*.1595.

vigour, suggesting that he is capable of powerful feelings, like Valentine.

Both Orsino (to some extent) and Proteus (to a greater extent) are set against embodiments of constancy in Viola and Julia. This emerges most clearly in the serenade scene of *The Two Gentlemen* (4.2) and the central scene of *Twelfth Night* (2.4), both of which focus on a song. In *The Two Gentlemen* the disguised Julia hears Proteus use 'Who is Silvia?' to woo her rival; in *Twelfth Night* the disguised Viola listens with Orsino to Feste singing 'Come away death'. Neither disguised heroine can speak of her love directly. Julia can only express her heartbreak at Proteus' betrayal through *double-entendres* in her dialogue with the Host (4.2.53–69), Viola her love for Orsino through the allegory of a sister who died of love but was silent:

> She never told her love,
> But let concealment, like a worm i'th' bud,
> Feed on her damask cheek. She pined in thought,
> And with a green and yellow melancholy
> She sat like patience on a monument,
> Smiling at grief.
>
> (2.4.110–15)

That final phrase encapsulates the mood, and the achievement, of *Twelfth Night*, smiles and tears inseparable. This is one—perhaps the supreme—example of Shakespeare's mastery as a writer of comedy. It would be idle to pretend that *The Two Gentlemen* achieves anything on that level. Even so, the disguised Julia's wooing of Silvia on Proteus' behalf brings out interesting connections, and equally interesting contrasts, with Viola's wooing Olivia on Orsino's behalf. Both heroines have a sense of humour which helps them cope with an emotionally demanding situation. When Viola realizes that Olivia is in love with her in her page's disguise, she comments: 'Poor lady, she were better love a dream!' (2.2.26). Nonetheless, as always, she determines to serve Orsino loyally: 'I'll do my best | To woo your lady' (1.4.40–1). But Julia takes a different line:

> Yet will I woo for him, but yet so coldly
> As, heaven it knows, I would not have him speed.
>
> (4.4.104–5)

And when she receives Silvia's portrait, she says she would

> have scratched out your unseeing eyes,
> To make my master out of love with thee.
>
> (4.4.201–2)

This might be considered a less successful attempt at a later achievement, but it is surely more useful to regard the dramatization of the heroines as different characters placed in a similar situation.

Perhaps the most striking resemblance between the two plays occurs in their final scenes, where a crisis, and a threat of violence, releases hitherto pent-up emotion. The attempted rape in *The Two Gentlemen* brings into the open Valentine's long-delayed declaration of love for Proteus: 'All that was mine in Silvia I give thee'; and Orsino's threat to kill Viola/Cesario, who appears to have betrayed him by marrying Olivia, draws from Viola the overt declaration of love that her page's disguise has prevented her from making throughout the play: she will follow Orsino,

> After him I love,
> More than I love these eyes, more than my life,
> More by all mores than e'er I shall love wife.
>
> (5.1.132–4)

Valentine's declaration of love must be explored further at the end of this introduction.

The Language(s) of Lovers

The lovers' language in *The Two Gentlemen of Verona* is on the whole clear, elegant, and lyrical, as in Proteus' famous quatrain

> O how this spring of love resembleth
> The uncertain glory of an April day,
> Which now shows all the beauty of the sun,
> And by and by a cloud takes all away.
>
> (1.3.84–7)

This lyrical utterance is often spiced with wit, which helps to establish the tone of a play that, initially, takes an ironic, or at least a lightweight, view of lovers' behaviour. Both the attitude and the style are economically established in the opening scene. Valentine mocks the clichés of romantic love,

> where scorn is bought with groans,
> Coy looks with heart-sore sighs, one fading moment's mirth
> With twenty watchful, weary, tedious nights.
>
> (1.1.29–31)

The light, mocking tone is also conveyed by the word-play of being 'over-boots in love' (25–8); and as Proteus and Valentine argue about the merits or otherwise of love, their echoing repetitions—

'Yet writers say . . . And writers say' (42–5)—employ a verbal patterning which is to be a major feature of the play's style. But underneath the elegance and wit, points are being made about the characters. The patterning reflects the competitiveness often easily, relaxedly expressed by close friends; and the language in general is very intimate—'my loving Proteus', 'Sweet Valentine', 'thy Proteus' (where 'thy' is the intimate form, 'you' the polite one), 'Sweet Proteus', and so on—so much so, in fact, that one could argue as accurately that the play dramatizes competing kinds of love as much as a debate between love and friendship, which is the more usual view. At any rate, this friendship is of an extremely close kind, so that a great deal is at stake when Proteus betrays it.

In the second scene, as Julia and Lucetta argue about the best way to express love, they exchange single lines in a way that develops the stylistic patterning of the opening scene. Julia starts it off by speaking of Proteus:

> JULIA
> Why, he of all the rest hath never moved me.
> LUCETTA
> Yet he of all the rest I think best loves ye.
> JULIA
> His little speaking shows his love but small.
> LUCETTA
> Fire that's closest kept burns most of all.
> JULIA
> They do not love that do not show their love.
> LUCETTA
> O, they love least that let men know their love.
> (1.2.27–32)

This balanced exchange also sets up a contrast between verbal volubility and silence, which is developed later in the play as events darken. But for the moment the mood is light and witty, and even more so when Julia tears up Proteus' letter, only to have to grovel on her hands and knees to piece it together again, with appropriate gestures and reactions, moving from

> Look, here is writ 'Kind Julia'—unkind Julia,
> As in revenge of thy ingratitude
> I throw thy name against the bruising stones,
> Trampling contemptuously on thy disdain

to the more tender and sensuous

> And here is writ 'Love-wounded Proteus'.
> Poor wounded name, my bosom as a bed
> Shall lodge thee till thy wound be throughly healed.
> (110–16)

This is an unfailingly effective scene of high comedy.

The contrast in the Julia/Lucetta exchange between speech and silence when communicating love recurs in 2.1 and 2.2. In 2.1, Silvia picks up Valentine's broken-off 'And yet —' and develops it into an elaborate speech which uses more of the patterning of the first two scenes:

> A pretty period. Well, I guess the sequel.
> And yet I will not name it; and yet I care not.
> And yet take this [the letter] again; and yet I thank you,
> Meaning henceforth to trouble you no more.

To which Speed with characteristic irony adds: 'And yet you will, and yet another yet' (2.1.106–11). By contrast, when Julia and Proteus part, the scene is very short, and Julia even leaves the stage without saying goodbye, upon which Proteus says:

> What, gone without a word?
> Ay, so true love should do: it cannot speak,
> For truth hath better deeds than words to grace it.
> (2.2.16–18)

It has indeed; and we soon see what Proteus' 'deeds' reveal about his vowed 'truth' to Julia.

When Proteus meets Silvia, Julia is 'quite forgotten' (2.4.193); and when he and Valentine are left alone, Valentine extends the lyrical language of the play into a new extravagance, which Proteus calls 'braggartism', in order to exalt Silvia at Julia's expense. Julia, he says,

> shall be dignified with this high honour,
> To bear my lady's train, lest the base earth
> Should from her vesture chance to steal a kiss
> And of so great a favour growing proud,
> Disdain to root the summer-swelling flower,
> And make rough winter everlastingly.
> (2.4.156–61)

This is probably the most hyperbolical speech in the play; and it has the effect, of course, of intensifying Proteus' interest in Silvia. In doing so, it interestingly connects with two of Shakespeare's later works. In his narrative poem *The Rape of Lucrece* (1594), Shakespeare makes the crucial point that it was the bragging of Lucrece's husband Collatine about his wife's qualities that drew the rapist Tarquin's attention to her in the first place: 'why is Collatine the publisher | Of that rich jewel he should keep unknown | From thievish ears . . . ?' (33–5); and at the other end of his career, in *Cymbeline* (1610), it is Posthumus' bragging about his wife's perfections that provokes Giacomo into wagering that he can seduce her: 'I make my wager rather against your confidence than her reputation' (1.4.108–9). In fact Innogen in *Cymbeline*, like Silvia, escapes rape, as Lucrece does not; but the combination of lyricism, extravagance, and potential sexual violence in what was probably Shakespeare's first play and one of his last testifies to his enduring interest in competitive sexuality. And the similarities with *Lucrece* and *Cymbeline* help to underline the way in which *The Two Gentlemen* begins to darken at this stage, as in Proteus' ensuing soliloquy:

> Is it mine eye, or *Valentine's praise*,
> Her true perfection, or my false transgression
> That makes me, reasonless, to reason thus?
> (2.4.194–6, my italics)

Just before he left, Valentine had apologized to Proteus:

> Forgive me that I do not dream on thee
> Because thou seest me dote upon my love.
> (170–1)

The intimacy (again) of the expression here helps to emphasize the growing tension between the demands of friendship and love, or between one kind of love and another, and Proteus underlines this tension in his soliloquy:

> Methinks my zeal to Valentine is cold,
> And that I love him not as I was wont.
> (201–2)

And in his next soliloquy (2.6), the patterned language from earlier on takes a sinister turn: 'Love bade me swear, and love bids me forswear' (6).

That speech provides an ironic context for Julia's plan to follow
her beloved to Milan disguised as a page. While Proteus' soliloquy
uses the patterning of earlier scenes to darker purpose, perhaps
Julia's language suggests that the play's lyricism can be more
functional than it seems at first. In this scene, she uses an
extended comparison to express her desire to follow Proteus:

> The current that with gentle murmur glides,
> Thou know'st, being stopped, impatiently doth rage.
> But when his fair course is not hinderèd
> He makes sweet music with th'enamelled stones,
> Giving a gentle kiss to every sedge
> He overtaketh in his pilgrimage.
>
> (2.7.25–30)

For Arthur Quiller-Couch ('Q'), who enjoyed the play 'as a light
and jocund Italianate comedy', this passage was nonetheless 'too
mellifluous . . . it keeps the speaker dallying luxuriously with an
image while the dramatic moment slips away';[1] and yet more
than one modern actress has been able, without sacrificing the
'mellifluous' lyricism of the speech, to use those lines as a means
of persuading Lucetta to let her have her way and help her to
follow Proteus. When played like that, Lucetta's anxious response
'Pray heaven he prove [faithful] when you come to him' (79)
reinforces the darker context of Proteus' preceding soliloquy,
casting a fleeting shadow by contrast with Julia's enthusiastic
eloquence, without destroying the human warmth and wit
with which the two of them enjoy discussing the details of Julia's
disguise.

Wooing (and Dramatic) Technique

Just as the play's language to some extent takes a wry view of
lovers' behaviour, so do the events on stage, particularly in 3.1,
where the Duke bit by bit lures Valentine into revealing his plan to
abduct Silvia, and 4.2, where Proteus serenades Silvia watched by
Julia in disguise. Both scenes also raise the issue of the limitations
or otherwise of Shakespeare's dramatic technique in this early
play.

---

[1] The New Shakespeare, 2nd edn. (Cambridge, 1955), pp. vii, x–xi.

The details of Valentine's planned elopement with Silvia employ the stock-in-trade of romance stories: the lady in the tower, the distant suitor, the daring climb to her window—so much so, indeed, that in Robin Phillips's production of 1970, Ian Richardson as Proteus was regularly convulsed with laughter at the idea of Valentine using a 'corded ladder'.[1] And the clichés of romantic behaviour are matched by the clichés with which Valentine urges the Duke to woo *his* lady. The Duke claims that he has 'long ago . . . forgot [how] to court', adding that 'the fashion of the time is changed' (3.1.85–6), and he asks Valentine to advise him about fashionable wooing. In fact, the fashions that Valentine recommends have a long history. When he advises the Duke to

> Win her with gifts, if she respect not words.
> Dumb jewels often in their silent kind
> More than quick words do move a woman's mind
> (89–91)

he echoes, for example, Ovid's *Ars Amatoria* (*The Art of Love*) 2.275–8: 'poems are praised, but costly gifts are sought . . . Now truly is the age of gold; by gold comes many an honour, by gold is affection gained.' And Valentine's implication that a woman coquettishly says the opposite of what she means, 'For "Get you gone" she doth not mean "Away"', finds a parallel in Lyly's *Sappho and Phao* 1.4.50–1: 'Where we cry "Away", do we not presently say "Go to" [i.e. "Come on"]?' The clunking couplet with which Valentine concludes this speech is a fitting climax to the cynical clichés of his advice to the Duke.

> That man that hath a tongue I say is no man
> If with his tongue he cannot win a woman.
> (93–105)

Those clichés are, of course, quite different from the romantic ones we have heard from Valentine earlier, to such an extent that Clifford Leech in his Arden edition says that they are 'difficult to reconcile with the romantic love that Valentine has been professing' (p. 58); but aren't his man-of-the-world sentiments simply telling the Duke what he thinks the Duke wants to hear? Even so, the dialogue is a bit halting in this scene: the Duke's 'How shall I

---

[1] For the possible origin of Valentine's 'anchoring hooks' (3.1.118), see the commentary.

fashion me to wear a cloak?' always sounds to me particularly lame: of course he knows how! But the stage action, as Valentine's embarrassment intensifies and his rope ladder is revealed (with nice ingenuity in the BBC television version, where he has it wrapped around himself) builds to an effective comic climax— before it all turns sour as the Duke denounces him for his upstart pretensions. Stanley Wells argues that this episode most clearly represents the unevenness of the play:

the comedy and the pathos are imperfectly fused. . . . Valentine stands revealed as a complete and utter ass, but his response to the Duke's subsequent sentence of banishment is so deeply felt, so touchingly idealistic, and so gracefully expressed as to require a complete shift in the actor's presentation of the character and in the audience's attitude to him.[1]

That impression of Valentine as an 'utter ass' is perhaps an inevitable consequence of the play's mockery of the absurdity of conventional lovers' behaviour; but it is also worth pointing out that in at least two modern stagings, David Thacker's in 1991 and Edward Hall's in 1998, the audiences audibly enjoyed Valentine's increasing discomfiture without, it seemed, losing sympathy with him. Richard Bonneville in Thacker's production, especially, was able with apparent ease to make the transition from a rather dim-witted hero to a very simple, genuine, convinced and convincing delivery of his soliloquy in response to his banishment, making much of the powerful phrase about Silvia: 'She is my essence' (3.1.182). He was beginning to grow up. Perhaps, then, despite its unevenness, the scene may be more playable than it seems at first; and the serenade scene, 4.2, is on an altogether higher level of accomplishment.

This scene, which re-introduces Julia to the action in her disguise as the page Sebastian, is the first in the play to make use of theatrical perspective. Julia and the Host, presumably near the front of the stage, watch Proteus and the musicians serenade Silvia at her window, presumably the balcony at the back of Elizabethan stages. As often in his comedies, Shakespeare uses music to make points about the characters and their relationships. The musicians presumably tune (l. 25) during the conversation

---

[1] *Shakespeare: The Poet and his Plays*, pp. 41–2.

between Julia and the Host (26–37). The song itself is a graceful assembly of the hyperboles of Elizabethan love poetry: Silvia is 'Holy', a goddess (l. 40); she can help cure Cupid's blindness (45–6); and she exceeds in value everything on earth (49–51). The language is well suited both to the attitude of the wooer and to the recipient, at least as he regards her. Line 55 suggests that Proteus himself sings the song, as in most modern productions,[1] and as in the source for the scene in Montemayor's *Diana*, where the musicians accompany 'the sweet voice of my Don Felix' (the heroine, Felismena, corresponding to Julia, is speaking). If the actor does sing (and accompany?) the song himself, that gives additional focus and edge both to his wooing of Silvia and to Julia's reactions. Again, the suggestion for these came from Felismena's next lines in the *Diana*: 'the great joy that I felt in hearing him cannot be imagined; for methought I heard him now as in that happy and past time of our loves. But after . . . seeing with mine eyes and hearing with mine ears that this music was bestowed upon another and not on me, God knows what a bitter death it was unto my soul' (p. 235). This was clearly the inspiration for the next exchange between Julia and the Host. He questions her about the music, and her replies enable her to express the depth of her disappointment in Proteus:

HOST How now, are you sadder than you were before? How do you, man?
　　The music likes you not.
JULIA You mistake: the musician likes me not.　　　　　　　(4.2.53–5)

Here the word-play points the emotional sense. The Host says, in effect, 'the music doesn't please you'; Julia replies that 'the musician doesn't love me'. Then a marked modulation in the music enables Julia to go further:

> HOST Hark what fine change is in the music.
> JULIA Ay, that 'change' is the spite.
> HOST You would have them always play but one thing?
> JULIA I would always have one play but one thing.
>
> 　　　　　　　　　　　　(4.2.66–9)

Shakespeare expands the situation that he found in Montemayor to involve Silvia in the scene, and her dialogue with Proteus is

---

[1] No contemporary music for the song exists. This edition offers a setting based on an Elizabethan melody in Appendix A.

punctuated by Julia's asides to the audience (the Host having fallen asleep). Silvia's response to Proteus' wooing is forthright: 'my will is even this, | That presently you hie you home to bed'. She is clearly unimpressed by the sentiments of the song:

> Think'st thou I am so shallow, so conceitless [unintelligent],
> To be seducèd by thy flattery,
> That hast deceived so many with thy vows?

When Proteus pretends that Julia is dead, Julia herself comments: ' 'Twere false if I should speak it, | For I am sure she is not burièd.' And when, still more desperately, Proteus claims that Valentine is also dead, Silvia responds in lines that, for the audience, echo Julia's aside:

> And so suppose am I, for in his grave,
> Assure thyself, my love is burièd.

In this passage, the patterned repetitions of the play's style take an interesting turn: Silvia's (unconscious) echo of Julia's words is an anticipation of her sympathy with Julia at 4.4.171–2, and of the way in which the two heroines come together in fellow-feeling. That later scene is also anticipated in the language of this one. Proteus asks for Silvia's portrait,

> For since the substance of your perfect self
> Is else [elsewhere] devoted, I am but a shadow,
> And to your shadow will I make true love.

Apart from emphasizing the emptiness, or at least superficiality, of Proteus' love for Silvia in that last line, this speech establishes the characteristically Shakespearian contrast between shadow and substance, illusion and reality, that is developed later. The reaction of the two heroines is similar, and tough. Julia immediately comments: 'If 'twere a substance, you would sure deceive it'; and Silvia goes further, using the language of the Sonnets discussed on p. 33 above:

> I am very loath to be your idol, sir . . .
> But . . . your falsehood shall become you well
> To worship shadows and adore false shapes.
>   (4.2.90–127)

Their triangular relationship is greatly developed in 4.4. In the exchange between Proteus and the disguised Julia, Proteus is immediately attracted to this 'youth', an unconscious re-awakening of his love for Julia:

> Sebastian, I have entertainèd thee
> . . . chiefly for thy face and thy behaviour,
> Which, if my augury deceive me not,
> Witness good bringing up, fortune, and truth.
> $(4.4.61-7)$

It might be argued that once again Proteus is judging by mere appearances; it might be more persuasively argued that he is responding to the person, Julia, beneath the page's disguise. And when Proteus and Julia/Sebastian discuss Julia's love for him, Julia transforms the earlier patterned style to express the intensity of her feelings:

> She dreams on him that has forgot her love;
> You dote on her that cares not for your love.
> 'Tis pity love should be so contrary.
> $(4.4.79-81)$

Now, love is not merely romantic, as it was earlier; it is 'contrary', perverse, difficult. Julia herself is maturing from the light comedy heroine who ostentatiously tore up her lover's letter and then had to re-assemble it on her hands and knees, or who so enthusiastically planned to follow her lover like a heroine of romance; she now has to face tough realities: betrayal, love not being ideal but 'contrary'— and having to serve her lover as his page and to advocate his suit to her rival.

In the soliloquy in which she comments on her situation, Julia again makes use of the play's patterned language to express her dilemma:

> Because he loves her, he despiseth me;
> Because I love him, I must pity him.

And when she says

> I am my master's true-confirmèd love,
> But cannot be true servant to my master
> Unless I prove false traitor to myself
> $(4.4.93-103)$

she echoes the phrasing of Proteus' soliloquy of betrayal in 2.6:

47

> I cannot now prove constant to myself
> Without some treachery used to Valentine.
>
> (2.6.31–2)

Julia, however, will use *her* 'treachery' to serve Proteus: it is interesting to see how Shakespeare is transforming the significance of
the language as he goes along. He does so again with the 'shadow'
and 'substance' of 4.2 in Julia's second soliloquy in this scene; but
before that there is a very telling exchange between Julia and
Silvia. At line 119, Julia gives Silvia a letter. It should be from
Proteus to Silvia, but of course it is the wrong letter. Julia has
given her a letter from Proteus to herself, perhaps that from 1.2,
'pieced together so that the audience could recognize it'.[1] Does
Julia deliberately give Silvia the wrong letter, as arguably she
deliberately gives Proteus the wrong ring in the final scene? If
so, Shakespeare's conception of Julia is of a character who is
resourceful and quick-witted as well as heartbroken. It is a perfectly possible interpretation, and one that chimes well with her
resolve at the end of her previous soliloquy:

> Yet will I woo for him, but yet so coldly
> As, heaven it knows, I would not have him speed.
>
> (4.4.104–5)

And in the soliloquy which ends the scene, her comparison of her
own fair hair to Silvia's auburn keeps the speech on a light level:

> If that be all the difference in his love,
> I'll get me such a coloured periwig.
>
> (187–8)

However heartbroken she may be, Julia maintains her sense of
humour; and so, at this stage, the play maintains a balance
between irony and intensity; but does it sustain that balance into
the finale? That is the crucial question of the play; but before
trying to answer it, a word is needed about those who put the
lovers' behaviour in perspective.

Lance, Speed, and Crab

The two gentlemen have hardly parted in the first scene before
Valentine's servant Speed arrives to engage Proteus in extended

---

[1] Harold Brooks, cited in Leech, p. xx.

word-play about 'laced muttons' (i.e. prostitutes) and to mock him about his love for Julia. His cross-talk act with Proteus (1.1.70–138), which lasts almost as long as the conversation between Valentine and Proteus that precedes it, reveals Speed as the pert, facetious page-boy from Lyly's comedies, and the part may have been taken by a boy actor, as it is in the BBC television version. The laborious witticisms of this exchange seem prime examples of what Dr Johnson meant when he said that 'a quibble was to [Shakespeare] the fatal Cleopatra for which he lost the world, and was content to lose it';[1] but what can seem dead on the page can work surprisingly well in performance, as it did in Edward Hall's 1998 production, where Proteus and a cocky manservant of a Speed took the whole exchange at great speed, scoring points off each other (and incidentally suggesting a reason for Speed's name), to the audible delight of the audience. And in the process they set up from the outset the way in which Speed and Lance provide an ironic commentary on the passions of their masters.

If Speed mocks the love affair between Proteus and Julia in this scene, he does the same, still more directly, for Valentine and Silvia later, openly mocking his master's love-sickness at 2.1.16– 29, and pointing out that Silvia, in asking Valentine to write a letter for her to send to a lover and then giving it to him, is declaring her love for him—something that Valentine has so far failed to notice. The irony that is verbal here is achieved by both verbal means and stage action in the next two scenes. As Proteus parts from Julia, he says:

> The tide is now. (*Julia weeps*) Nay, not thy tide of tears,
> That tide will stay me longer than I should.
>
> (2.2.14–15)

And in the next scene, a weeping Lance uses the same pun as he and his dog part from his family:

PANTHINO Away, ass, you'll lose the tide if you tarry any longer.
LANCE It is no matter if the tied were lost, for it is the unkindest tied that ever any man tied.
PANTHINO What's the unkindest tide?
LANCE Why, he that's tied here, Crab my dog.   (2.3.34–9)

---

[1] Preface to Johnson's edition of Shakespeare's *Plays* (1765), i. 23–4.

On a more extended scale, Lance's catalogue of the virtues and vices of the milkmaid whom he proposes to marry clearly counterpoint, on a more prosaic level, the love affairs in the main plot. And if the conclusion is ultimately dictated by financial considerations, so is the Duke's plan to marry Silvia to Thurio, and Lance's materialism does not compare unfavourably with his master's treachery and betrayal. Indeed, in some ways, as Stanley Wells observes, Lance is 'a figure of unsophisticated but basic human decency',[1] particularly when he instinctively mistrusts Proteus' treatment of Valentine (he cannot *know* of his betrayal) at 3.1.260–1—'I am but a fool, look you, and yet I have the wit to think my master is a kind of a knave'—and when he takes the whipping intended for Crab (4.4.24–9). Furthermore, the devotion of Lance for the undeserving Crab obviously parallels Julia's for the undeserving Proteus.

The prose of Lance's two great monologues (2.3.1–31, 4.4.1–38) offsets the lyrical verse of the lovers, and is arguably the finer achievement in theatrical terms, which is no doubt why some commentators have felt that Lance's role is a later addition. In addressing the audience so directly, both speeches are in the great tradition of English popular entertainers, extending from Richard Tarlton, as I have suggested above, via the Victorian music hall to the stand-up comics of our own time. One of the finest of these, Frankie Howerd, played Lance for BBC radio in 1958; he was a master of timing, and in this part timing is all. The elaborately balanced phrasing of these monologues provides a prosaic counterpoint to the patterning of the verse discussed so far. In his analysis of the first monologue, Peter Hall, who directed Patrick Wymark's classic performance of Lance at Stratford-upon-Avon in 1960, points out that the effect of the speech depends upon its 'strong rhythmic base'; this is initially 'partly produced by antithesis, partly by alliteration': 'I have received my proportion, like the prodigious son, and am going with Sir Proteus to the Imperial's court' (2.3.3–5). Later, the prose becomes more colloquial, to accompany the by-play with the shoes that represent Lance's father and mother (14–19). But the language, confident as it is, constitutes only half of the total impact; the other is provided by the dog playing Crab. As Hall says, 'the dog becomes the

---

[1] *Shakespeare: The Poet and his Plays*, p. 44.

8. Lance and Crab, by Richard Westall (1765–1836).

straight man in a cross-talk act. He is the stooge. If he does nothing, the actor can time the laugh off the dog's lack of reaction. And if he makes any movement—rolling his eyes, scratching his ears, wagging his tail—there is likely to be an even bigger laugh.' In short, Shakespeare has brilliantly written the speech so that the actor can use *anything* the dog does. As Hall concludes, 'the dog gives the scene an immediacy and a danger which is a comic contrast to the high-flown emotions of the young lovers.'[1]

This technique is developed further in Lance's second monologue. As in his first, it comments on the preceding scene, which introduces Sir Eglamour, who, in true chivalric style, proclaims himself Silvia's 'servant'; but even before we discover (5.3.6) that he will desert Silvia in the forest, his knight errantry seems a faded, remote affair as soon as we hear Lance's colloquial voice cutting across the centuries.[2] He, too, has a 'servant', of a very different kind from Silvia's: 'When a man's servant shall play the cur with him, look you, it goes hard. One that I brought up of a puppy, one that I saved from drowning when three or four of his blind brothers and sisters went to it' (4.4.1–5). As Lance develops his account of the ungrateful Crab's misdemeanours, and his own self-sacrifice to save him from the consequences, he continues to involve the audience by direct address: 'You shall judge' (4.4.15); 'How many masters would do this for his servant?' (27–8). But then, unlike his previous monologue, he turns to Crab and talks directly to him— 'Thou think'st not of this now' (33)—as he builds to Crab's crowning offence of urinating over Silvia's skirt: no wonder she thought the 'dog was a cur' (47). As he does so, the actor invites the dog to react to him; but as before, whether Crab *does* react (some do) or not, the actor can use whatever he does.

All this prepares for the dialogue that follows between Lance and Proteus. Proteus apparently sent Silvia a tiny lap-dog as a present, which was stolen from Lance, so he offered her Crab instead. Proteus is appalled—'didst thou offer her *this* from me?' (52)—and fires Lance, appointing the disguised Julia in his place. This situation has two interesting implications. First, it reinforces the connection between Lance and Julia: a man who is faithful to an undeserving servant, and a woman who is loyal to an undeserving master. But it also raises a wider issue. This is Lance's last appearance in the play; neither he nor Speed appears in the final scene.[3] The reason is not far to seek. If either servant

---

[1] *Shakespeare's Advice to the Players* (2003), pp. 69–75.

[2] Michael Dobson extends this point when he says that Crab's presence exploits 'the breach of dramatic decorum constituted by putting a real dog among pretend people' ('A Dog at All Things', *Performance Research* 5 (2), (2000), 116–24; p. 118).

[3] In 1998, Edward Hall rationalized Speed's absence by having Valentine dismiss Speed when he joined the outlaws.

extended their ironic commentary, whether verbally or by a raised eyebrow—or if Crab yawned—at the events of the finale, the impact of the final reconciliation would be even more precarious than it is now.[1]

'In love / Who respects friend?': the Final Scene

Modern opinion about the final scene is fairly represented by Stanley Wells when he writes: 'The basic problem of this scene is that Shakespeare is too obviously manipulating his characters, huddling events together in order to bring the action to a conclusion in which the claims of love and friendship will be reconciled, without fully articulating the emotions his characters are required to undergo.'[2] Most commentators feel that the action is carried out with indecent haste, so much so that it has been suspected that the scene was abbreviated. In their New Shakespeare edition of 1921, for example, Arthur Quiller-Couch and John Dover Wilson argue that the scene has been truncated and adapted by another hand. The difficulty with this argument is that there is no sign of abbreviation in the Folio text itself, none of those tell-tale broken verse lines, except perhaps for Proteus' irregular line 'My shame and guilt confounds me' (5.4.73)—and for that, there are strong dramatic reasons, as will emerge. Otherwise, Proteus' attempted rape and Valentine's forgiveness are expressed in regular iambic verse (which in itself perhaps exacerbates adverse reaction to them). We must work with the text that we have, and try to discover, with the help of modern stagings, what is actually going on in this scene.

As Silvia resists Proteus' ever-intensifying attentions, she accuses him of being a 'counterfeit to thy true friend'. His reply, 'In love | Who respects friend?' is the crunch-point of the scene and perhaps of the play. It exposes the raw nerve at the heart of the central relationships, the dark reality lurking beneath the wit and lyricism with which the play has in general presented lovers' behaviour and their absurdities. And Silvia gives him his answer: 'All men but Proteus' (5.4.53–4). It is this unsparing statement of

---

[1] Compare Leech: 'a glance from Launce to Crab or a pert comment from Speed would have too obviously deflated the romancing of the two gentlemen' (p. lxxiii).

[2] *Shakespeare: The Poet and his Plays*, pp. 45–6.

9. Valentine rescuing Silvia from Proteus, by William Holman Hunt (1827–1910), 1851.

truth that provokes the attempted rape and Valentine's inter-
vention. His reaction is initially expressed in an outburst
which might be taken as the other side of his earlier romantic
extravagance:

> Thou common friend, that's without faith or love,
> For such is a friend now. Treacherous man,
> Thou hast beguiled my hopes. . . .
>
> (62–4)

But as his speech of disappointment intensifies, it leads to a simple
phrase that perhaps cuts through more painfully than anything
else in the play: 'The private wound is deepest.' Proteus' reply is
the one irregular verse line in the exchange, suggesting a pause
before it: 'My shame and guilt confounds me.' After his three and
a half lines of repentance, Valentine forgives him, picking up and
completing his verse line, so that there is no room for a pause; his
response is immediate:

> I do as truly suffer
> As e'er I did commit.
> VALENTINE   Then I am paid.

And there follow Valentine's controversial lines of forgiveness:

> And that my love may appear plain and free,
> All that was mine in Silvia I give thee.
>
> (5.4.71–83)

These are the lines that have provoked especial outrage; but what
exactly do they imply? That Valentine is handing Silvia over to
Proteus? That, presumably, is what Julia thinks, if her swoon is
genuine (or even if it isn't). What Silvia thinks we have no means
of knowing, since she remains silent for the rest of the play. Is she
traumatized by Proteus' attempt to rape her? Or is she shocked at
Valentine's giving her to her would-be rapist? Or both?

Theatre productions have responded to these issues in a number
of ways. From the eighteenth century to the mid nineteenth (and
often thereafter, including sometimes in the early twentieth
century) Valentine's offer was simply omitted. It has been included
in most modern productions, though with different emphases.
In Robin Phillips's 1970 version, for example, Valentine, before
making his offer, kissed Silvia and then kissed Proteus. The line
clearly meant 'the love that I have given to Silvia I also extend to

you'—which is what I think it *does* mean, and how it was interpreted in Leon Rubin's 1984 Ontario production and in the BBC television one. David Thacker in 1991 involved Silvia herself in the situation; and since his handling of the denouement was widely considered to be especially successful, it deserves to be examined in some detail.

As in Phillips's production, Proteus' attempted rape was graphically staged. Valentine had to drag Proteus violently off Silvia, and a fight developed, a harsher version of the friendly horseplay in which they had engaged in their first scene. Taking the hint suggested by the incomplete verse line, Proteus held a huge pause before saying 'My shame and guilt confounds me'. This pause provoked a great deal of discussion, especially from Robert Smallwood in his review: 'At some performances that little enigmatic flicker of a smile seemed to be discernible before he began to speak. When it was, the repentance was clearly a pure sham, and they were all being duped; when it was not, we had genuine penitence and thus the possibility of a comic ending'.[1] Since my recollection of this moment did not entirely correspond with either of Smallwood's alternatives—I recalled a clenching of the mouth that spoke of inner tension, even resentment—I asked the actor of Proteus, Finbar Lynch,[2] no doubt unfairly, to cast his mind back fifteen years to that moment. He generously did so, and said that while he was sure that his performance varied from night to night, both he and his director believed that Proteus' repentance was genuine. He added that David Thacker had encouraged them to play each emotion for all it was worth, pushing each to extremes, and to experience each fully as it came, including Valentine's offer of Silvia to Proteus. After Proteus' 'I do as truly suffer | As e'er I did commit' (76–7), there was a silence in which, says Smallwood, 'one was aware of Silvia looking very hard at Valentine, willing him to accept this apology . . ., the first to forgive him. The notorious "All that was mine in Silvia I give thee" thus came to mean something like "the mutual love and trust between Silvia and me is something in which you can now share", and even as we were taking this in, Julia collapsed and we

---

[1] 'Shakespeare Performed', *SQ* 43 (1992), p. 352.
[2] In 1991, he was Barry Lynch. 'Barry', he explained, is a standard diminutive of 'Finbar'.

were into the mechanical unwinding of the plot that concludes the play. It was a daring and in many ways brilliant solution to what has so often been regarded, on the page, as an intractable problem.' I admired it too; but the objections are, first, as Small-wood admits, that in transforming Silvia's silence into the 'motor' for Valentine's forgiveness, the character 'had become the chattel of the director's sentimental invention', and second, more prosaically, that, as Shakespeare has written the scene, there is *no* pause, no 'silence', in which Silvia can intervene, because Valentine's 'Then I am paid' completes Proteus' half-line of repentance. For all that, there was a sense of the whole play being enlarged, taken on to a higher plane of experience, as if the characters were transformed by their experiences from the callow to the heartfelt, as at the end the two gentlemen took hands again.

Edward Hall is emphatically not a director who is given to sentimentality, still less to allowing Shakespeare's verse-structure to be disrupted by unwritten pauses. As I said earlier, his 1998 production was one of the best-spoken of those I have seen, and that helped greatly in dealing with this tricky scene. Like Thacker, he encouraged his cast to think hard about each line before delivering it, never to let either repentance or forgiveness become automatic. Also like Thacker, he pushed the emotions in this final scene to extremes, as in the attempted rape, when Proteus 'ran on stage with Silvia, manhandling her obscenely and apparently about to expose himself as she struggled and cringed, coat ripped and stockings torn. Valentine's arrival was only just in the nick of time'.[1] But if the rape was pushed to an extreme, so were the heartfelt penitence and forgiveness. And Hall built on the sympathetic coming together of Julia and Silvia in 4.4.130–75 to create an interesting final tableau. The two ladies took hands, partly as a defence mechanism for being to some extent excluded by the intensity of the reconciliation between the two men, but not, ultimately, to the exclusion of the men, to whom they extended their hands, so that Valentine's last line of reunion, 'One feast, one house, one mutual happiness' did not emerge as something irredeemably hollow.

---

[1] Robert Smallwood, 'Shakespeare Performances in England, 1998', *SS* 52 (1999), p. 231.

That ending, however, depends on what happens *after* Valentine's offer. Does Julia, for example, actually faint or pretend to? If the former, that will prolong the intensity of the preceding episode; if the latter, that will help ease the scene towards its 'happy' ending. Unfortunately, the text gives no clear guidance. Julia's movement into prose at 5.4.87–8 might indicate the grogginess of a recovery from a fainting fit; but it might equally suggest that Julia is deliberately improvising, giving Proteus the wrong ring, in order to pave the way to revealing herself to him (as perhaps at 4.4.119–21 she deliberately gave the wrong letter to Silvia). This would not imply a scheming, contriving Julia, simply a resourceful heroine with her wits about her, who realizes that she needs to prise Proteus away from Valentine as much as from Silvia. And it is by focusing upon Julia's disguise that the play is able to conclude on a lighter note than the Valentine/Proteus exchange:

> VALENTINE
> What think you of this page, my lord?
> DUKE
> I think the boy hath grace in him, he blushes.
> VALENTINE
> I warrant you, my lord, more grace than boy.
> DUKE What mean you by that saying?
>
> (5.4.162–5)

Some productions have Julia reveal her sex at this point, others have the Duke see through her disguise and appreciate the joke, as Eric Porter did at Stratford-upon-Avon in 1960. This enables Valentine's reference to Proteus' 'penance' for his betrayal to achieve an appropriately light touch, and for a reasonably happy ending to be achieved. But it is a close-run thing, and a convincing close depends much upon the playing. Benedict Nightingale concluded his review of Edward Hall's production, in which he found the end 'surprisingly moving': 'Could there be life and happiness after the ending of what is, on the face of it, one of the Bard's most perfunctory romances? Maybe' (*The Times*, 23 December 1998).

Perhaps one could build on that tentative 'Maybe' and suggest something a little more positive by proposing that *The Two Gentlemen* is about a learning process, about growing up. Julia's development from an idealistic, romantically-inclined girl to a woman who has to witness her lover's attempt to rape another woman is only the most considerable of the play's journeys. Proteus and Valentine move from a mocking attitude to love to a crisis in which they are forced to declare their love for one another, and at the same time to come to an understanding with their future wives. Those wives have to accept, because it is so overtly presented to them, that they do not have exclusive claims on the love of their husbands. To put it like that is perhaps to subject a lightweight, lyrical, witty comedy to undue strain—but no more than the play itself does in its final scene.

The Text

The Two Gentlemen of Verona first appeared in print in the First Folio of Shakespeare's plays in 1623. It was entered in the Stationers' Register on 8 November 1623, together with the fifteen other plays not previously registered for publication. The Folio text presents few difficulties, though it exhibits the characteristics, and sometimes the eccentricities, of Ralph Crane, the professional scribe who, it is generally agreed, prepared the text for the Folio. Because of the fortunate survival of certain plays, notably Thomas Middleton's *A Game at Chess*, both in the dramatist's manuscripts and in transcripts by Crane, we have a great deal of valuable information about Crane's scribal characteristics and about how he handled an author's text.[1] The most noticeable feature of the Folio text of *The Two Gentlemen* is its 'massed entrances'—that is, the listing at the start of each scene of everyone who appears in it, with no indication of where a character enters within the scene or (mostly; there are exceptions) leaves. This feature alone makes it clear that Crane was not transcribing a prompt-book, since such a procedure would be useless for practical performance. Crane's transcription was aimed not at performers but at readers, and was almost certainly based on the 'classical' layout of Ben Jonson's *Works* in 1616. Trevor Howard-Hill has demonstrated how Crane edited 'the raw material of Middleton's dramatic manuscripts into finished literary texts

---

[1] F. P. Wilson, 'Ralph Crane, Scrivener to the King's Players', *The Library*, 4th series, 7 (1926–7), 194–215; T. H. Howard-Hill, *Ralph Crane and Some Shakespeare First Folio Comedies* (Charlottesville, 1972), and 'Shakespeare's Earliest Editor, Ralph Crane', *SS 44* (Cambridge, 1992), 113–29.

designed to allow readers to create freshly a performance of the play in the theatre of their imagination'. He explains how Crane did this: he 'imposed a decorum on his copy that was . . . textual in its marking of emphasis and . . . the use of italics and parentheses, and persistently reformative by means of . . . emendation of the text, and attention to matters which might be distressing to readers'.[1] In other words, he interfered substantially with his author's text.

He did not do so lightly or irresponsibly. As Howard-Hill says, 'Crane was disposed to get things right.' But his procedure inevitably raises problems of editorial interpretation, especially since he was not consistent in his practice. Not every transcript shows evidence of all of Crane's scribal habits; but the Folio text of *The Two Gentlemen* contains enough of them to leave no doubt that it is based on a Crane transcript. His punctuation was heavy. His transcripts show a liberal use of parentheses (round brackets), hyphens, superfluous apostrophes, and colons. It is not always possible to be sure how many of these features derive from Crane's copy and how many from the compositors who had to set it in type, since neither spelling nor punctuation was standardized at this time; but what makes Crane's presence virtually certain is the sheer number of his habits here.

The first few lines reveal his generous use of parentheses where this edition simply uses commas, as at 1.1.7 / TLN 10: '(liuing dully sluggardiz'd at home)'.[2] His uses of parenthesis and redundant apostrophe are combined in '(hap'ly)' (1.1.12 / TLN 15), a good illustration of what E. A. J. Honigmann calls Crane's 'partiality for placing single words in brackets, a less common phenomenon than the use of brackets in general'.[3] Crane's liking for hyphenated compounds occurs, for example, at 'Corded-ladder' (2.6.33 / TLN 962) and 'gentleman-like-dogs' (4.4.16–17 / TLN 1836); and his characteristic spellings in 'Sirha' (e.g. 2.1.7 / TLN 404), 'guift' (4.4.56 / TLN 1875), and 'ceazed' (5.4.33 / TLN 2152).

---

[1] 'Shakespeare's Earliest Editor' (see previous note), p. 124.

[2] For convenience of reference, quotations in this section are keyed both to this edition and to the through line numbering (TLN) provided by Charlton Hinman in *The Norton Facsimile of The First Folio of Shakespeare*, 2nd edn. (1996), conveniently re-issued by the Folio Society, 2006.

[3] *The Texts of 'Othello' and Shakespearian Revision* (1996), p. 59.

Why did Crane choose to use the annoying and theatrically inconvenient device of massed entries for *The Two Gentlemen* but not, for example, for his Folio texts of *The Tempest* or *Measure for Measure*? Howard-Hill points out that one of Middleton's two manuscripts of *A Game at Chess* is rudimentary in what it provides, so that Crane may have looked upon it 'as simply the occasion for preparation of a readable text'.[1] So if he was faced with the 'foul papers', that is Shakespeare's original manuscript of *The Two Gentlemen*, with all its inconsistencies and confusions, he may have felt the freedom, and even the necessity, to impose his own editorial habits and improvements upon it, for the benefit of his readership. We do not *know* that Crane was transcribing Shakespeare's foul papers. Stanley Wells notes that 'the naming of the characters in speech-prefixes exhibits none of the variability that seems often to have been present in Shakespeare's foul papers',[2] but that is easily explained by Crane's conscientious efforts to regularize his text.[3]

On three occasions, however, Crane may be responsible for slight changes in the text. There is some evidence that the play may have been censored: 'save you' at 1.1.70, a standard abbreviation for 'God save you' (where the Folio text has an apostrophe before 'save'), and 'bless the mark', for 'God bless the mark', at 4.4.18. If so, and if this was to conform with the 1606 Act forbidding the name of God to be spoken on stage, that would imply a late revival of *The Two Gentlemen*. But if Crane was, as I have suggested, transcribing Shakespeare's original manuscript, then he himself did the censoring. This is probable. Howard-Hill shows that 'Crane apparently did not approve of swearing of any kind. He also shows a certain sensitivity to sexual and scatological references'.[4] The latter may well be responsible for the (to me) clear misreading at 2.3.48 / TLN 642, where the Folio reading 'thy Taile' for 'my tail' (see the commentary) may therefore be less an error than a deliberate removal of a reference to a sexual practice of which Crane did not approve. Howard-Hill says that *The Two Gentlemen* has no examples of Crane's habit of marking an elision

---

[1] 'Shakespeare's Earliest Editor', p. 116.

[2] *TC*, p. 166.

[3] There are a mere two slips, in the speech-prefixes to 5.2.7 / TLN 2046 and 13 / TLN 2052 (and perhaps to 2.4.114 / TLN 767).

[4] 'Shakespeare's Earliest Editor', p. 122.

with an apostrophe but still spelling the syllable to be elided, and so far as the printed text is concerned, that is true. I suspect, however, that one such lay behind 2.4.162 (see the commentary). Last, and more significant, Crane may be responsible for a variant at 3.2.14 / TLN 1459. This page of the Folio (sig. C4) exists in both a corrected and an uncorrected state. The uncorrected version reads 'heauily', the corrected 'grieuously'.[1] Charlton Hinman shows that some readings of the corrected page almost certainly represent a consultation of the copy (in my interpretation, of Shakespeare's foul papers),[2] and 'heavily', which like 'grievously' means 'sorrowfully', is very likely to be an example of Crane's tendency to replace a word in his copy with another that is broadly synonymous.[3]

Crane probably provided the division into acts and scenes, and the list of characters, in the Folio. He may have done something more far-reaching. *The Two Gentlemen* is an unusually short play. Dover Wilson, whose New Shakespeare edition in 1921 preceded F. P. Wilson's identification of Crane (see p. 59 n. 1), speculated that 'at least 600 lines of the original have disappeared' (p. 81). Howard-Hill shows that Crane 'skilfully reduced' the text of Middleton's *A Game at Chess* in its Trinity manuscript 'by about 787 lines' to create a play which he presumably considered 'more powerful by condensation'.[4] Did he make similar cuts in *The Two Gentlemen*? And if so, why? Without such evidence as exists for *A Game at Chess*, I am reluctant to venture along that treacherous speculative path. On the whole, I think Crane tried to 'get things right', and that such inconsistencies and confusions as remain in the play should be laid at the young Shakespeare's door rather than at Crane's.

---

[1] Both uncorrected and corrected states are usefully reproduced in Hinman's *Facsimile*, pp. 912–13.

[2] *The Printing and Proof-Reading of the First Folio of Shakespeare*, 2 vols. (Oxford, 1963), i. 255.

[3] Howard-Hill, *Ralph Crane and Some Shakespeare First Folio Comedies*, p. 57.

[4] 'Shakespeare's Earliest Editor', pp. 123–4.

EDITORIAL PROCEDURES

THIS edition follows the Editorial Procedures established for the series by Stanley Wells and summarized in Gary Taylor's Oxford Shakespeare edition of *Henry V* (1982), pp. 75–81. In accordance with them, passages from Shakespeare's contemporaries quoted in the introduction and commentary are also modernized even when they are taken from editions using old spelling; as Taylor says, 'If modernizing is valid for Shakespeare's text it is equally valid for passages quoted only to illuminate that text'. Old spelling is reserved for the collations and for passages in the textual introduction where the original printing is relevant: the early use of u, v, i, and j is retained, but not long 's'.

Stage directions such as 'aside' or 'to' a character are all editorial, and are not collated. All changes in directions for stage action are collated, but where the specified action is clearly implied by the dialogue, the change is neither bracketed in the text nor attributed to an earlier editor. Disputable directions are printed in broken brackets.

Quotations from classical works are from the Loeb editions. References to plays by Shakespeare's contemporaries are to the Revels editions, and those to other works by Shakespeare to the Oxford *Complete Works* (second edition, 2005).

Abbreviations and References

The following references are used in the introduction, in the collations, and in the commentary. In all bibliographical references, the place of publication is London, unless otherwise specified.

EDITIONS OF SHAKESPEARE

F, F1	The First Folio, 1623
F2	The Second Folio, 1632
F3	The Third Folio, 1663
F4	The Fourth Folio, 1685

Bond	R. Warwick Bond, *The Two Gentlemen of Verona*, The Arden Shakespeare (1906)
Boswell	James Boswell, *Plays and Poems*, 21 vols. (1821)
Cambridge	W. G. Clark and W. A. Wright, *Works*, The Cambridge Shakespeare, 9 vols. (Cambridge, 1863–6)
Capell	Edward Capell, *Comedies, Histories, and Tragedies*, 10 vols. (1767–8)
Carroll	William C. Carroll, *The Two Gentlemen of Verona*, The Arden Shakespeare, Third Series (2004)
Collier	John Payne Collier, *Works*, 8 vols. (1842–4)
Dover Wilson	Arthur Quiller-Couch and John Dover Wilson, *The Two Gentlemen of Verona*, The New Shakespeare (Cambridge, 1921; 2nd edn., 1955)
Dyce	Alexander Dyce, *Works*, 6 vols. (1857)
Dyce 1868	Alexander Dyce, *Works*, 9 vols., 2nd edn. (1868)
Halliwell	James O. Halliwell, *Works*, 16 vols. (1853–65)
Hanmer	Thomas Hanmer, *Works*, 6 vols. (Oxford, 1743–4)
Johnson	Samuel Johnson, *Plays*, 8 vols. (1765)
Keightley	Thomas Keightley, *Plays*, 6 vols. (1864)
Knight	Charles Knight, *Comedies, Histories, Tragedies, and Poems*, Pictorial Edition, 7 vols. (1838–43)
Leech	Clifford Leech, *The Two Gentlemen of Verona*, The Arden Shakespeare, Second Series (1969)
Malone	Edmond Malone, *Plays and Poems*, 10 vols. (1790)
Norton	*The Norton Shakespeare Based on the Oxford Edition* (New York, 1997)
Oxford	Stanley Wells, Gary Taylor, John Jowett and William Montgomery, *Complete Works* (Oxford, 1986; 2nd edn., 2005)
Pope	Alexander Pope, *Works*, 6 vols. (1723–5)
Rowe	Nicholas Rowe, *Works*, 6 vols. (1709)
Sanders	Norman Sanders, *The Two Gentlemen of Verona*, The Penguin Shakespeare (1968; reissued 2005)
Schlueter	Kurt Schlueter, *The Two Gentlemen of Verona*, The New Cambridge Shakespeare (Cambridge, 1990)
Singer	Samuel W. Singer, *Dramatic Works*, 10 vols. (1856)
Sisson	Charles J. Sisson, *Complete Works* (1954)
Theobald	Lewis Theobald, *Works*, 7 vols. (1733)

OTHER ABBREVIATIONS

Abbott	E. A. Abbott, *A Shakespearian Grammar*, 2nd edn. (1870), cited by paragraph
Bullough	Geoffrey Bullough, *Narrative and Dramatic Sources of Shakespeare*, 8 vols. (1957–75)
Dent	R. W. Dent, *Shakespeare's Proverbial Language: An Index* (Berkeley, 1981)
Moore	Anthony Telford Moore, unpublished research into *The Two Gentlemen of Verona*
OED	*The Oxford English Dictionary*, 2nd edn., 20 vols. (Oxford, 1989)
Onions	C. T. Onions, *A Shakespeare Glossary*, 2nd edn., with enlarged addenda (Oxford, 1953)
Re-Editing	Stanley Wells, *Re-Editing Shakespeare for the Modern Reader* (Oxford, 1984)
Schmidt	Alexander Schmidt, *Shakespeare Lexicon*, 3rd edn., 2 vols. (Berlin, 1902; Dover reprint, New York, 1971)
Shaheen	Naseeb Shaheen, *Biblical References in Shakespeare's Plays* (Newark, Delaware, 1999)
SQ	*Shakespeare Quarterly*
SS	*Shakespeare Survey*
TC	Stanley Wells, Gary Taylor, John Jowett, and William Montgomery, *William Shakespeare: A Textual Companion* (Oxford, 1987)
Tilley	M. P. Tilley, *A Dictionary of the Proverbs in England in the Sixteenth and Seventeenth Centuries* (Ann Arbor, 1950)
Williams	Gordon Williams, *A Glossary of Shakespeare's Sexual Language* (1997)
Wright	Joseph Wright, *The Dialect Dictionary*, 6 vols. (1898–1905)

The Two Gentlemen of Verona

THE PERSONS OF THE PLAY

VALENTINE ⎫
PROTEUS ⎭ two young gentlemen of Verona

SPEED, Valentine's page

JULIA, in love with Proteus

LUCETTA, her waiting-woman

ANTONIO, Proteus' father

PANTHINO, his servant

The DUKE of Milan

SILVIA, his daughter

THURIO, her wealthy suitor

LANCE, Proteus' servant

CRAB, his dog

HOST of an inn, where Julia lodges

EGLAMOUR, Silvia's accomplice in her escape

OUTLAWS

Servants, musicians

THE PERSONS OF THE PLAY *The Two Gentlemen of Verona* is one of only seven Folio texts to give a list of characters (at the end of the play). Several of these plays were set from transcripts by the scrivener Ralph Crane (see Introduction, pp. 59–62), and he was almost certainly responsible for the lists. As his list is not entirely accurate, it is not followed here.

PANTHINO, THURIO Some editions read 'Pantino' and 'Turio', on a supposed analogy with F's 'Protheus'. But since at *Richard Duke of York* (*3 Henry VI*) 3.2.192 F spells the name 'Proteus', the original spellings were indifferent, and the modern form is

'Proteus'. There are no such parallels for the other two names, so F's spellings are retained. In some stage directions, and in F's list of characters, Panthino is called 'Panthion'; but when he is addressed at 1.3.1 (his first appearance) he is called 'Panthino'—correctly, as the verse stresses make clear. F's 'Panthmo' at 1.3.76 looks like a compositorial misreading, and is corrected in F2. 'Panthion' probably originates with Ralph Crane (see previous note) but R. W. Bond suggests that Shakespeare may have used both forms (p. 2).

The Two Gentlemen of Verona

1.1 *Enter Valentine and Proteus*

VALENTINE

Cease to persuade, my loving Proteus;
Home-keeping youth have ever homely wits.
Were't not affection chains thy tender days
To the sweet glances of thy honoured love,
I rather would entreat thy company   5
To see the wonders of the world abroad
Than, living dully sluggardized at home,
Wear out thy youth with shapeless idleness.
But since thou lov'st, love still, and thrive therein,
Even as I would, when I to love begin.   10

1.1.0.1 *Enter . . . Proteus*] *Valentine: Protheus*, and *Speed*. F

Title It is only from this that we know that
the play opens in Verona, which is not
mentioned in the text until 3.1.81, where
it is misleading (see note).

1.1.0.1 *Valentine, Proteus* The two gentlemen are given appropriate names.
St Valentine, a conflation of two early
Italian saints, was the patron saint
of lovers, and 'a Valentine' became a
byword for a true lover, as at 3.1.192.
Proteus was a classical sea-god famous
for changing his shape, described by Ovid
at *Metamorphoses* 2.9 and 8.730–7; in his
translation of 1567, Arthur Golding calls
him 'unstable Proteus', which nicely
catches the significance of the name for
an unstable, changeable character.

1 **Cease to persuade** The play begins in
mid-conversation, sometimes with Valentine's luggage carried on to the stage.
loving This probably establishes their affectionate relationship (compare 'Sweet'
at l. 11) rather than suggesting mockery
of Proteus' love for Julia.
Proteus The verse requires three syllables here, but two elsewhere (e.g. at
l. 56)—though even in those cases it is
possible to pronounce the full name
without losing the rhythm.

2 **Home-keeping . . . wits** Travel was,
then as now, supposed to broaden the
mind. In *The Taming of the Shrew*, which
probably followed *The Two Gentlemen* in
order of composition, Lucentio comes to
study in Padua, 'nursery of arts' (1.1.2),
and Petruccio leaves Verona, 'Where
small experience grows', in order 'to see
the world' (1.2.51, 57). In both plays,
Shakespeare seems to see Verona as a
kind of backwater to be left behind: was
he thinking of Stratford-upon-Avon?
Compare the proverbial 'He who still
keeps home knows nothing' (Dent N274).
ever always
homely simple

3 **Were't not** if it were not for the fact that
affection passion, love
tender young, immature. *OED*'s earliest
example of the phrase 'tender years' is
from 1610 (*adj.* 4). The youth of the two
gentlemen is stressed from the start.

6 **abroad** away from home

7 **sluggardized** made lazy (like a 'sluggard')

8 **shapeless** aimless, without purpose

9 **still** constantly

71

PROTEUS

Wilt thou be gone? Sweet Valentine, adieu.
Think on thy Proteus when thou haply seest
Some rare noteworthy object in thy travel.
Wish me partaker in thy happiness
When thou dost meet good hap; and in thy danger—   15
If ever danger do environ thee—
Commend thy grievance to my holy prayers;
For I will be thy beadsman, Valentine.

VALENTINE

And on a love-book pray for my success?

PROTEUS

Upon some book I love I'll pray for thee.   20

VALENTINE

That's on some shallow story of deep love:
How young Leander crossed the Hellespont.

PROTEUS

That's a deep story of a deeper love,
For he was more than over-shoes in love.

VALENTINE

'Tis true, for you are over-boots in love,   25
And yet you never swam the Hellespont.

PROTEUS

Over the boots? Nay, give me not the boots.

26 swam] F (swom)

12 **haply** by chance (or perhaps 'happily')
15 **hap** fortune
17 **Commend thy grievance** entrust your trouble (Moore)
18 **beadsman** one who prays for another, counting the prayers on the 'beads' of his rosary (a Roman Catholic custom)
19 **love-book** 'Manual of courtship or a romance' (Sanders), rather than the rosary of the previous line.
21 **shallow story of deep love** The word-play on *shallow* (superficial) and *deep* (intense) and on shallow and deep water prepares for the use of the story of Hero and Leander that follows (see next note).
22 **How . . . Hellespont** Hero and Leander were lovers who lived on either side of the Hellespont; swimming across to her, Leander was drowned and became 'one of the patterns of love' mocked by

Rosalind at *As You Like It* 4.1.93–9. The story was familiar in Elizabethan England from Ovid's *Heroides* 18 and 19. Marlowe's poem on the subject was not printed until 1598, but Shakespeare may have seen it in manuscript, although since it was not entered in the Stationers' Register until 28 September 1593, after Marlowe's death, this gives no clue as to when it was written. See note to 3.1.119–20.
23–4 **deep . . . deeper . . . over-shoes** Leander was both deeply in love, and in such deep water that it covered his shoes.
25 **over-boots** Mockingly picks up *over-shoes*, and alludes to the proverbial 'over shoes over boots' (Dent S379).
27 **give . . . boots** don't mock me (proverbial: Dent B537)

VALENTINE

No, I will not; for it boots thee not.

PROTEUS   What?

VALENTINE

To be in love, where scorn is bought with groans,
Coy looks with heart-sore sighs, one fading moment's
    mirth   30
With twenty watchful, weary, tedious nights.
If haply won, perhaps a hapless gain;
If lost, why then a grievous labour won;
However, but a folly bought with wit,
Or else a wit by folly vanquishèd.   35

PROTEUS

So by your circumstance you call me fool.

VALENTINE

So by your circumstance I fear you'll prove.

PROTEUS

'Tis love you cavil at, I am not love.

VALENTINE

Love is your master, for he masters you,
And he that is so yokèd by a fool   40
Methinks should not be chronicled for wise.

PROTEUS

Yet writers say, as in the sweetest bud

---

28 **boots** profits (quibbling on *boots* in the previous line)

29–35 **To be in love . . . vanquishèd** This speech establishes the play's ironic tone in presenting lovers' behaviour, at least to start with, made up, in Sanders's apt summary, 'of Renaissance common-places about romantic love'; it 'contains most of the conventional attitudes attributed to the lover at this period'. Compare Lyly's *Campaspe* 3.5.52–3: 'deep and hollow sighs, sad and melancholy thoughts, wounds and slaughters of conceits'.

30 **Coy** disdainful (Schmidt)

31 **watchful** wakeful (and so keeping watch; compare Sonnet 61.12: 'To play the watchman ever for thy sake.')

32 **haply . . . hapless** Quibbling on 'by chance' and 'unfortunate'.

33 **If lost . . . won** i.e. if the love-suit is

unsuccessful, the lover has gained only grievous labour (Moore)

34 **However** whatever the case
but . . . wit i.e. all that the intellect (*wit*) has obtained through the love-suit is *folly*

36 **circumstance** circumlocution, as at *Merchant* 1.1.154: 'To wind about my love with circumstance'.
you So far, the two friends have used the intimate 'thou' or 'thee'; but in using the formal *you* perhaps Proteus is expressing annoyance at being called a fool. He reverts to 'thee' at l. 55.

37 **circumstance** situation

40 **yokèd** put in a yoke (like a beast of burden)

41 **chronicled for** reputed (as if in a historical chronicle) as

42, 45 **writers say** For the patterned style, see Introduction, p. 39.

The eating canker dwells, so doting love
Inhabits in the finest wits of all.

VALENTINE

And writers say, as the most forward bud   45
Is eaten by the canker ere it blow,
Even so by love the young and tender wit
Is turned to folly, blasting in the bud,
Losing his verdure even in the prime,
And all the fair effects of future hopes.   50
But wherefore waste I time to counsel thee
That art a votary to fond desire?
Once more adieu; my father at the road
Expects my coming, there to see me shipped.

---

43 doting] OXFORD; eating F

42–3 **writers say . . . canker dwells** The
  writers include Shakespeare (compare
  Sonnet 70.7: 'canker vice the sweetest
  buds doth love'), but the idea was proverbial: 'The canker soonest eats the
  fairest rose' (Dent C56).
43 **canker** canker-worm, caterpillar
  doting F has 'eating'. Wells (*Re-Editing*,
  pp. 43–4) comments: 'The double use of
  "eating" may be deliberate' but 'though
  "eating" is appropriate to a "Canker", it is
  so only in the most figurative sense to
  "Loue" . . . and "doting" seems far more
  appropriate to the metaphor sustained in'
  lines 45–50. The slip could be compositorial, or 'Ralph Crane's transcription of
  Shakespeare's handwriting' (see Introduction, pp. 59–62).
43–4 **doting . . . all** Proverbial: 'The finest
  wits are soonest subject to love' (Dent
  W576).
44 **Inhabits** dwells
45–50 The idea, and the language, anticipate *Hamlet* 1.3.39–40: 'The canker galls
  the infants of the spring | Too oft before
  their buttons be disclosed'.
45 **forward** well advanced, early
46 **ere** before
  blow blossom
48 **blasting** withering. Another anticipation
  of the language of *Hamlet*, where Ophelia
  says that Hamlet's 'blown youth' is
  'Blasted with ecstasy [madness]'
  (3.1.162–3).
49 **verdure** greenness, i.e. freshness

49 **prime** spring (of life, as in modern 'prime
  of life')
50 **effects** fulfilment
51 **counsel** advise
52 **votary to** addicted to, with the religious
  overtone implying 'worshipping'
  (Sanders)
  fond doting (with the critical overtone
  'foolish')
53 **adieu** farewell (French, but common in
  English usage)
  road 'sheltered piece of water near the
  shore where vessels may lie at anchor'
  (*OED sb.* 3a). This sense is used more frequently at this period than *OED* suggests:
  Shakespeare uses it again at 2.4.185;
  Shrew 2.1.371, *Errors* 3.2.153, and
  Merchant 5.1.288; and Marlowe at e.g.
  Jew of Malta (pre-1593) 1.1.50, 86.
54 **shipped** Shakespeare has been much
  mocked since Dr Johnson's time (see
  Introduction, p. 22) for sending his hero
  by sea between two inland towns. He may
  have known of the system of water-
  courses in Italy, just as he seems to have
  known (from travellers' tales?) about
  what he calls, with surprising precision,
  'the traject, . . . the common ferry |
  Which trades to Venice' (*Merchant*
  3.4.53–4; see the revised Penguin edition
  (2005), pp. xlix, 137). But it could simply
  be Shakespeare's geographical ignor-
  ance; for the geographical confusion in
  the play, see Introduction, p. 22.

PROTEUS

And thither will I bring thee, Valentine.   55

VALENTINE

Sweet Proteus, no. Now let us take our leave.

To Milan let me hear from thee by letters

Of thy success in love, and what news else

Betideth here in absence of thy friend;

And I likewise will visit thee with mine.   60

PROTEUS

All happiness bechance to thee in Milan.

VALENTINE

As much to you at home; and so farewell.   *Exit*

PROTEUS

He after honour hunts, I after love.

He leaves his friends to dignify them more,

I leave myself, my friends, and all, for love.   65

Thou, Julia, thou hast metamorphosed me,

Made me neglect my studies, lose my time,

War with good counsel, set the world at naught;

Made wit with musing weak, heart sick with thought.

    Enter Speed

---

65 leave] POPE; loue F   66 metamorphosed] F (metamorphis'd)   69.1 *Enter Speed*] *not in* F

---

57 **Milan** (stressed, as usual in Shakespeare, on the first syllable, unlike modern prose usage)

58 **Of thy success** how you fare (not necessarily well)

59 **Betideth** takes place

60 **visit** communicate with (figurative use: *OED v.* 8a)

61 **bechance** come

62 **you** There seems no point in Valentine's answering Proteus' intimate *thee* in the previous line with the polite *you*, so it probably implies 'all of you'.

64 **dignify** bring honour to (by his advancement)

66 **metamorphosed** transformed (as he will be again later, from Julia to Silvia). The word is obviously relevant to Proteus' changeable nature; but in view of the fact that Ovid's *Metamorphoses* was Shakespeare's favourite reading (to judge from the number of times he alludes to it), it is surprising that he only uses the

word here, at 2.1.28, and at *Two Noble Kinsmen* 5.5.84. (The book itself is brought on stage at *Titus* 4.1.42.) F's spelling 'metamorphis'd' 'had a comparatively short life simultaneously with the *-ose* form which has become standard. . . . There seems no point in retaining the obsolete spelling' (*TC*, p. 166).

67 **lose** waste

68 **good counsel** sensible advice
   set . . . naught care nothing for worldly matters

69 **musing** (excessive) contemplation
   thought anxiety or distress of mind (*OED sb.* 5a)

69.1 **Speed** In its list of characters, F describes Speed as 'a clownish servant to Valentine'—misleadingly, since Speed is not a clown but a pert page-boy, contrasted with Lance, whom F describes as 'the like to Proteus', missing the contrast: this is one reason for suspecting that F's list does not derive from Shakespeare.

SPEED

   Sir Proteus, save you. Saw you my master?   70

PROTEUS

   But now he parted hence to embark for Milan.

SPEED

   Twenty to one, then, he is shipped already,

   And I have played the sheep in losing him.

PROTEUS

   Indeed, a sheep doth very often stray,

   An if the shepherd be a while away.   75

SPEED

   You conclude that my master is a shepherd, then, and I

     a sheep?

PROTEUS   I do.

SPEED

   Why then, my horns are his horns, whether I wake or

     sleep.

PROTEUS   A silly answer, and fitting well a sheep.

SPEED   This proves me still a sheep.   80

PROTEUS   True, and thy master a shepherd.

SPEED   Nay, that I can deny by a circumstance.

PROTEUS   It shall go hard but I'll prove it by another.

---

70 save] F4; 'saue FI   76 a sheep] F2; Sheepe FI

70–138 For a discussion of this exchange,
see Introduction, p. 49. Beneath the
word-play, there are three simple facts:
Valentine may have left without Speed;
Proteus is trying to discover Julia's
answer to his message; and Speed is
trying to get a tip from Proteus, having
failed to get one from Julia (or, as it turns
out, Lucetta).

70 **Sir Proteus** *Sir* here is a courtesy title; it
does not imply that Proteus is a knight;
but the frequency with which it is used
in the play—Sir Valentine, Sir Thurio,
Sir Eglamour—does have the effect of
recalling medieval knights like Malory's
Sir Lancelot, and reminding the audience
that these are aristocrats participating in
(to some extent) a courtly romance.

   save you A standard abbreviation of
'God save you', a common greeting of the
period. Indeed, the original may have

read 'God save you'; see Introduction,
p. 61.

72–3 **shipped, sheep** This *ship/sheep* quibble
(the words were pronounced similarly)
leads into the extended word-play about
sheep and shepherds that follows. Shakespeare obviously enjoyed it: he also uses it
at *Errors* 4.1.93–4 and *Love's Labour's
Lost* 2.1.219–23.

74–5 Proverbial (Dent S312).

75 **An if** Emphatic form of 'if'.

78 **my horns are his horns** i.e. if I am a
sheep, my horns belong to my master.
There is probably what Sanders calls a
'pointless' allusion to the ever-popular
joke about the horns of a cuckold. Proteus rightly calls it a *silly answer*.

82 **circumstance** detailed argument

83 **go hard** be to my disadvantage (*OED*,
hard, *adv*. 2c)

SPEED The shepherd seeks the sheep, and not the sheep the
    shepherd; but I seek my master, and my master seeks   85
    not me; therefore I am no sheep.

PROTEUS The sheep for fodder follow the shepherd, the
    shepherd for food follows not the sheep; thou for wages
    followest thy master, thy master for wages follows not
    thee; therefore thou art a sheep.   90

SPEED Such another proof will make me cry 'baa'.

PROTEUS But dost thou hear: gav'st thou my letter to Julia?

SPEED Ay, sir. I, a lost mutton, gave your letter to her, a
    laced mutton, and she, a laced mutton, gave me, a lost
    mutton, nothing for my labour.   95

PROTEUS Here's too small a pasture for such store of
    muttons.

SPEED If the ground be overcharged, you were best stick her.

PROTEUS Nay, in that you are astray. 'Twere best pound
    you.   100

SPEED Nay sir, less than a pound shall serve me for carry-
    ing your letter.

PROTEUS You mistake; I mean the pound, a pinfold.

SPEED

From a pound to a pin? Fold it over and over

---

91 **make me cry 'baa'** i.e. demonstrate that
I am a sheep (and Proteus has won the
argument) or, if there is a quibble on
'bah!', that Speed rejects the argument.
At *Love's Labour's Lost* 5.1.48 Mote, a pert
page like Speed, uses a similar proof to
mock the pedantic schoolmaster: 'Ba,
most silly sheep, with a horn!'

92 **gav'st . . . Julia** Proteus tries to bring the
conversation back to business—in vain,
as Speed's reply indicates.

93 **Ay** yes. *OED* says that 'ay' appeared suddenly around 1575, of unknown origin.
It was usually spelt 'I' (as in the Folio text
here), which indicates the pronunciation.
It survives in English dialects and
regional accents.

93–4 **lost mutton . . . laced mutton** Speed
resumes the sheep jokes, moving them
into obscenity. *Laced mutton* was slang for
a prostitute, either referring to the tight
lacing of her bodice, or to a 'Bridewell

lacing', the marks of a whipping at
Bridewell prison (Williams).

94–5 **gave me . . . labour** Speed reminds
Proteus, beneath all the quibbles, that he
has not been paid.

96 **store** abundance

98 **overcharged** over-full, has too many
(sheep)
stick her (a) kill the excess sheep; (b)
penetrate Julia

98 **pound** put in an enclosure for stray
sheep, a *pinfold*, as Proteus explains at l.
103 (with a quibble on 'beat')

99 **pound** Speed tries to raise the issue of
payment again with a pun.

104 **From a pound to a pin** Speed picks up
the *pin* from Proteus' *pinfold*, and turns it
into what he will receive for carrying Proteus' letter: not a pound, but something
that was proverbially worthless: 'Not
worth a pin' (Dent P334).
Fold multiply. Speed now picks up on the
second half of *pinfold*.

'Tis threefold too little for carrying a letter to your lover.   105
PROTEUS But what said she?
SPEED (*nods, then says*) Ay.
PROTEUS Nod-ay? Why, that's 'noddy'.
SPEED You mistook, sir. I say she did nod, and you ask me
  if she did nod, and I say 'Ay'.   110
PROTEUS And that set together is 'noddy'.
SPEED Now you have taken the pains to set it together, take
  it for your pains.
PROTEUS No, no, you shall have it for bearing the letter.
SPEED Well, I perceive I must be fain to bear with you.   115
PROTEUS Why, sir, how do you bear with me?
SPEED Marry, sir, the letter very orderly, having nothing
  but the word 'noddy' for my pains.
PROTEUS Beshrew me, but you have a quick wit.
SPEED And yet it cannot overtake your slow purse.   120
PROTEUS Come, come, open the matter in brief. What said
  she?
SPEED Open your purse, that the money and the matter
  may be both at once delivered.
PROTEUS (*giving money*) Well, sir, here is for your pains.   125
  What said she?
SPEED Truly, sir, I think you'll hardly win her.
PROTEUS Why? Couldst thou perceive so much from her?
SPEED Sir, I could perceive nothing at all from her, no, not
  so much as a ducat for delivering your letter. And being   130
  so hard to me, that brought your mind, I fear she'll

107 *nods, then says*] *not in* F   125 *giving money*] *not in* F

---

107 The inserted stage direction is needed to
  account for Proteus' reply.
108 **Nod-ay** Speed says that Julia merely
  nodded, then that she said 'yes'; no
  wonder Proteus is confused.
  noddy simpleton
115 **fain** willing
  bear put up
117 **Marry . . . orderly** Speed quibbles on
  bear (put up with) and *bear* (carry the
  letter), bringing the exchange back to
  payment, or the lack of it.
  Marry A mild oath, originally by the
  'Virgin Mary'.

117 **orderly** dutifully
119 **Beshrew me** Another mild oath ('a
  curse on me').
121 **open the matter** tell me what
  happened
128 **perceive** receive (an obsolete sense:
  OED v. 8b)
130 **ducat** A gold coin of varying value, but
  clearly Speed is angling for a large tip.
131 **hard** ungenerous
  mind message

prove as hard to you in telling your mind. Give her no
token but stones, for she's as hard as steel.

PROTEUS What said she? Nothing?

SPEED No, not so much as 'Take this for thy pains'. To   135
testify your bounty, I thank you, you have testerned me;
in requital whereof, henceforth carry your letters yourself. And so, sir, I'll commend you to my master.

⌈*Exit*⌉

PROTEUS

Go, go, be gone, to save your ship from wreck,
Which cannot perish having thee aboard,   140
Being destined to a drier death on shore.
I must go send some better messenger.
I fear my Julia would not deign my lines,
Receiving them from such a worthless post.   *Exit*

I.2 *Enter Julia and Lucetta*

JULIA

But say, Lucetta, now we are alone,
Wouldst thou then counsel me to fall in love?

LUCETTA

Ay, madam, so you stumble not unheedfully.

JULIA

Of all the fair resort of gentlemen

136 testerned] F2 (*subs.*); cestern'd FI   138.1 *Exit*] *not in* F   139 wreck] F (wrack)

132 **in telling your mind** when you tell her
     in person
133 **stones** i.e. precious stones (with a pun
     on 'testicles')
136 **testify** bear witness to
     testerned rewarded with a *tester*, or six-
     pence (much less than the ducat he
     wanted)
138.1 *Exit* Speed probably leaves here (no
     exit is given in F), in which case Proteus
     calls his next three lines after him; but
     Proteus might speak them directly to
     Speed, who would then leave after l. 141.
139–418 These lines allude to the proverbial
     'He that is born to be hanged (drowned)
     shall never be drowned (hanged)' (Dent
     B139), as at *Tempest* 1.1.28–9: 'he hath

no drowning mark upon him; his complexion is perfect gallows'.
143 **deign** accept graciously
144 **post** (a) messenger; (b) door-post, i.e.
     blockhead
I.2.0.1 *Julia* Her name may have been sug-
     gested by the heroine of Arthur Brooke's
     Romeus and Juliet. See Introduction, p. 18.
     Lucetta Italian diminutive of 'Lucy'.
  3 **stumble** (playing on Julia's *fall* in the
     previous line)
     unheedfully carelessly
4–24 For the similarities and differences
     between this discussion and that between
     Portia and Nerissa at *Merchant* 1.2, see
     Introduction, p. 29.
  4 **resort** company

That every day with parle encounter me,   5
In thy opinion which is worthiest love?

LUCETTA

Please you repeat their names, I'll show my mind
According to my shallow simple skill.

JULIA

What think'st thou of the fair Sir Eglamour?

LUCETTA

As of a knight well spoken, neat, and fine,   10
But were I you, he never should be mine.

JULIA

What think'st thou of the rich Mercatio?

LUCETTA

Well of his wealth, but of himself, so-so.

JULIA

What think'st thou of the gentle Proteus?

LUCETTA

Lord, lord, to see what folly reigns in us!   15

JULIA

How now? What means this passion at his name?

LUCETTA

Pardon, dear madam, 'tis a passing shame

---

5 **parle** conversation
6 **worthiest love** most worthy to be loved
7 **Please you** if you will
   mind opinion (as in modern 'speak my mind')
9–14 **Eglamour, Mercatio, Proteus** It is interesting that Julia's suitors recur, in different ways, as Silvia's. Proteus, of course; Mercatio, whose only virtue lies in his wealth, anticipates Thurio; and Eglamour's name, at least, is given to Silvia's accomplice in her escape from Milan.
9 **Eglamour** The name suggests a chivalric hero, as in *Sir Eglamour of Artois* (1500), though Bond, citing Dekker's *Satiromastix*, thinks it had come to imply a mere carpet-knight, i.e. one knighted for courtly rather than military reasons. He certainly *is* courtly, as the next line makes clear—and so is the Eglamour who appears later in the play. Shakespeare may have intended initially to make them the same character, but changed his mind as he wrote. In some productions, they *are* the same character,

as in the BBC television version, which begins with Eglamour, satirically treated, presenting Julia with a scroll setting out his ancestry.
10 **neat** elegant (but with a hint of mockery, as in Hotspur's account of the popinjay lord, 'neat and trimly dressed' (*1 Henry IV* 1.3.32))
   fine refined, courtly
12 **Mercatio** Since he is 'rich', this may be a significant name, from Italian *mercato*, market. But it may equally be a simple compositorial misreading of the name 'Mercutio' in Brooke's and Shakespeare's versions of the Romeo and Juliet story, to which it is very tempting to emend it.
14 **gentle** well-born (with the modern meaning as well, indicating Julia's affection for Proteus)
15 **reigns** in rules, controls
16 **How now** An exclamation of surprise, an abbreviation of 'how is it now?', very common in Shakespeare.
   passion emotional outburst
17 **passing** surpassing

That I, unworthy body as I am,
Should censure thus on lovely gentlemen.

JULIA
Why not on Proteus, as of all the rest?   20

LUCETTA
Then thus: of many good, I think him best.

JULIA Your reason?

LUCETTA
I have no other but a woman's reason:
I think him so because I think him so.

JULIA
And wouldst thou have me cast my love on him?   25

LUCETTA
Ay, if you thought your love not cast away.

JULIA
Why, he of all the rest hath never moved me.

LUCETTA
Yet he of all the rest I think best loves ye.

JULIA
His little speaking shows his love but small.

LUCETTA
Fire that's closest kept burns most of all.   30

JULIA
They do not love that do not show their love.

LUCETTA
O, they love least that let men know their love.

JULIA
I would I knew his mind.

LUCETTA (*giving Proteus' letter*)
Peruse this paper, madam.

34   *giving Proteus' letter*] not in F

19 **censure** pass judgement
20 **of** on
23 **a woman's reason** Proverbial: 'Because
    is woman's reason' (Dent B179).
25 **cast** bestow
26 **cast away** thrown away, wasted
27 **moved me** (a) declared his love to me; (b)
    stirred love in me. Both these senses are
    present in her anxious 'I would I knew
    his mind' (l. 33).
28 **ye** Though used interchangeably with
    'you', *ye* occurs far more frequently in the
    earlier plays, and especially in this play,

or, later, in the plays of collaborative
authorship (e.g. *All is True*, *Kinsmen*),
implying that Shakespeare came to
favour it less as his career developed. Here
it is probably chosen for the rhyme.

29–32 These patterned lines draw upon
proverbs (Dent F265, L165) which Shakespeare transmutes into concrete dramatic
situations, both in this play and in Shakespearian comedy in general, especially in
the contrast between Orsino's language
and Viola's in *Twelfth Night*. See Introduction, pp. 35–8.

JULIA

'To Julia'—say, from whom?   35

LUCETTA

That the contents will show.

JULIA

Say, say, who gave it thee?

LUCETTA

Sir Valentine's page; and sent, I think, from Proteus.

He would have given it you, but I being in the way

Did in your name receive it. Pardon the fault, I pray.   40

JULIA

Now, by my modesty, a goodly broker.

Dare you presume to harbour wanton lines?

To whisper, and conspire against my youth?

Now trust me, 'tis an office of great worth,

And you an officer fit for the place.   45

There, take the paper, see it be returned,

   She gives Lucetta the letter

Or else return no more into my sight.

LUCETTA

To plead for love deserves more fee than hate.

JULIA

Will ye be gone?

LUCETTA   That you may ruminate.   *Exit*

JULIA

And yet I would I had o'erlooked the letter.   50

It were a shame to call her back again

And pray her to a fault for which I chid her.

What fool is she, that knows I am a maid

And would not force the letter to my view,

46.1 *She . . . letter*] *not in* F 53 fool] F4; 'foole F1

---

36 **contents** (stressed on the second
  syllable)
38–40 **Sir . . . receive it** So it was Lucetta,
  not Julia, whom Speed met and whom he
  describes to Proteus in the previous
  scene.
41 **broker** go-between, pander
42 **harbour wanton lines** receive love
  letters (or perhaps more censorious: 'give
  a home to immodest messages')

49 **That** so that
  ruminate meditate
52 **to** to commit
53 **What fool** what a fool (as F indicates
  by its apostrophe before 'fool'). 'A was
  sometimes omitted after "what", in the
  sense of "what kind of"' (Abbott 86).

Since maids in modesty say 'No' to that   55
Which they would have the profferer construe 'Ay'.
Fie, fie, how wayward is this foolish love
That like a testy babe will scratch the nurse
And presently, all humbled, kiss the rod.
How churlishly I chid Lucetta hence   60
When willingly I would have had her here.
How angerly I taught my brow to frown
When inward joy enforced my heart to smile.
My penance is to call Lucetta back
And ask remission for my folly past.   65
What ho! Lucetta!
        Enter Lucetta
LUCETTA   What would your ladyship?
JULIA
Is't near dinner-time?
LUCETTA   I would it were,
That you might kill your stomach on your meat
And not upon your maid.
        She drops and picks up the letter
JULIA   What is't that you
Took up so gingerly?   70
LUCETTA Nothing.

66 *Enter Lucetta*] not in F   69 *She . . . letter*] not in F

55–6 **Since maids . . . 'Ay'** Proverbial (Dent
   W660), and used as such by Valentine at
   3.1.101.
56 **profferer** him who makes the offer
   construe interpret (stressed on the first
   syllable)
57 **Fie, fie** (an expression of impatience)
58 **testy** peevish, fretful
59 **presently** immediately (the standard
   Elizabethan meaning)
   kiss the rod Proverbial (Dent R156);
   Elizabethan children were apparently
   required to kiss the stick with which they
   were beaten.
62 **angerly** angrily (formed from the noun
   rather than the adjective; Abbott 447)
64 **penance** Used in its strict religious sense
   of 'penitence undertaken in repentance
   for sin' at 5.2.36, this is an example of
   religious language used in a context
   of love, as at 2.4.127 and 5.4.168.

65 **remission** pardon
68 **stomach** (a) appetite; (b) anger. The
   stomach was regarded as the seat of the
   emotions.
   meat food
69 ***She drops . . . letter*** That Lucetta drops
   the letter here is supported by the corresponding passage in *Diana*, where the
   maid 'of purpose . . . let the letter closely
   fall, which, when I perceived, "What is
   that that fell down?" said I, "let me see
   it." "It is nothing, mistress," said she'
   (Bullough, p. 231). If Lucetta drops it
   earlier, at her exit at l. 49, as sometimes
   suggested, Julia would obviously pick
   it up and so not need her soliloquy at
   ll. 50–65.
70 **gingerly** cautiously. This anticipates
   OED's first recorded example (*OED adv.* b)
   of 1607.

JULIA Why didst thou stoop then?

LUCETTA

  To take a paper up that I let fall.

JULIA

  And is that paper nothing?

LUCETTA

  Nothing concerning me.   75

JULIA

  Then let it lie for those that it concerns.

LUCETTA

  Madam, it will not lie where it concerns,

  Unless it have a false interpreter.

JULIA

  Some love of yours hath writ to you in rhyme.

LUCETTA

  That I might sing it, madam, to a tune,   80

  Give me a note; your ladyship can set.

JULIA

  As little by such toys as may be possible.

  Best sing it to the tune of 'Light o' love'.

LUCETTA

  It is too heavy for so light a tune.

JULIA

  Heavy? Belike it hath some burden, then?   85

LUCETTA

  Ay, and melodious were it, would you sing it.

JULIA

  And why not you?

---

83 o' love] THEOBALD; *O, Loue* F

76–7 **lie . . . lie** remain; speak falsely

77 **concerns** is of importance

80–98 This dialogue plays on musical terms to reflect the situation, particularly Julia's changing moods and attitudes to Lucetta.

80 **That** so that

81–2 **set. | As little** Lucetta asks Julia to choose a (musical) note; Julia twists it to mean 'set little store by'.

82 **toys** trifles

83 **Light o' love** A popular Elizabethan tune, also mentioned at *Much Ado*

3.4.40, and ironically relevant to Julia's lover Proteus and to Julia's own subsequent development from flirtatiousness to sombre awareness of love's problems.

84 **heavy** serious

85 **burden** (a) bass line of a song; (b) emotional weight

86 **melodious . . . sing it** it would be melodious if you were to sing it

87 **I cannot reach so high** (a) it is beyond my vocal range; (b) I am unworthy of someone as noble as Proteus

LUCETTA   I cannot reach so high.

JULIA

Let's see your song.

⌜*She tries to take the letter*⌝

How now, minion!

LUCETTA

Keep tune there still; so you will sing it out.

⌜*Julia strikes her*⌝

And yet methinks I do not like this tune.   90

JULIA You do not?

LUCETTA

No, madam, 'tis too sharp.

JULIA

You, minion, are too saucy.

LUCETTA

Nay, now you are too flat,

And mar the concord with too harsh a descant.   95

There wanteth but a mean to fill your song.

JULIA

The mean is drowned with your unruly bass.

LUCETTA

Indeed, I bid the base for Proteus.

JULIA

This bauble shall not henceforth trouble me.

---

88 *She . . . letter*] *not in* F   89.1 *Julia strikes her*] *not in* F   97 your] F2; you FI   99 bauble]
F (babble)

88, 93 **minion** Almost always a term of
contempt in Shakespeare.
89 **Keep tune** (a) stay in tune; (b) don't lose
your temper
sing it out (a) finish singing; (b) stop
being angry
89.1 *Julia strikes her* Some such action is
needed to motivate Lucetta's next line.
90 **tune** (a) melody; (b) mood
92 **sharp** (a) out of tune, too high in pitch;
(b) painful
94 **flat** (a) too low in pitch; (b) blunt
95 **concord** harmony (both musical and
between us)
descant (a) improvised counterpoint
on the theme; (b) Julia's temperamental
moods
96 **wanteth but** lacks only

mean (a) correct pitch, neither *sharp*
(l. 92) nor *flat* (l. 94); (b) tenor (probably
referring to Proteus); middle part of a
musical arrangement
97 **bass** (a) lowest vocal line; (b) bad
behaviour
98 **bid the base** challenge on behalf of.
Lucetta picks up 'bass' from the previous
line, and transfers the sense to the
game of prisoner's base, which involves
running between two 'bases' or opposing
camps. She will be Proteus' champion.
99 **bauble** trifle (the letter). Of F's 'babble',
Dover Wilson says: 'both "babble" and
"bauble" could be spelt "bable" in the six-
teenth century'. 'Bauble' makes better
sense in the context (*TC*, p. 166).

Here is a coil with protestation.   100
    She tears the letter and drops the pieces
Go, get you gone, and let the papers lie.
You would be fing'ring them to anger me.

LUCETTA

She makes it strange, but she would be best pleased
To be so angered with another letter.   *Exit*

JULIA

Nay, would I were so angered with the same.   105
O hateful hands, to tear such loving words;
Injurious wasps, to feed on such sweet honey
And kill the bees that yield it with your stings.
I'll kiss each several paper for amends.
    She picks up some of the pieces of paper
Look, here is writ 'Kind Julia'—unkind Julia,   110
As in revenge of thy ingratitude
I throw thy name against the bruising stones,
Trampling contemptuously on thy disdain.
And here is writ 'Love-wounded Proteus'.
Poor wounded name, my bosom as a bed   115
Shall lodge thee till thy wound be throughly healed;
And thus I search it with a sovereign kiss.
But twice or thrice was 'Proteus' written down.
Be calm, good wind, blow not a word away
Till I have found each letter in the letter   120
Except mine own name. That, some whirlwind bear

100.1 *She . . . pieces*] *not in* F   104 *Exit*] *not in* F   109.1 *She . . . paper*] *not in* F

100 **coil with protestation** fuss about a
    vow of love
103–4 These lines look like an aside, spoken
    directly to the audience; but it is an
    Elizabethan convention that asides are
    not heard by others on stage, and since
    Julia picks up Lucetta's *angered* in her
    following speech, Lucetta presumably
    projects them so that Julia can hear
    them.
103 **makes it strange** pretends not to care
107 **Injurious** unjust
    wasps i.e. her fingers
109 **several** separate
115–16 **my bosom . . . Shall lodge thee** Julia

puts the fragment of the letter into 'the
small pocket which Elizabethan women's
gowns had located in the inside of
the bodice between the breasts. It is
frequently alluded to as a receptacle for
letters, love-tokens and sentimental
mementoes' (Sanders).
116 **throughly** thoroughly
117 **search** probe (the wound in order to
    cleanse and cure it)
    sovereign of supreme healing quality
    (*OED a.* 3)
121 **mine own** Shakespeare often uses *mine*
    instead of 'my' before a vowel for greater
    fluency of delivery (Abbott 237).

Unto a ragged, fearful, hanging rock
And throw it thence into the raging sea.
Lo, here in one line is his name twice writ:
'Poor forlorn Proteus', 'passionate Proteus',   125
'To the sweet Julia'—that I'll tear away.
And yet I will not, sith so prettily
He couples it to his complaining names.
Thus will I fold them, one upon another.
Now kiss, embrace, contend, do what you will.   130
    Enter Lucetta

LUCETTA
Madam, dinner is ready, and your father stays.
JULIA Well, let us go.
LUCETTA
What, shall these papers lie like telltales here?
JULIA
If you respect them, best to take them up.
LUCETTA
Nay, I was taken up for laying them down.   135
Yet here they shall not lie, for catching cold.
JULIA
I see you have a month's mind to them.
LUCETTA
Ay, madam, you may say what sights you see.
I see things too, although you judge I wink.
JULIA Come, come, will't please you go?   *Exeunt*   140

130.1 *Enter Lucetta*] *not in* F

122 **raggèd** rugged. At 3 *Henry VI* 5.4.27, Queen Margaret compares her enemy the future Richard III to 'a raggèd fatal rock' upon which her army will founder. 'Probably from the same root as *rugged*, but *OED* keeps the forms distinct, and *ragged* has several meanings not included in modern *rugged*' (*TC*, p. 166).
    hanging over-hanging
125 **forlorn** (stressed on the first syllable)
127 **sith** since
128 **complaining** (of his suffering in love)
129–30 Julia wittily and suggestively makes

the papers do what she would like to do with Proteus.
131 **stays** waits
134 **respect** value
    best to take it were best that you take
135 **taken up** rebuked
136 **for** for fear of
137 **a month's mind** liking, inclination, originally derived from the custom of saying a mass for someone for a month after their death (*OED*, *month's mind*, 1a, 2).
139 **wink** close my eyes

1.3 *Enter Antonio and Panthino*

ANTONIO

Tell me, Panthino, what sad talk was that
Wherewith my brother held you in the cloister?

PANTHINO

'Twas of his nephew Proteus, your son.

ANTONIO

Why, what of him?

PANTHINO   He wondered that your lordship
Would suffer him to spend his youth at home   5
While other men, of slender reputation,
Put forth their sons to seek preferment out:
Some to the wars, to try their fortune there,
Some to discover islands far away,
Some to the studious universities.   10
For any or for all these exercises
He said that Proteus your son was meet,
And did request me to importune you
To let him spend his time no more at home,
Which would be great impeachment to his age   15
In having known no travel in his youth.

ANTONIO

Nor need'st thou much importune me to that
Whereon this month I have been hammering.
I have considered well his loss of time,

1.3.0.1 *Enter . . . Panthino*] *Enter Antonio and Panthino. Protheus.* F

1.3.0.1 *Enter Antonio and Panthino* F's
stage direction reads '*Enter Antonio and
Panthino. Protheus.*' This appears to
follow the general pattern of this text,
listing all the characters in a scene at the
start, regardless of when they appear.
This edition accordingly follows others
in bringing on Proteus after l. 43; but
it is possible that, in this instance, F
reflects what was in the manuscript that
Ralph Crane was transcribing: perhaps,
as in the 1957 Old Vic production, the
Proteus enters at the same time as the
others but remains apart, absorbed in
Julia's letter, while the other two discuss
his future.
Panthino For the forms of his name in F,

see the commentary to 'The Persons of
the Play'.
1 **sad** serious
2 **cloister** colonnade (without necessarily
suggesting a religious building, as now)
5 **suffer** allow
6 **slender reputation** small repute
7 **Put forth** send out into the world
preferment advancement
12 **meet** fit
13, 17 **importune** urge (stressed on the
second syllable)
15 **impeachment** to detriment in
18 **hammering** pondering, deliberating
(with a hint of laborious mental effort, as
in Richard II's soliloquy in prison (5.5.5))

And how he cannot be a perfect man,   20
Not being tried and tutored in the world.
Experience is by industry achieved,
And perfected by the swift course of time.
Then tell me, whither were I best to send him?

PANTHINO

I think your lordship is not ignorant   25
How his companion, youthful Valentine,
Attends the Emperor in his royal court.

ANTONIO I know it well.

PANTHINO

'Twere good, I think, your lordship sent him thither.
There shall he practise tilts and tournaments,   30
Hear sweet discourse, converse with noblemen,
And be in eye of every exercise
Worthy his youth and nobleness of birth.

ANTONIO

I like thy counsel; well hast thou advised,
And that thou mayst perceive how well I like it,   35
The execution of it shall make known.
Even with the speediest expedition
I will dispatch him to the Emperor's court.

PANTHINO

Tomorrow, may it please you, Don Alfonso,
With other gentlemen of good esteem,   40
Are journeying to salute the Emperor
And to commend their service to his will.

---

20 **perfect** complete
21 **tried** tested
23 **perfected** made complete (stressed on the first syllable, as usual in Shakespeare)
24 **whither were I best** where would it be best for me
27 **Emperor** He is called 'Duke' later. All references to him as Emperor occur early in the play, suggesting that Shakespeare had not yet made up his mind about the character's rank.
30 **tilts and tournaments** Although these were the chief pastime of the military aristocracy in the Middle Ages, there was a significant revival of such chivalric modes at the courts of Elizabeth I and James I. In Montemayor's *Diana*, the equivalent of Proteus, Felix, attracts the

attention of Felismena (Julia) 'by tilt and tourneys' (Bullough, p. 230).
31 **discourse** conversation (stressed on the second syllable, as throughout the play)
32 **in eye** the witness
33 **Worthy** worthy of
34 **counsel** advice
35–6 The construction changes from 'so that you may see how much I like your advice' to 'the way I adopt your advice will show my approval of it'.
37 **expedition** urgency, speed
39 **Don** Properly a title for a Spanish nobleman, but probably here a 'general title of rank' (Bond), perhaps suggested by the Spanish source.
41 **salute** greet
42 **commend** commit

ANTONIO

  Good company; with them shall Proteus go.

    Enter Proteus with a letter. He does not see Antonio
    and Panthino

  And in good time; now will we break with him.

PROTEUS

  Sweet love, sweet lines, sweet life!   45

  Here is her hand, the agent of her heart;

  Here is her oath for love, her honour's pawn.

  O that our fathers would applaud our loves

  To seal our happiness with their consents.

  O heavenly Julia!   50

ANTONIO

  How now, what letter are you reading there?

PROTEUS

  May't please your lordship, 'tis a word or two

  Of commendations sent from Valentine,

  Delivered by a friend that came from him.

ANTONIO

  Lend me the letter. Let me see what news.   55

PROTEUS

  There is no news, my lord, but that he writes

  How happily he lives, how well beloved

  And daily gracèd by the Emperor,

  Wishing me with him, partner of his fortune.

ANTONIO

  And how stand you affected to his wish?   60

PROTEUS

  As one relying on your lordship's will,

  And not depending on his friendly wish.

ANTONIO

  My will is something sorted with his wish.

  Muse not that I thus suddenly proceed,

43.1–2 *Enter . . . Panthino*] *not in* F   50 O] F2; *Pro.* Oh F1

44 **in good time** at the right moment (a common phrase of the period)
  break with broach the matter to
46 **hand** handwriting
47 **pawn** pledge
48 **applaud** approve of
53 **commendations** greetings

58 **gracèd** honoured
59 **fortune** success
60 **stand you affected** are you disposed
63 **something sorted** somewhat in agreement
64 **Muse not** do not wonder

For what I will, I will, and there an end.   65
I am resolved that thou shalt spend some time
With Valentinus in the Emperor's court.
What maintenance he from his friends receives,
Like exhibition thou shalt have from me.
Tomorrow be in readiness to go.   70
Excuse it not, for I am peremptory.

PROTEUS

My lord, I cannot be so soon provided.
Please you deliberate a day or two.

ANTONIO

Look what thou want'st shall be sent after thee.
No more of stay; tomorrow thou must go.   75
Come on, Panthino; you shall be employed
To hasten on his expedition.

Exeunt Antonio and Panthino

PROTEUS

Thus have I shunned the fire for fear of burning
And drenched me in the sea where I am drowned.
I feared to show my father Julia's letter   80
Lest he should take exceptions to my love,
And with the vantage of mine own excuse
Hath he excepted most against my love.

---

76 Panthino] F2; *Panthmo* F1   77.1 *Exeunt . . . Panthino*] *not in* F

65 **there an end** that's that (proverbial: Dent E113.1)
66 **thou** As he becomes more *peremptory* (l. 71), Antonio moves from the polite 'you' to the brusque 'thou'.
67 **Valentinus** The Latin form provides a regular verse line; it may also 'suit Antonio's ponderous style', as Moore suggests.
68 **maintenance** subsidy
   friends relatives
69 **Like exhibition** the same allowance
71 **Excuse it not** do not make excuses (for not going)
   peremptory fully resolved (stressed on the first syllable, as usual in Shakespeare)

72 **provided** equipped
74 **Look what** whatever. This was a common Elizabethan idiom, perhaps derived from 'some non-literary dialect' (*OED v.* 4b). Shakespeare uses *look what* several times, usually for emphasis, as at *Measure for Measure* 2.2.53: 'Look what I will not, that I cannot do.'
   want lack, i.e. need
75 **No more of stay** no more talk of delay
77 **expedition** journey
81 **take exceptions** make objections
82 **the vantage . . . excuse** i.e. my own lie (about Valentine's letter) gave him the opportunity
83 **excepted . . . against** objected to

O how this spring of love resembleth
   The uncertain glory of an April day,   85
Which now shows all the beauty of the sun,
   And by and by a cloud takes all away.
         Enter Panthino
PANTHINO
   Sir Proteus, your father calls for you.
   He is in haste, therefore I pray you go.
PROTEUS
   Why, this it is. My heart accords thereto,   90
   And yet a thousand times it answers 'No'.   *Exeunt*

2.1 *Enter Valentine and Speed*
SPEED (*offering Valentine a glove*)
   Sir, your glove.
VALENTINE   Not mine; my gloves are on.
SPEED
   Why then this may be yours, for this is but one.
VALENTINE
   Ha, let me see; ay, give it me, it's mine:
   Sweet ornament, that decks a thing divine.
   Ah, Silvia, Silvia!   5
SPEED Madam Silvia, Madam Silvia!
VALENTINE How now, sirrah?
SPEED She is not within hearing, sir.
VALENTINE Why, sir, who bade you call her?

87.1 *Enter . . . Panthino*] *not in* F   88 father] F2; Fathers F1   91 *Exeunt*] ROWE; *Exeunt. Finis.* F

  2.1.0.1 *Enter . . . Speed*] *Enter Valentine, Speed, Siluia.* F   1 *offering . . . glove*] *not in* F

84–7 The changeableness of the April day
    was proverbial (Dent L92a) and Shake-
    speare often alludes to it, e.g. in Sonnets
    33 and 34, and at *All's Well* 5.3.34–5:
    'thou mayst see a sunshine and a hail |
    In me at once.' It perfectly catches
    Proteus' own changeability. As Proteus
    expresses his emotional situation, he
    moves into rhyme: for the use of lyrical
    language as an expression of feeling in
    the play, see Introduction, pp. 38–9.
90–1 **My heart . . . 'No'** 'suggesting that he
    is divided between desire to go and desire
    to stay' (Norton)
90 **accords thereto** agrees to it

2.1.2 **but** only
    one Speed quibbles upon *on* in the previ-
    ous line: the words were pronounced
    alike.
4 **decks** adorns
7 **sirrah** fellow (address to a social
    inferior, often expressing annoyance, as
    here). See next note.
9 **who . . . her** Both the servant's pre-
    sumption and the master's annoyance
    recur at *Merchant* 2.5.6–7: 'SHYLOCK
    Why, Jessica, I say! LANCELOT Why,
    Jessica! | SHYLOCK Who bids thee call? I
    do not bid thee call.'
    bade ordered

SPEED Your worship, sir, or else I mistook.   10
VALENTINE Well, you'll still be too forward.
SPEED And yet I was last chidden for being too slow.
VALENTINE Go to, sir. Tell me, do you know Madam Silvia?
SPEED She that your worship loves?
VALENTINE Why, how know you that I am in love?   15
SPEED Marry, by these special marks: first, you have
     learned, like Sir Proteus, to wreath your arms, like a
     malcontent; to relish a love-song, like a robin redbreast;
     to walk alone, like one that had the pestilence; to sigh,
     like a schoolboy that had lost his ABC; to weep, like a   20
     young wench that had buried her grandam; to fast, like
     one that takes diet; to watch, like one that fears robbing;
     to speak puling, like a beggar at Hallowmas. You were
     wont, when you laughed, to crow like a cock; when
     you walked, to walk like one of the lions. When you   25
     fasted, it was presently after dinner; when you looked
     sadly, it was for want of money. And now you are

11 **still** always
    forward presumptuous
13 **Go to** A common expression of impa-
    tience: 'Come, come!'
16–29 In this bravura speech, Speed mock-
    ingly describes the conventional attitudes
    of the lover, as Mote does at *Love's
    Labour's Lost* 3.1.10–24: the two speeches
    are linked in style, content, and virtuoso
    display.
16 **special marks** At *As You Like It* 3.2.360–
    71, Rosalind too provides a mocking
    account of a lover's *marks*.
17–18 **wreath . . . malcontent** fold your
    arms like a melancholy lover. This was a
    standard pose for a man in love, as in the
    celebrated portrait of John Donne (see
    fig. 7). In the speech about the lover from
    Love's Labour's Lost mentioned in the
    note to 16–29, Mote speaks of 'your arms
    crossed on your thin-belly doublet'
    (3.1.16–17).
18 **relish** sing (probably with enjoyment;
    *OED v.*² *Obs.*, citing *Lucrece* 1126: 'Relish
    your nimble notes to pleasing ears').
    Compare Mote again (see previous note):
    'sigh a note and sing a note' (3.1.12–13).
    like a robin redbreast In winter,
    a solitary robin's plaintive notes often

provide the only birdsong to be heard.
Sanders suggests 'Perhaps . . . Valentine
spends his time alone and disconsolate
like a robin in winter'; if so, that would
lead naturally into the next phrase.
19 **pestilence** plague. Anyone with the
    plague was shunned.
20 **ABC** primer or spelling book. It was
    pronounced 'absey' in Shakespeare's
    day, but productions nowadays usually
    pronounce it 'A-B-C', which makes the
    meaning clearer for a modern audience.
21 **grandam** grandmother
22 **takes diet** follows a diet for one's
    health
    watch stay awake. See note to 1.1.31.
23 **puling** whiningly
    like . . . Hallowmas Hallowmas was All
    Saints' Day or All Hallows (1 November),
    on which beggars traditionally sought for
    alms.
24, 67 **wont** accustomed
24 **crow like a cock** i.e. make a raucous
    noise (unlike the sighing and whining he
    uses now)
25 **like one of the lions** i.e. strut proudly.
    Probably an allusion to the famous lions
    kept in the Tower of London, also men-
    tioned at Webster's *White Devil* 5.6.266.

metamorphosed with a mistress, that when I look on
you I can hardly think you my master.

VALENTINE Are all these things perceived in me?   30

SPEED They are all perceived without ye.

VALENTINE Without me? They cannot.

SPEED Without you? Nay, that's certain, for without you
were so simple, none else would. But you are so without
these follies that these follies are within you, and shine   35
through you like the water in an urinal, that not an eye
that sees you but is a physician to comment on your
malady.

VALENTINE But tell me, dost thou know my lady Silvia?

SPEED She that you gaze on so as she sits at supper?   40

VALENTINE Hast thou observed that? Even she I mean.

SPEED Why sir, I know her not.

VALENTINE Dost thou know her by my gazing on her, and
yet know'st her not?

SPEED Is she not hard-favoured, sir?   45

VALENTINE Not so fair, boy, as well favoured.

SPEED Sir, I know that well enough.

VALENTINE What dost thou know?

SPEED That she is not so fair as, of you, well favoured.

VALENTINE I mean that her beauty is exquisite but her   50
favour infinite.

SPEED That's because the one is painted and the other out
of all count.

VALENTINE How painted? And how out of count?

---

28 **metamorphosed** See note to 1.1.66.
with by

31 **without ye** in your external appearance

32 **Without me** in my absence
cannot (be)

33 **Without . . . without** outside . . . unless

34 **would** 'would be so simple' (Johnson) or
'would perceive them' (Bond)
without Now implying both 'outside'
and 'lacking'.

36 **urinal** A transparent glass used by
doctors to test urine, a standard Elizabethan medical procedure for diagnosing
illness, hence the next phrase.

42 **know** Perhaps punning on *know* sexu-

ally. If so, Valentine characteristically
misses the point.

45 **hard-favoured** ugly

46 **Not . . . well favoured** 'Silvia's beauty is
surpassed by her charm of manner'
(Sanders).

49 **of you, well favoured** looked on with
favour by you

50–1 **The balanced phrasing is very like John
Lyly's courtly manner; see Introduction,
p. 18.

51 **favour** graciousness

52 **painted** using make-up

52–3 **out of all count** beyond calculation,
boundless (proverbial: Dent C704.1)

SPEED Marry, sir, so painted to make her fair that no man   55
counts of her beauty.

VALENTINE How esteem'st thou me? I account of her
beauty.

SPEED You never saw her since she was deformed.

VALENTINE How long hath she been deformed?   60

SPEED Ever since you loved her.

VALENTINE I have loved her ever since I saw her, and still I
see her beautiful.

SPEED If you love her you cannot see her.

VALENTINE Why?   65

SPEED Because love is blind. O that you had mine eyes, or
your own eyes had the lights they were wont to have
when you chid at Sir Proteus for going ungartered.

VALENTINE What should I see then?

SPEED Your own present folly and her passing deformity;   70
for he being in love could not see to garter his hose, and
you being in love cannot see to put on your hose.

VALENTINE Belike, boy, then you are in love, for last morning you could not see to wipe my shoes.

SPEED True, sir. I was in love with my bed. I thank you,   75
you swinged me for my love, which makes me the bolder
to chide you for yours.

VALENTINE In conclusion, I stand affected to her.

SPEED I would you were set. So your affection would cease.

---

56 **counts of** esteems

57 **account of** appreciate

59–60 **deformed** Speed means 'changed
from her true shape' (Bond) because seen
through the lover's falsifying eyes; Valentine thinks he means 'physically
misshapen'.

66 **love is blind** Proverbial: Dent L506.
Cupid, classical god of love, was trad-
itionally blind, and so, therefore, are
lovers, as at Sonnet 137.1–2: 'Thou blind
fool love, what dost thou to mine eyes |
That they behold and see not what they
see?'

67 **lights** power to see clearly

68 **chid at** criticized

going ungartered A traditional sign
of the love-sick man, as at *As You Like

It* 3.2.366: 'your hose should be ungartered'; and when Hamlet is feigning
love-madness, he appears with 'his stockings . . . Ungartered' (2.1.80–1). *Hose*
(stockings) were held up by garters above
or below the knee.

70 **passing** surpassing, exceeding

75 **I was . . . bed** In Montemayor's *Diana*,
the servant Fabius criticizes 'those
troublesome loves, which makes us run
up and down more, and sleep less, than
we would' (Bullough, p. 239).

76 **swinged** beat

78 **stand affected to** am in love with.
Speed takes *stand* in its bawdy sense
('have an erection') in his reply.

79 **set** Literally 'seated', but figuratively
'sexually satisfied'.

VALENTINE Last night she enjoined me to write some lines   80
  to one she loves.
SPEED And have you?
VALENTINE I have.
SPEED Are they not lamely writ?
VALENTINE No, boy, but as well as I can do them. Peace,   85
  here she comes.
      Enter Silvia
SPEED (*aside*) O excellent motion! O exceeding puppet!
  Now will he interpret to her.
VALENTINE
  Madam and mistress, a thousand good-morrows.
SPEED (*aside*) O, give ye good e'en! Here's a million of   90
  manners.
SILVIA
  Sir Valentine and servant, to you two thousand.
SPEED (*aside*) He should give her interest, and she gives it
  him.
VALENTINE
  As you enjoined me, I have writ your letter   95
  Unto the secret, nameless friend of yours;
  Which I was much unwilling to proceed in
  But for my duty to your ladyship.
      He gives her a letter
SILVIA
  I thank you, gentle servant, 'tis very clerkly done.

86.1 *Enter Silvia*] *not in* F   90 give] DYCE; 'giue F   e'en] F (ev'n)   98.1 *He . . . letter*] *not in* F

90, 95 **enjoined** commanded
84 **lamely** 'lacking the correct number of
  metrical feet' (Sanders), hence the pun
  on 'lame'.
87–8 **motion . . . puppet . . . interpret** A
  motion was a puppet-show (*OED sb.* 13a,
  citing *Winter's Tale* 4.3.95–6: 'a motion of
  the Prodigal Son'), in which Valentine is
  the *puppet*. Puppeteers interpreted, com-
  mented on, their puppet-shows, as *Hamlet* 3.2.234–5 makes clear: 'I could interpret between you and your love if I could
  see the puppets dallying.'
89–90 **thousand . . . million** Valentine uses
  the extravagant language of the conventional lover; Speed mocks him by

reducing it to arithmetic. Even before
Valentine and Silvia begin their courtly
banter, we approach them from Speed's
satirical viewpoint.
90 **give . . . e'en** may God give you a good
  evening (a common greeting)
92 **servant** Silvia replies to Valentine's
  greeting with the language of courtly
  love: she is the *mistress*, he the *servant*.
93–4 **He . . . him** Valentine should give her
  even more compliments, but instead Silvia increases his *thousand* (l. 89) to *two
  thousand* (l. 92), and so gives him financial *interest*.
99 **clerkly done** well written (either as a
  clerk or a scholar or both)

VALENTINE

Now trust me, madam, it came hardly off;   100

For being ignorant to whom it goes

I writ at random, very doubtfully.

SILVIA

Perchance you think too much of so much pains?

VALENTINE

No, madam. So it stead you I will write,

Please you command, a thousand times as much.   105

And yet—

SILVIA

A pretty period. Well, I guess the sequel.

And yet I will not name it; and yet I care not.

And yet take this again;

    She offers him the letter

                    and yet I thank you,

Meaning henceforth to trouble you no more.   110

SPEED (*aside*)

And yet you will, and yet another yet.

VALENTINE

What means your ladyship? Do you not like it?

SILVIA

Yes, yes; the lines are very quaintly writ,

But since unwillingly, take them again.

    She presses the letter upon him

Nay, take them.

VALENTINE   Madam, they are for you.   115

SILVIA

Ay, ay; you writ them, sir, at my request,

But I will none of them; they are for you.

I would have had them writ more movingly.

---

104 stead] F (steed)   109 *She . . . letter*] *not in* F   114.1 *She . . . him*] *not in* F

---

100 **came hardly off** was difficult to write
102 **doubtfully** uncertainly
104 **So it stead** if it helps
106 **And yet—**He presumably breaks off because he doesn't want to write more to her unknown admirer.
107 **period** full stop, hesitation

108–11 **And yet . . . another yet** Silvia picks up Valentine's broken-off *And yet* and lightly mocks him with her repetitions; Speed in turn mocks both of them in his response, which is in verse, presumably to echo theirs.
113 **quaintly** skilfully, ingeniously

VALENTINE

  Please you, I'll write your ladyship another.

SILVIA

  And when it's writ, for my sake read it over,   120

  And if it please you, so; if not, why, so.

VALENTINE

  If it please me, madam, what then?

SILVIA

  Why, if it please you, take it for your labour.

  And so good morrow, servant.   *Exit*

SPEED (*aside*)

  O jest unseen, inscrutable, invisible   125

  As a nose on a man's face or a weathercock on a steeple.

  My master sues to her, and she hath taught her suitor,

  He being her pupil, to become her tutor.

  O excellent device, was there ever heard a better?—

  That my master, being scribe, to himself should write

      the letter.   130

VALENTINE How now, sir—what, are you reasoning with
yourself?

SPEED Nay, I was rhyming. 'Tis you that have the reason.

VALENTINE To do what?

SPEED To be a spokesman from Madam Silvia.   135

VALENTINE To whom?

SPEED To yourself. Why, she woos you by a figure.

VALENTINE What figure?

SPEED By a letter, I should say.

VALENTINE Why, she hath not writ to me.   140

---

131 what, are] What are F

125–30 Speed slips into doggerel verse to
mock the courtliness of the lovers.

125–6 O jest . . . steeple i.e. however subtle
Silvia's device seems, it is in fact blatantly
obvious. 'As plain as the nose on a man's
face' was proverbial (Dent N215).

131 what, are F's 'What are' makes sense,
'but elsewhere Shakespeare seems to use
"reason with" only as an intransitive
verb' (*TC*, p. 167).

131–3 reasoning . . . rhyming Playing on
the proverbial juxtaposition 'neither
rhyme nor reason' (Dent R98). Shakespeare uses it again at *Errors* 2.2.47–8
and *As You Like It* 3.2.384–5.

131 reasoning with talking to

137–8 figure device (i.e. indirectly)

SPEED What need she, when she hath made you write to
    yourself? Why, do you not perceive the jest?
VALENTINE No, believe me.
SPEED No believing you indeed, sir. But did you perceive
    her earnest?   145
VALENTINE She gave me none, except an angry word.
SPEED Why, she hath given you a letter.
VALENTINE That's the letter I writ to her friend.
SPEED And that letter hath she delivered, and there an end.
VALENTINE I would it were no worse.   150
SPEED I'll warrant you, 'tis as well.
    For often have you writ to her, and she in modesty
    Or else for want of idle time could not again reply,
    Or fearing else some messenger that might her mind
        discover,
    Herself hath taught her love himself to write unto her
        lover.   155
    — All this I speak in print, for in print I found it. Why
    muse you, sir? 'Tis dinner-time.
VALENTINE I have dined.
SPEED Ay, but hearken, sir. Though the chameleon love
    can feed on the air, I am one that am nourished by my   160
    victuals, and would fain have meat. O, be not like your
    mistress—be moved, be moved!   *Exeunt*

---

145 **earnest** (a) down payment; (b) serious
    intention
152–5 This time Speed's doggerel verse is in
    old-fashioned 'fourteeners', so called
    because they contain fourteen syllables.
    Shakespeare uses them again in the play
    scene of *A Midsummer Night's Dream*
    (5.1) and for the apparitions in *Cymbeline*
    (5.5.124–86). Speed is again mocking
    Silvia's use of the letter as an indirect
    way of wooing.
156 **in print** precisely
    for . . . I found it Editors have con-
    jectured that this refers to some un-
    known printed source; but surely it's yet
    another ironical reference to the letter?
157 **muse** ponder, dream

158 **dined** (on love)
159–60 **chameleon . . . air** Because this
    lizard can go without food for long
    periods, it was proverbially thought to
    feed on air (Dent M226); and because it
    was reputed to change its colour, it was
    often associated, as here, with the
    changeable behaviour of lovers. Compare
    2.4.24–7.
161 **victuals** food. *OED* notes that the pro-
    nunciation, *vittles*, reflects the word's Old
    French origin.
    fain gladly
    meat food
162 **be moved** (a) have compassion; (b) go in
    to dinner

2.2 *Enter Proteus and Julia*

PROTEUS

Have patience, gentle Julia.

JULIA

I must where is no remedy.

PROTEUS

When possibly I can I will return.

JULIA

If you turn not, you will return the sooner.

    She gives him a ring

Keep this remembrance for thy Julia's sake.   5

PROTEUS

Why then, we'll make exchange. Here, take you this.

    He gives her a ring

JULIA

And seal the bargain with a holy kiss.

    ⌈*They kiss*⌉

PROTEUS

Here is my hand for my true constancy.

And when that hour o'erslips me in the day

Wherein I sigh not, Julia, for thy sake,   10

The next ensuing hour some foul mischance

Torment me for my love's forgetfulness.

My father stays my coming; answer not.

The tide is now. (*Julia weeps*) Nay, not thy tide of tears,

That tide will stay me longer than I should.   15

2.2.0.1 *Enter . . . Julia*] *Enter Protheus, Iulia, Panthion.* F   4.1 *She . . . ring*] *not in* F   6.1 *He . . . ring*] *not in* F   7.1 *They kiss*] *not in* F   14 *Julia weeps*] *not in* F

2.2.1–2 **Have . . . remedy** These lines draw on the proverbs 'What cannot be cured must be endured' (Dent C922) and 'There is no remedy but patience' (Dent R71).

2 **where is** where there is

4 **turn not** are constant, not unfaithful

5–8 It is sometimes suggested that the exchange of rings, and Proteus giving his hand, represents a formal, legally binding Elizabethan betrothal ceremony, a 'contracting'. But 'though couples could pledge themselves in private, the preferred formula had them "contract . . . before honest and credible witnesses"'

(David Cressy, *Birth, Marriage, and Death* (Oxford, 1997), p. 273). This is what happens at *As You Like It* 4.1.116–32, where Rosalind and Orlando exchange binding promises, with Celia as witness. Here, by comparison, such a contracting ceremony is, at most, hinted at.

8 **constancy** For a discussion of 'constant' and 'constancy' in the play, see the Introduction, pp. 34–5.

9 **o'erslips** passes by

13 **stays** awaits

14 **now** suitable for sailing

Julia, farewell.   *Exit Julia*
          What, gone without a word?
Ay, so true love should do: it cannot speak,
For truth hath better deeds than words to grace it.
     Enter Panthino

PANTHINO
Sir Proteus, you are stayed for.
PROTEUS   Go, I come, I come.—
Alas, this parting strikes poor lovers dumb.   *Exeunt*   20

2.3 *Enter Lance with his dog Crab*

LANCE (*To the audience*) Nay, 'twill be this hour ere I have
     done weeping. All the kind of the Lances have this
     very fault. I have received my proportion, like the
     prodigious son, and am going with Sir Proteus to the
     Imperial's court. I think Crab, my dog, be the sourest-   5
     natured dog that lives. My mother weeping, my father
     wailing, my sister crying, our maid howling, our cat
     wringing her hands, and all our house in a great per-
     plexity, yet did not this cruel-hearted cur shed one tear.

16 *Exit Julia*] not in F   18.1 *Enter Panthino*] not in F
  2.3.0.1 *Enter . . . Crab*] *Enter Launce, Panthion.* F

16–18 Proverbial: 'Whom we love best, to
    them we say least' (Dent L165); see note
    to 1.2.29–32.
2.3.0.1 *Lance* The Folio spelling is 'Launce',
    but 'Lance' is the modern form. The
    name may be a comic version of King
    Arthur's knight Sir Lancelot (compare
    Lancelot Gobbo in *Merchant*) and may
    suggest the jousting weapon—not to
    mention the phallus.
1–31 For a discussion of dogs on stage, see
    Introduction, p. 24; and of Lance's
    monologues, pp. 50–2.
  1 **Nay** Not a negative, but used for
    emphasis, to launch the monologue. It
    is a Lance mannerism: he uses it in his
    second soliloquy, at 4.4.28, 33.
    this hour ere an hour before
  2 **kind** family
  3 **very** exact
    proportion Lance's mistake for 'por-
    tion', inheritance. See next note.
  4 **prodigious** Another malapropism, a

mistake for 'prodigal'. In the biblical parable of the Prodigal Son (Luke 15:12), the
younger son asks his father for his 'por-
tion' as he leaves home.
  5 **Imperial's** Lance's slip for 'Emperor's', a
    misuse he shares with another Clown, at
    Titus 4.4.40. For the Emperor, see note to
    1.3.27.
5–6 **sourest-natured** This explains Crab's
    name, since the crab-apple is sour, bitter.
    Compare *Shrew* 2.1.226–7: 'You must not
    look so sour. | It is my fashion when I see
    a crab.' In *Tarlton's Jests* (see Introduc-
    tion, p. 24), the famous clown Richard
    Tarlton knelt to his father and asked his
    blessing, upon which a 'fellow' in the
    audience threw an apple at him. Tarlton
    commented 'for an apple he hath cast a
    Crab' (sig. B2v); this incident may have
    suggested the dog's name and nature.
  9 **cur** Both literal and contemptuous: 'a
    worthless, low-bred, or snappish dog'
    (*OED* 1).

He is a stone, a very pebble-stone, and has no more pity   10
in him than a dog. A Jew would have wept to have seen
our parting. Why, my grandam, having no eyes, look
you, wept herself blind at my parting. Nay, I'll show you
the manner of it. This shoe is my father. No, this left
shoe is my father. No, no, this left shoe is my mother.   15
Nay, that cannot be so, neither. Yes, it is so, it is so: it
hath the worser sole. This shoe with the hole in it is my
mother, and this my father. A vengeance on't, there 'tis.
Now, sir, this staff is my sister, for, look you, she is as
white as a lily and as small as a wand. This hat is Nan   20
our maid. I am the dog. No, the dog is himself, and I am
the dog. O, the dog is me, and I am myself. Ay, so, so.
Now come I to my father. 'Father, your blessing.' Now
should not the shoe speak a word for weeping. Now
should I kiss my father. Well, he weeps on. Now come I   25
to my mother. O that she could speak now, like a wood

26 wood] F (would); moved OXFORD

10–11 **no . . . dog** Proverbial: 'To have as much pity as a dog' (Dent D510.1).

11–12 **A Jew . . . parting** Proverbial: 'It would make a Jew rue' (Dent J50.1). As Leech points out, 'this seems to strengthen the link' between Lance and Lancelot Gobbo in *Merchant*, especially his tearful parting from Shylock's daughter Jessica at 2.3.1–14. And see note to 2.1.9.

12 **having no eyes** i.e. being blind

12–13 **look you** This is a favourite catch-phrase of Lance's: he uses it again at l. 19; 2.5.26; 3.1.260, 274; and 4.4.2. It is a colloquialism, used for emphasis: 'listen to me' (*OED*, *look*, *v.* 4a), now particularly associated with Welsh idiom.

13–29 **Nay . . . makes** Lance re-stages his parting from his family as a comic routine, complete with props: shoe, hat, and dog.

17–18 **worser sole . . . mother** Lance puns on the *sole* of the shoe and his mother's soul: 'the female has the inferior "soul" to the male, according to misogynistic tradition' (Carroll). Then he confirms that the shoe must represent his mother because, like her, it has a *hole*.

18 **A vengeance . . . 'tis** curse it, that is how it is (Moore)

20 **white . . . lily** Proverbial (Dent L296). **small** slim

21–2 **I am the dog . . . myself** As when deciding which shoe should represent which parent, Lance becomes confused in the casting here, first casting himself as the dog, then realizing there is a better candidate standing beside him—only to lead to further confusion.

22 **so, so** that's it

26–7 **wood woman** madwoman, 'crazy, frantic with grief' (Theobald, who proposed this reading of F's 'would-woman'). Sanders, reading 'old woman', rejects Theobald's as 'inappropriate in the context', but it seems to me perfectly apt: Lance's mother is driven mad with grief at the parting. *Wood* has also been rejected as graphically implausible, but in the Quarto text of *Merry Wives*, the spellings 'would' and 'wood' are used indifferently: 'Would you wood helpe me to beare it' (2.2.178), as Carroll points out. And *wood* meaning mad occurs at *Dream* 2.1.192: 'And here am I, and wood within this wood'. So I have not felt the need to follow Oxford's 'moved' (*Re-Editing*, p. 36).

woman. Well, I kiss her. Why, there 'tis. Here's my
mother's breath up and down. Now come I to my sister;
mark the moan she makes.—Now the dog all this while
sheds not a tear nor speaks a word; but see how I lay the   30
dust with my tears.
    Enter Panthino
PANTHINO Lance, away, away, aboard. Thy master is
  shipped, and thou art to post after with oars. What's the
  matter? Why weep'st thou, man? Away, ass, you'll lose
  the tide if you tarry any longer.   35
LANCE It is no matter if the tied were lost, for it is the
  unkindest tied that ever any man tied.
PANTHINO What's the unkindest tide?
LANCE Why, he that's tied here, Crab my dog.
PANTHINO Tut, man, I mean thou'lt lose the flood, and in   40
  losing the flood, lose thy voyage, and in losing thy voy-
  age, lose thy master, and in losing thy master, lose thy
  service, and in losing thy service—
    Lance puts his hand over Panthino's mouth
  Why dost thou stop my mouth?
LANCE For fear thou shouldst lose thy tongue.   45
PANTHINO Where should I lose my tongue?
LANCE In thy tale.

31.1 *Enter Panthino*] *not in* F   43.1 *Lance . . . mouth*] *not in* F

---

27 **there 'tis** that's it (a colloquialism also
   used by Falstaff at *1 Henry IV* 3.3.12:
   'there is it')
28 **up and down** in every respect, com-
   pletely (*OED adv.* 6a)
30–1 **lay . . . tears** Lance's *lay* [settle] *the dust*
   is *OED*'s first example of the phrase (*lay,*
   v.[1] 3a).
33 **post** hurry
   with oars in a rowing-boat
34–5 **lose the tide** Together with Lance's
   weeping, the extended play on *tide* and
   tied that follows is clearly an ironic
   counterpart to the parting of Julia and
   Proteus, and especially her 'tide of tears',
   in the preceding scene (ll. 14–15).

34 **lose** miss
35 **if . . . longer** Echoing the proverb 'The
   tide tarries for no man' (Dent T323).
36 **tied** Lance shifts the sense from *tide* = sea
   or river to the tied-up Crab, releasing the
   word-play that follows. It also occurs in
   Lyly's *Endymion* (1588?): 'it is said, the
   tide tarrieth no man. . . . A monstrous
   lie; for I was tied two hours, and tarried
   for one to unloose me' (4.2.9–12).
40 **lose the flood** miss the favourable tide
43 **service** employment
45, 46 **lose** A quibble on 'lose' and 'release'
   (i.e. keep on talking). Both are spelt
   'loose' in F.

PANTHINO In my tail!

LANCE Lose the tide, and the voyage, and the master, and
   the service, and the tied? Why, man, if the river were   50
   dry, I am able to fill it with my tears. If the wind were
   down, I could drive the boat with my sighs.

PANTHINO Come, come away, man, I was sent to call thee.

LANCE Sir, call me what thou darest.

PANTHINO Wilt thou go?   55

LANCE Well, I will go.   *Exeunt*

2.4 *Enter Valentine, Silvia, Thurio, and Speed*

SILVIA Servant!

VALENTINE Mistress?

SPEED (*to Valentine*) Master, Sir Thurio frowns on you.

VALENTINE Ay, boy, it's for love.

SPEED Not of you.   5

VALENTINE Of my mistress, then.

SPEED 'Twere good you knocked him.   ⌈*Exit*⌉

SILVIA (*to Valentine*) Servant, you are sad.

VALENTINE Indeed, madam, I seem so.

THURIO Seem you that you are not?   10

VALENTINE Haply I do.

THURIO So do counterfeits.

VALENTINE So do you.

THURIO What seem I that I am not?

VALENTINE Wise.   15

---

48 my] DYCE 1868 (*conj.* Hanmer); thy F

2.4.0.1 *Enter . . . Speed*] *Enter Valentine, Siluia, Thurio, Speed, Duke, Protheus.* F   7 *Exit*] *not in* F

48 **In my tail!** Hanmer's proposed emendation of F's 'thy' to 'my' is needed to bring
out the (obscene) sense of the remark.
Lance's 'In thy tale' in the previous line
means 'you will lose/loose your tongue in
talking so much'; Panthino takes him to
mean 'rimming', anal penetration with
the tongue (*OED*, *rim*, *v.*³ 1a), hence his
outrage (F's spelling differentiates
between Lance's 'Tale' and Panthino's
'Taile'). Compare *Shrew* 2.1.216: 'What,
with my tongue in your tail?' F's reading
probably reflects Ralph Crane's censoring: see Introduction, p. 61.

53, 54 **call . . . call** Panthino means
'summon', Lance 'call names, insult'.

2.4.1 **Servant** See note to 2.1.92.

7 **knocked** struck. Speed has nothing
more to say in this scene. 'As Valentine's
page, he could remain in silent attend-
ance' (*TC*, p. 167), but it is hard to believe
that so loquacious a character would
say nothing for a long scene; so I follow
the Cambridge editors in removing him,
especially since he has a strong exit line.

11 **Haply** perhaps

12 **counterfeits** deceivers

THURIO What instance of the contrary?

VALENTINE Your folly.

THURIO And how quote you my folly?

VALENTINE I quote it in your jerkin.

THURIO My 'jerkin' is a doublet.   20

VALENTINE Well then, I'll double your folly.

THURIO How!

SILVIA What, angry, Sir Thurio? Do you change colour?

VALENTINE Give him leave, madam, he is a kind of
chameleon.   25

THURIO That hath more mind to feed on your blood than
live in your air.

VALENTINE You have said, sir.

THURIO Ay, sir, and done too, for this time.

VALENTINE I know it well, sir, you always end ere you   30
begin.

SILVIA A fine volley of words, gentlemen, and quickly shot
off.

VALENTINE 'Tis indeed, madam, we thank the giver.

SILVIA Who is that, servant?   35

VALENTINE Yourself, sweet lady, for you gave the fire. Sir
Thurio borrows his wit from your ladyship's looks, and
spends what he borrows kindly in your company.

THURIO Sir, if you spend word for word with me, I shall
make your wit bankrupt.   40

VALENTINE I know it well, sir. You have an exchequer of
words, and, I think, no other treasure to give your followers; for it appears by their bare liveries that they live
by your bare words.

16 **instance** evidence

18, 19 **quote** observe, note (often written
and pronounced 'cote', hence the pun
with 'jerkin')

19 **jerkin** long jacket worn over, or in place
of, a doublet (see next note)

20 **doublet** short jacket

21 **double** (punning on *doublet* in the previous line, i.e. 'double it')

22 **How!** An expression of annoyance,
hence Silvia's response.

23–7 **change colour . . . air** See note to
2.1.159–60.

28–9 **said . . . done** Playing on the proverb 'no sooner said than done' (Dent
S117).

30–1 **end ere you begin** (implying
cowardice)

32–3 **A fine . . . shot off** Compare the
Princess at *Love's Labour's Lost* 5.2.29:
'Well bandied, both; a set of wit well
played.' Silvia's imagery (*volley*, *shot off*)
is of gunfire, picked up in the next lines.

34 **giver** one who directs the aim (and so
'inspirer')

38 **kindly** gratefully, naturally

41 **exchequer** treasury

43–4 **bare . . . bare** threadbare, mere.
Compare the accusation that Don
Armado's followers 'are but lightly
rewarded' (*Love's Labour's Lost* 1.2.144).

43 **liveries** uniforms

SILVIA No more, gentlemen, no more. Here comes my   45
    father.

    Enter the Duke

DUKE

  Now, daughter Silvia, you are hard beset.

  Sir Valentine, your father is in good health;

  What say you to a letter from your friends

  Of much good news?

VALENTINE   My lord, I will be thankful   50

  To any happy messenger from thence.

DUKE

  Know ye Don Antonio, your countryman?

VALENTINE

  Ay, my good lord, I know the gentleman

  To be of worth, and worthy estimation,

  And not without desert so well reputed.   55

DUKE Hath he not a son?

VALENTINE

  Ay, my good lord, a son that well deserves

  The honour and regard of such a father.

DUKE You know him well?

VALENTINE

  I knew him as myself, for from our infancy   60

  We have conversed, and spent our hours together,

  And though myself have been an idle truant,

  Omitting the sweet benefit of time

  To clothe mine age with angel-like perfection,

  Yet hath Sir Proteus—for that's his name—   65

  Made use and fair advantage of his days:

  His years but young, but his experience old;

  His head unmellowed, but his judgement ripe.

46.1 *Enter the Duke*] *not in* F   60 knew] F; know HANMER

47 **beset** pressed, besieged
49 **say you to** what would you say if I told you of
51 **happy messenger** bringer of good news
52 **Don** See note to 1.3.39.
54 **worthy estimation** worthy of esteem
55 **desert** deserving, justification
60 **knew** Perhaps an example of the simple past sense being used for the complete present (Abbott 347), but Hanmer's emendation 'know' might be clearer in performance.
61 **conversed** kept company
63 **Omitting** neglecting
68 **unmellowed** without grey hair

And in a word—for far behind his worth
Comes all the praises that I now bestow—   70
He is complete in feature and in mind,
With all good grace to grace a gentleman.

DUKE

Beshrew me, sir, but if he make this good
He is as worthy for an empress' love
As meet to be an emperor's counsellor.   75
Well, sir, this gentleman is come to me
With commendation from great potentates,
And here he means to spend his time awhile.
I think 'tis no unwelcome news to you.

VALENTINE

Should I have wished a thing it had been he.   80

DUKE

Welcome him then according to his worth.
Silvia, I speak to you, and you, Sir Thurio;
For Valentine, I need not cite him to it.
I will send him hither to you presently.   *Exit*

VALENTINE

This is the gentleman I told your ladyship   85
Had come along with me, but that his mistress
Did hold his eyes locked in her crystal looks.

SILVIA

Belike that now she hath enfranchised them
Upon some other pawn for fealty.

---

84 *Exit*] *not in* F

70 **Comes all the praises** A singular verb with a plural subject is common in Shakespeare (Abbott 335).
71 **complete** perfect
   feature appearance
73 **make this good** prove this to be true
74–5 **empress . . . emperor** These may be general terms, rather than referring to Silvia and the Duke himself (the former recurs at 5.4.139), though Shakespeare may still be hovering between 'Emperor' and 'Duke'. See note to 1.3.27.
75 **meet** fit
77 **potentates** Literally 'rulers', though Shakespeare may simply be thinking of the 'gentlemen of good esteem' with

whom Proteus travelled to Milan (1.3.40).
80 **a thing** anything
83 **cite** incite
84 **hither** here
   presently straightaway
86 **Had** would have
87 **eyes . . . looks** Perhaps this refers to objects displayed in glass. Compare *Love's Labour's Lost* 2.1.242–3: 'his senses were locked in his eye, | As jewels in crystal'.
88 **Belike** it is likely
   enfranchised set free
89 **pawn for fealty** pledge of (Proteus') fidelity

VALENTINE

  Nay, sure, I think she holds them prisoners still.   90

SILVIA

  Nay, then he should be blind, and being blind

  How could he see his way to seek out you?

VALENTINE

  Why, lady, love hath twenty pair of eyes.

THURIO

  They say that Love hath not an eye at all.

VALENTINE

  To see such lovers, Thurio, as yourself.   95

  Upon a homely object love can wink.

SILVIA

  Have done, have done; here comes the gentleman.

     Enter Proteus

VALENTINE

  Welcome, dear Proteus. Mistress, I beseech you

  Confirm his welcome with some special favour.

SILVIA

  His worth is warrant for his welcome hither,   100

  If this be he you oft have wished to hear from.

VALENTINE

  Mistress, it is; sweet lady, entertain him

  To be my fellow-servant to your ladyship.

SILVIA

  Too low a mistress for so high a servant.

PROTEUS

  Not so, sweet lady, but too mean a servant   105

97.1 *Enter Proteus*] *not in* F

---

94 **They say . . . at all** Another reference
to the blindness of Cupid: see note to
2.1.66.

96 **homely** plain

97 **Have done** stop arguing

98 **beseech** beg

99 **favour** privilege or mark of favour, but
perhaps also in the more specific chivalric
sense of a glove or other object to be
worn by a knight as a mark of his lady's
affection (*OED sb.* 7a).

100 **warrant** guarantee

102–3 **entertain . . . ladyship** Valentine
is again using the language of courtly
love, asking Silvia to take Proteus into
her service—a dangerous request, as
will emerge. The courtly language is
sustained in the following lines.

104 **low . . . high** insignificant . . .
distinguished

105 **mean** lowly

To have a look of such a worthy mistress.

VALENTINE

Leave off discourse of disability.

Sweet lady, entertain him for your servant.

PROTEUS

My duty will I boast of, nothing else.

SILVIA

And duty never yet did want his meed.   110

Servant, you are welcome to a worthless mistress.

PROTEUS

I'll die on him that says so but yourself.

SILVIA

That you are welcome?

PROTEUS   That you are worthless.

⌜*Enter a Servant*⌝

⌜SERVANT⌝

Madam, my lord your father would speak with you.

SILVIA

I wait upon his pleasure.   ⌜*Exit the Servant*⌝

Come, Sir Thurio,   115

Go with me. Once more, new servant, welcome.

I'll leave you to confer of home affairs.

When you have done, we look to hear from you.

PROTEUS

We'll both attend upon your ladyship.

Exeunt Silvia and Thurio

VALENTINE

Now tell me, how do all from whence you came?   120

---

106 worthy] F2; worthy a F   113.1 *Enter a Servant*] *not in* F   114 SERVANT] THEOBALD;
Thur. F   115 *Exit the Servant*] *not in* F   119.1 *Exeunt . . . Thurio*] *not in* F

---

106 **have a look of** deserve a glance from
107 **disability** unworthiness. Even Valentine is finding their courtliness excessive.
110 **want his meed** lack its reward
112 **die on him** die fighting against
114 SERVANT F gives this line to Thurio, but since he is on stage, he is in no position to know the Duke's wishes, so this edition follows Theobald's sensible introduction of a servant to deliver the message.
117 **confer of** talk about

120–1 **you . . . Your** When they were last together, in the opening scene, the two friends normally used the intimate 'thou' and 'thy'. Does their use of the more formal *you* indicate a slight distancing (perhaps because they are both now absorbed in other people), or is Shakespeare unconsciously thinking ahead to what is to happen? Valentine reverts to 'thou' at l. 153, but Proteus continues to use *you*.

PROTEUS

   Your friends are well, and have them much
      commended.

VALENTINE

   And how do yours?

PROTEUS   I left them all in health.

VALENTINE

   How does your lady, and how thrives your love?

PROTEUS

   My tales of love were wont to weary you,

   I know you joy not in a love-discourse.   125

VALENTINE

   Ay, Proteus, but that life is altered now.

   I have done penance for contemning love,

   Whose high imperious thoughts have punished me

   With bitter fasts, with penitential groans,

   With nightly tears and daily heart-sore sighs;   130

   For in revenge of my contempt of love

   Love hath chased sleep from my enthrallèd eyes,

   And made them watchers of mine own heart's sorrow.

   O gentle Proteus, love's a mighty lord,

   And hath so humbled me as I confess   135

   There is no woe to his correction,

   Nor to his service no such joy on earth.

   Now, no discourse except it be of love;

   Now can I break my fast, dine, sup, and sleep

   Upon the very naked name of love.   140

PROTEUS

   Enough, I read your fortune in your eye.

   Was this the idol that you worship so?

---

121 **have . . . commended** sent their good
    wishes, commendations

124 **were wont** used

127 **contemning** despising

128 **imperious** domineering (the influence
    of Cupid the god)

129–40 These lines echo 1.1.29–35 and
    2.1.16–29 as an elaborate statement
    of the standard behaviour of the con-
    ventional lover.

132 **enthrallèd** enslaved

135 **as** that

136 **to his correction** compared to his
    punishment

140 **very naked** mere

142–5 **idol . . . saint . . . divine** For the use
    of religious language to express love,
    compare Sonnet 31.5–6: 'How many a
    holy and obsequious tear | Hath dear
    religious love stol'n from mine eye'. For
    further discussion, see Introduction,
    p. 33.

VALENTINE

  Even she; and is she not a heavenly saint?

PROTEUS

  No, but she is an earthly paragon.

VALENTINE

  Call her divine.

PROTEUS   I will not flatter her.   145

VALENTINE

  O flatter me; for love delights in praises.

PROTEUS

  When I was sick you gave me bitter pills,

  And I must minister the like to you.

VALENTINE

  Then speak the truth by her; if not divine,

  Yet let her be a principality,   150

  Sovereign to all the creatures on the earth.

PROTEUS

  Except my mistress.

VALENTINE   Sweet, except not any,

  Except thou wilt except against my love.

PROTEUS

  Have I not reason to prefer mine own?

VALENTINE

  And I will help thee to prefer her, too.   155

  She shall be dignified with this high honour,

  To bear my lady's train, lest the base earth

  Should from her vesture chance to steal a kiss

143–4 **heavenly saint . . . earthly paragon**
  The distinction recurs at *Cymbeline*
  3.6.42–3, where the heroine is called 'an
  angel—or, if not, | An earthly paragon'.

149 **by** of

150 **principality** A spiritual being, one of
  the nine orders of angels (*OED sb.* 5).

151 **Sovereign** superior

152 **Sweet** In the very act of praising his
  mistress as a divine being, Valentine slips
  into the intimate *Sweet* used by Patroclus
  to his male lover Achilles at *Troilus*
  3.3.215, and then in the next line shifts
  from his previous use of *you* to the more
  affectionate *thou*, which he continues to
  use up to his exit line. It emphasizes the
  closeness of the relationship—which
  Proteus is about to betray.

152–3 **except . . . Except . . . except** Valentine picks up Proteus' *Except* earlier in the
  line, where it is used in the normal modern sense, and plays variations on it,
  moving from 'exclude' in l. 152 to 'unless
  you take exception to' in l. 153.

154–5 **prefer . . . prefer** Another quibble: the
  first means 'have a preference for', the
  second 'promote'.

157 **train** the elaborate, extended skirt of a
  ground-length dress

157–61 **lest . . . everlastingly** Valentine's
  elaborate personification is characteristic
  of much of the style of this play, at once
  artificial and lyrically beautiful. See
  Introduction, pp. 40–1.

157 **base** lowly

158 **vesture** garment

And of so great a favour growing proud,
Disdain to root the summer-swelling flower,   160
And make rough winter everlastingly.

PROTEUS

Why, Valentine, what braggartism's this?

VALENTINE

Pardon me, Proteus, all I can is nothing
To her whose worth makes other worthies nothing.
She is alone.

PROTEUS   Then let her alone.   165

VALENTINE

Not for the world. Why man, she is mine own,
And I as rich in having such a jewel
As twenty seas, if all their sand were pearl,
The water nectar, and the rocks pure gold.
Forgive me that I do not dream on thee   170
Because thou seest me dote upon my love.
My foolish rival, that her father likes
Only for his possessions are so huge,
Is gone with her along, and I must after;
For love, thou know'st, is full of jealousy.   175

---

162 braggartism's] This edition; Bragadisme is F   164 makes] F2; make F1

160 **root** establish or nourish the roots of
summer-swelling which will grow,
blossom, in summer
161 **rough** harsh, stormy. Compare *Winter's Tale* 3.2.211–12: 'still [everlasting] winter | In storm perpetual'.
162 **braggartism's this** F reads 'Bragadisme is this'; but Ralph Crane, the scribe who probably prepared the Folio text, had a habit of marking elisions but still spelling out the word. I suspect he wrote 'Bragadisme'is' and the compositor omitted the apostrophe rather than the 'i'. My reading not only regularizes the line but makes it more speakable and (I think) more effective.
braggartism ostentatious boasting. F's spelling is an indifferent variant: see *OED*, where this line is the earliest example. It is also Shakespeare's only use of the word.
163 **can** can say

164 **To** compared to
worthies excellences
165 **She is alone** She is unique—a claim Proteus deflates in his reply, i.e. 'then leave her alone'.
167 **jewel** This may be the language of lovers, but that need not imply any lack of genuine feeling: compare Innogen in *Cymbeline*, parting from her husband, Posthumus: she is 'not comforted to live | But that there is this jewel in the world' (1.1.91–2).
170 **I . . . thee** 'pay attention to you' (Norton), or, stronger, 'you are no longer my sole occupation' (Richard Proudfoot, in Carroll), which fits very well with the intimate *thee*.
173 **for** because
175 **love . . . jealousy** Proverbial: 'Love is never without jealousy' (L510).
jealousy suspicion (*OED* 5)

PROTEUS But she loves you?

VALENTINE

    Ay, and we are betrothed. Nay more, our marriage hour,

    With all the cunning manner of our flight,

    Determined of: how I must climb her window,

    The ladder made of cords, and all the means   180

    Plotted and 'greed on for my happiness.

    Good Proteus, go with me to my chamber,

    In these affairs to aid me with thy counsel.

PROTEUS

    Go on before; I shall enquire you forth.

    I must unto the road, to disembark   185

    Some necessaries that I needs must use,

    And then I'll presently attend you.

VALENTINE Will you make haste?

PROTEUS I will.   *Exit Valentine*

    Even as one heat another heat expels,   190

    Or as one nail by strength drives out another,

    So the remembrance of my former love

    Is by a newer object quite forgotten.

    Is it mine eye, or Valentine's praise,

    Her true perfection, or my false transgression   195

    That makes me, reasonless, to reason thus?

---

189 *Exit Valentine*] F (*Exit.*, after l. 188)   194 Is it] F2; It is FI   mine eye] THEOBALD; mine F

---

179 **Determined of** decided on

180 **cords** rope (perhaps suggested by Brooke's *Romeus and Juliet*: see Introduction, p. 18)

183 **counsel** advice (as at 1.3.34)

184 **before** ahead

    enquire you forth seek you out

185 **road** harbour (as at 1.1.53)

187 **presently** at once

190–1 **Even as . . . another** Shakespeare combines two proverbs here 'One fire/nail drives out another' (Dent F277, N17), as he does in one incisive line at *Coriolanus* 4.7.54: 'One fire drives out one fire, one nail one nail.'

193 **by** because of

194 Something has gone wrong with F, which reads 'It is mine, or *Valentines* praise?' 'It is' is easily corrected to 'Is it', as F2 does, but though there are many other lines in Shakespeare of eight syllables and four stresses, this one does not scan. Theobald emended 'mine' to 'mine eye', and C. J. Sisson supports this by reference to a similar slip at Sonnet 113.14 (*New Readings in Shakespeare*, 2 vols. (Cambridge, 1956), i. 56). *Valentines* is sometimes emended to 'Valentinus'', as at 1.3.67, where it arguably suits the speaker (see note); but 'a mid-line pause gives weight to the antithesis' (*TC*, p. 167, where Gary Taylor also conjectures 'Valentine his').

196 **reasonless** irrational

She is fair, and so is Julia that I love—
That I *did* love, for now my love is thawed,
Which like a waxen image 'gainst a fire
Bears no impression of the thing it was.   200
Methinks my zeal to Valentine is cold,
And that I love him not as I was wont.
O, but I love his lady too-too much,
And that's the reason I love him so little.
How shall I dote on her with more advice,   205
That thus without advice begin to love her?
'Tis but her picture I have yet beheld,
And that hath dazzlèd my reason's light.
But when I look on her perfections
There is no reason but I shall be blind.   210
If I can check my erring love I will,
If not, to compass her I'll use my skill.   *Exit*

2.5 *Enter Speed, and Lance with his dog Crab*
SPEED Lance, by mine honesty, welcome to Milan.
LANCE Forswear not thyself, sweet youth, for I am not
   welcome. I reckon this always, that a man is never
   undone till he be hanged, nor never welcome to a

---

208 dazzelèd] ROWE; dazel'd F   212 *Exit*] F2; *Exeunt.* FI
   2.5.0.1 *with . . . Crab*] *not in* F   I Milan] POPE; *Padua* F

---

200 **impression** image produced by a
   stamp or signet ring
201 **zeal** love
202 **was wont** used to
203 **too-too** excessively. For the verbal
   mannerism, compare Don Armado at
   Love's Labour's Lost 5.2.525–6: 'the
   schoolmaster is . . . too-too vain'.
205 **advice** consideration, deliberation
207 **picture** outward appearance. Some
   productions (Old Vic 1957, Stratford-
   upon-Avon 1998) have emphasized this
   by showing Silvia having her portrait
   painted earlier in the scene, and Proteus
   making reference to it here.
208 **dazzlèd** (three syllables: dazzelèd)
   reason's light clarity of mind

209 **perfections** inner qualities (as opposed
   to her outward appearance at l. 207)
210 **no reason but** no doubt that
212 **compass** obtain
2.5.1 **Milan** F says 'Padua', but they are in
   fact in Milan. Shakespeare's mind in this
   play is wandering between various Italian
   cities. 'Perhaps "Padua" is a first thought,
   rejected but not cancelled in the manuscript; Padua had a famous university to
   which Valentine might appropriately
   have been sent' (Wells, *Re-Editing*, p. 49);
   compare *Shrew* I.I.2: 'fair Padua,
   nursery of arts'.
2 **Forswear** perjure
4 **undone** ruined

place till some certain shot be paid and the hostess say   5
'Welcome'.

SPEED Come on, you madcap. I'll to the alehouse with you
presently, where, for one shot of five pence, thou shalt
have five thousand welcomes. But sirrah, how did thy
master part with Madam Julia?   10

LANCE Marry, after they closed in earnest they parted
very fairly in jest.

SPEED But shall she marry him?

LANCE No.

SPEED How then, shall he marry her?   15

LANCE No, neither.

SPEED What, are they broken?

LANCE No, they are both as whole as a fish.

SPEED Why then, how stands the matter with them?

LANCE Marry, thus: when it stands well with him it stands   20
well with her.

SPEED What an ass art thou! I understand thee not.

LANCE What a block art thou, that thou canst not! My
staff understands me.

SPEED What thou sayst?   25

LANCE Ay, and what I do too. Look thee, I'll but lean,
and my staff under-stands me.

SPEED It stands under thee indeed.

LANCE Why, stand-under and under-stand is all one.

5 **certain** particular
  shot Wright says that *shot* was 'in general dialect and colloquial use' for a bill or
  reckoning, 'especially used of tavern
  accounts' (*Dialect Dictionary, sb.*[1] I). *Shot*
  occurs again in a context of hanging (see
  previous line) at *Cymbeline* 5.5.247–50.
  Compare also Falstaff at 1 *Henry IV*
  5.3.30–1, in another context of death:
  'Though I could scape shot-free at London, I fear the shot here.'

11 **closed** (a) agreed; (b) embraced

17 **broken** no longer engaged

18 **as . . . fish** Lance takes *broken* in the previous line to mean 'in pieces' and replies
  with a proverb meaning 'whole, sound'
  (Dent F301).

19 **how . . . them** how are things between
  them?

20 **when . . . him** (a) when it goes well with
  him; (b) when he has an erection

20–1 **it . . . her** she is pleased when he is
  erect

23 **block** blockhead

26 **Look thee** A colloquial, familiar variant
  on Lance's regular catchphrase 'look you'
  (see note to 2.3.12–13). Compare the Old
  Shepherd at *Winter's Tale* 3.3.109–10:
  'look thee here, boy'.

27–9 **my staff . . . one** The laborious word-
  play on 'understands' is handled more
  incisively at *Twelfth Night* 3.1.78–9: 'My
  legs do better understand me, sir, than I
  understand what you mean . . .'

28 **stands under thee** (perhaps another
  erection joke)

29 **all one** one and the same thing

115

SPEED But tell me true, will't be a match?   30

LANCE Ask my dog. If he say 'Ay', it will. If he say 'No', it
    will. If he shake his tail and say nothing, it will.

SPEED The conclusion is, then, that it will.

LANCE Thou shalt never get such a secret from me but by a
    parable.   35

SPEED 'Tis well that I get it so. But Lance, how sayst thou
    that my master is become a notable lover?

LANCE I never knew him otherwise.

SPEED Than how?

LANCE A notable lubber, as thou reportest him to be.   40

SPEED Why, thou whoreson ass, thou mistak'st me.

LANCE Why, fool, I meant not thee, I meant thy master.

SPEED I tell thee my master is become a hot lover.

LANCE Why, I tell thee I care not, though he burn himself
    in love. If thou wilt, go with me to the alehouse. If not,   45
    thou art an Hebrew, a Jew, and not worth the name of a
    Christian.

SPEED Why?

LANCE Because thou hast not so much charity in thee as to
    go to the ale with a Christian. Wilt thou go?   50

SPEED At thy service.   *Exeunt*

37 that] F2; that that F1   45 wilt,] KNIGHT; wilt∧ F

34 **Thou . . . me** Leech sees this as an ironic
    comment on the lovers in the main plot:
    'the obligation of secrecy was a heritage
    from the courtly love code.'
34–5 **by a parable** i.e. indirectly
36 **how sayst thou** what do you say about
    the fact
40 **lubber** clumsy lout (also used at Lyly's
    Campaspe 3.2.19 and by Feste at *Twelfth
    Night* 4.1.13). *OED* suggests that this
    derives ultimately from Old French *lobeor*,
    'swindler', modified by association with
    lob, a word of Teutonic origin meaning
    'clown' or 'lout', as at *Dream* 2.1.16,
    where Robin Goodfellow is called 'thou
    lob of spirits'.
41 **whoreson** A general term of abuse,
    literally 'son of a whore'.

42 **meant not thee** Lance (mis)under-
    stands Speed's *mistak'st me* (misunder-
    stands me) in the previous line to
    mean 'takes me for someone else', i.e.
    Valentine.
43 **hot** ardent
44–5 **burn . . . love** (probably by contract-
    ing venereal disease)
46 **an Hebrew, a Jew** See the note to
    2.3.11–12.
50 **ale** alehouse (or the ale itself). Perhaps,
    in view of *charity* (l. 49), a reference to
    'holy-ales', fund-raising church festivals,
    as, arguably, at *Pericles* Sc. 1.6, though
    the phrase is not recorded elsewhere.
    OED 2a cites an example of the phrase 'to
    the ale' as early as *c*.1500.

2.6 *Enter Proteus*

PROTEUS

To leave my Julia shall I be forsworn;
To love fair Silvia shall I be forsworn;
To wrong my friend I shall be much forsworn.
And e'en that power which gave me first my oath
Provokes me to this threefold perjury.   5
Love bade me swear, and love bids me forswear.
O sweet-suggesting love, if thou hast sinned,
Teach me, thy tempted subject, to excuse it.
At first I did adore a twinkling star,
But now I worship a celestial sun.   10
Unheedful vows may heedfully be broken,
And he wants wit that wants resolvèd will
To learn his wit t'exchange the bad for better.
Fie, fie, unreverent tongue, to call her bad
Whose sovereignty so oft thou hast preferred   15
With twenty thousand soul-confirming oaths.
I cannot leave to love, and yet I do.

2.6.0.1 *Enter Proteus*] *Enter Protheus solus.* F   1, 2 forsworn;] THEOBALD; forsworne? F
4 e'en] F (ev'n)

2.6.1–43 In this speech, in which Proteus
persuades himself to break his vow of
love to Julia in the interests of another
love, there are several parallels with an
important scene in *Love's Labour's Lost*
(4.3) where Biron uses an elaborate
argument about the power of love to
'excuse' his and his companions' breaking of an earlier oath. Details are given in
the notes below.
1, 2 **forsworn** guilty of perjury
 4 **e'en that** even that very
 power i.e. love
 6 **forswear** break my oath. Compare
Biron's argument at *Love's Labour's Lost*
4.3.287–341.
 7 **sweet-suggesting**   sweetly   seductive
(Onions)
 sinned (in tempting him to break his
oath)
9–10 **star . . . sun** This contrast between
Julia and Silvia anticipates that between
Rosaline and the Princess at *Love's
Labour's Lost* 4.3.228–9: 'her mistress is a
gracious moon, | She an attending star,
scarce seen a light.'

11 **Unheedful . . . broken** This echoes the
proverbial 'An unlawful oath is better
broken than kept' (Dent O7) and perhaps
the Homily 'Against Swearing and
Perjury': 'how damnable a thing it is,
either to forswear ourselves, or to keep an
unlawful and an unadvised oath'
(Shaheen, p. 84).
 Unheedful rash, ill-considered
 heedfully   advisedly,   upon   further
consideration
12 **wit . . . will** Proteus plays on the traditional opposition of *wit* (intelligence)
and *will* (determination); compare Feste's
'Wit, an't be thy will' at *Twelfth Night*
1.5.29.
 wants lacks
 resolvèd decided, firm of purpose
13 **learn** teach
 t'exchange . . . better Proverbial (Dent
B26).
14 **unreverent** irreverent
15 **preferred** recommended
16 **soul-confirming**   sworn   by   my   soul,
devout
17 **leave to love** stop loving (Julia)

But there I leave to love where I should love.
Julia I lose, and Valentine I lose.
If I keep them I needs must lose myself.   20
If I lose them, thus find I by their loss
For Valentine, myself; for Julia, Silvia.
I to myself am dearer than a friend,
For love is still most precious in itself,
And Silvia—witness heaven that made her fair—   25
Shows Julia but a swarthy Ethiope.
I will forget that Julia is alive,
Rememb'ring that my love to her is dead,
And Valentine I'll hold an enemy,
Aiming at Silvia as a sweeter friend.   30
I cannot now prove constant to myself
Without some treachery used to Valentine.
This night he meaneth with a corded ladder
To climb celestial Silvia's chamber-window,
Myself in counsel his competitor.   35
Now presently I'll give her father notice
Of their disguising and pretended flight,
Who, all enraged, will banish Valentine;
For Thurio he intends shall wed his daughter.
But Valentine being gone, I'll quickly cross   40
By some sly trick blunt Thurio's dull proceeding.
Love, lend me wings to make my purpose swift,
As thou hast lent me wit to plot this drift.   *Exit*

---

20 **If . . . myself** Compare *Love's Labour's
Lost* 4.3.337–8: 'Let us once lose our
oaths to find ourselves, | Or else we
lose ourselves to keep our oaths' (the
climax of Biron's using love to justify
oath-breaking, referred to in the head-
note).

needs necessarily

24 **still** always

26 **but** merely

Ethiope black African. This was a common Elizabethan term, used as the
antithesis of fair-skinned beauty, derived
ultimately from the fair-haired Queen
Elizabeth herself. Compare *Love's Labour's
Lost* 4.3.113–16: 'Do not call it sin in me |
That I am forsworn for thee, | Thou for
whom great Jove would swear | Juno but
an Ethiope were'.

27–30 In these lines, Proteus makes his
decision: he will abandon Julia, and
betray Valentine.

30 **sweeter friend** (than his former *friend*,
Valentine; but *friend* could also mean
'lover' in the period)

33 **corded** rope

35 **in . . . competitor** his secret accomplice.
This is the common Shakespearian use,
as at *Love's Labour's Lost* 2.1.82: 'he and
his competitors in oath'.

37 **pretended** intended

40 **cross** thwart

41 **blunt** stupid

dull proceeding awkward conduct
(i.e. his wooing)

42 **lend me wings** Cupid was a winged god.
make . . . swift quickly achieve my aim

43 **drift** scheme

2.7 *Enter Julia and Lucetta*

JULIA

Counsel, Lucetta. Gentle girl, assist me,
And e'en in kind love I do conjure thee,
Who art the table wherein all my thoughts
Are visibly charactered and engraved,
To lesson me, and tell me some good mean   5
How with my honour I may undertake
A journey to my loving Proteus.

LUCETTA

Alas, the way is wearisome and long.

JULIA

A true-devoted pilgrim is not weary
To measure kingdoms with his feeble steps.   10
Much less shall she that hath love's wings to fly,
And when the flight is made to one so dear,
Of such divine perfection as Sir Proteus.

LUCETTA

Better forbear till Proteus make return.

JULIA

O, know'st thou not his looks are my soul's food?   15
Pity the dearth that I have pinèd in
By longing for that food so long a time.
Didst thou but know the inly touch of love
Thou wouldst as soon go kindle fire with snow
As seek to quench the fire of love with words.   20

2.7.2, 52 e'en] F (eu'n)

2.7.1 **Counsel** (give me) advice
2, 52 **e'en** even (F has 'eu'n')
 2 **conjure** entreat
 3 **table** tablet, notebook. Shakespeare often associates a *table* with mental processes, as at *Hamlet* 1.5.98: 'the table of my memory', and Sonnet 122.1: 'Thy gift, thy tables, are within my brain'.
 4 **charactered** written down (in 'characters', alphabetical letters); stressed on the second syllable. Compare Sonnet 122.2 (see previous note): 'Full charactered with lasting memory' (where, however, *charactered* is stressed on the

first syllable, such is the flexibility of Shakespearian verse).
 5 **lesson** instruct
   mean means
 6 **with my honour** without sacrificing my reputation
10 **measure** travel across
11 **she . . . fly** Ironically juxtaposed with the phrasing of her lover's plan to abandon her in the previous scene (l. 42).
18 **inly** inward
19–20 Proverbial: 'To force fire from snow' (Dent F284).

LUCETTA

I do not seek to quench your love's hot fire,
But qualify the fire's extreme rage,
Lest it should burn above the bounds of reason.

JULIA

The more thou damm'st it up, the more it burns.
The current that with gentle murmur glides,   25
Thou know'st, being stopped, impatiently doth rage.
But when his fair course is not hinderèd
He makes sweet music with th'enamelled stones,
Giving a gentle kiss to every sedge
He overtaketh in his pilgrimage.   30
And so by many winding nooks he strays
With willing sport to the wild ocean.
Then let me go, and hinder not my course.
I'll be as patient as a gentle stream,
And make a pastime of each weary step   35
Till the last step have brought me to my love.
And there I'll rest as after much turmoil
A blessèd soul doth in Elysium.

LUCETTA

But in what habit will you go along?

JULIA

Not like a woman, for I would prevent   40
The loose encounters of lascivious men.
Gentle Lucetta, fit me with such weeds
As may beseem some well-reputed page.

22 **qualify** moderate
  fire's (two syllables)
  extreme (stressed on the first syllable)
24 **thou damm'st** you try to block it, as a
  dam does a river. Bond, anxious to avoid
  a mixed metaphor, interprets 'banking
  up a fire by heaping fuel upon it'; but that
  damm'st has its normal meaning is made
  clear by the elaborate, and lyrical, passage that follows; and Bond himself cites
  the parallel combination of fire and water
  at *Venus* 331–2: 'An oven that is stopped,
  or river stayed, | Burneth more hotly,
  swelleth with more rage.' Schlueter notes
  that Julia is 'returning the proverbial
  wisdom she has learned earlier from
  Lucetta' at 1.2.30.
28 **enamelled** i.e. having the hardness and
  polish of enamel (Moore)

29 **sedge** 'grassy, rush-like or flag-like
  plants growing in wet places' (*OED sb.*[1] 1)
32 **wild** open, unenclosed (as at *Errors*
  2.1.21: 'wild wat'ry seas')
38 **Elysium** (the heaven of classical
  mythology)
39 **habit** clothing
40–1 Julia's motive here anticipates
  Rosalind's at *As You Like It* 1.3.107–21;
  she is the first of several other cross-
  dressed heroines in Shakespeare: Portia,
  Viola, Innogen.
  prevent . . . men i.e. avoid being raped.
  It is ironical that her beloved Proteus will
  turn out to be one of these *lascivious men*,
  though in another direction.
42 **fit** equip
  weeds clothes
43 **beseem** become

LUCETTA

Why then, your ladyship must cut your hair.

JULIA

No, girl, I'll knit it up in silken strings,   45

With twenty odd-conceited true-love knots.

To be fantastic may become a youth

Of greater time than I shall show to be.

LUCETTA

What fashion, madam, shall I make your breeches?

JULIA

That fits as well as 'Tell me, good my lord,   50

What compass will you wear your farthingale?'

Why, e'en what fashion thou best likes, Lucetta.

LUCETTA

You must needs have them with a codpiece, madam.

JULIA

Out, out, Lucetta, that will be ill-favoured.

LUCETTA

A round hose, madam, now's not worth a pin   55

Unless you have a codpiece to stick pins on.

JULIA

Lucetta, as thou lov'st me let me have

What thou think'st meet and is most mannerly.

But tell me, wench, how will the world repute me

45 **knit it up** bind with knots
silken strings The phrase recurs at *Titus* 2.4.46, where it refers to the strings of a lute.

46 **odd-conceited** curiously imagined
true-love knots 'A kind of knot, of a complicated and ornamental form . . . used as a symbol of true love' (*OED*).

47 **fantastic** fanciful

48 **Of greater time** older
show appear

51 **compass** fullness
farthingale A hooped structure of bone or wire, used to support and pad out Elizabethan women's skirts.

52 **thou . . . likes** Shakespeare often uses this construction (and not *likest*) for fluency of delivery (Abbott 340).

53 **codpiece** An elaborately decorated pouch worn outside men's breeches or hose to emphasize their genitalia.

54 **Out, out** (an expression of reproof)
ill-favoured unseemly

55 **round . . . pin** A *round hose* was a description of puffed-out, round breeches. Lucetta's implication that the *round hose* is going out of fashion is sustained by Portia's mockery of the clothes of her English suitor at *Merchant* 1.2.70–3, including his 'round hose'.
not worth a pin without value (proverbial: Dent P334)

56 **to . . . on** Apparently an Elizabethan fashion; compare Webster, *The White Devil* 5.3.100: 'Look you his codpiece is stuck full of pins'. Lucetta turns the figurative 'worth a pin' of the previous line into actual pins.

58 **meet** fit
mannerly seemly

59 **wench** Often, as here, an intimate mode of address.
how . . . repute me what will the world think of my action

For undertaking so unstaid a journey?   60
I fear me it will make me scandalized.

LUCETTA

If you think so, then stay at home, and go not.

JULIA Nay, that I will not.

LUCETTA

Then never dream on infamy, but go.
If Proteus like your journey when you come,   65
No matter who's displeased when you are gone.
I fear me he will scarce be pleased withal.

JULIA

That is the least, Lucetta, of my fear.
A thousand oaths, an ocean of his tears,
And instances of infinite of love   70
Warrant me welcome to my Proteus.

LUCETTA

All these are servants to deceitful men.

JULIA

Base men, that use them to so base effect;
But truer stars did govern Proteus' birth.
His words are bonds, his oaths are oracles,   75
His love sincere, his thoughts immaculate,
His tears pure messengers sent from his heart,
His heart as far from fraud as heaven from earth.

LUCETTA

Pray heaven he prove so when you come to him.

---

60 **unstaid** immodest, reckless

61, 67 **fear me** am afraid. The *me* here is the 'ethic dative', in which *me* originally meant 'for me'. By Shakespeare's time, it had become little more than an intensifier, as here.

61 **scandalized** disgraced

64 **infamy** disgrace

67, 79 Lucetta here is the voice of shrewd, worldly wisdom; but her apparent suspicion of Proteus conflicts a little with her advocacy of his love for Julia at 1.2.28, 98.

67 **withal** An emphatic form of 'with it', used at the end of a sentence (Abbott 196).

70 **infinite** an infinity. *Infinite* as a noun was common at the time; but this may simply be an example of Shakespeare characteristically using one part of speech for another (here an adjective as a noun).

71 **Warrant** guarantee

74 **truer . . . birth** The stars under which one was born were supposed to govern one's actions.

75 **His . . . bonds** Proverbial: 'An honest man's word is as good as his bond' (Dent M458).

oracles i.e. like statements of the gods

76 **immaculate** pure

JULIA

  Now, as thou lov'st me, do him not that wrong   80
  To bear a hard opinion of his truth.
  Only deserve my love by loving him,
  And presently go with me to my chamber
  To take a note of what I stand in need of
  To furnish me upon my longing journey.   85
  All that is mine I leave at thy dispose,
  My goods, my lands, my reputation;
  Only in lieu thereof dispatch me hence.
  Come, answer not, but to it presently.
  I am impatient of my tarriance.   *Exeunt*   90

3.1 *Enter Duke, Thurio, and Proteus*

DUKE

  Sir Thurio, give us leave, I pray, awhile;
  We have some secrets to confer about.   *Exit Thurio*
  Now tell me, Proteus, what's your will with me?

PROTEUS

  My gracious lord, that which I would discover

3.1.0 *Enter . . . Proteus*] *Enter Duke, Thurio, Protheus, Valentine, Launce, Speed.* F   2 *Exit Thurio*] *not in* F

85 **longing** prompted by longing
86 **dispose** in your care, at your disposal. This seems to ignore the fact that Julia is said to have a father at 1.2.131. Perhaps this is Shakespeare's inconsistency; or perhaps Julia is concealing her flight from him.
88 **in lieu thereof** in exchange for
  dispatch me hence send me quickly away
90 **tarriance** delay
3.1 This is much the longest scene in the play, and a great deal happens in it. Proteus takes the decisive step and betrays Valentine; the Duke tricks Valentine into revealing his attempted abduction of Silvia and banishes him; Proteus hypocritically sympathizes with Valentine; and Lance and Speed provide an ironic perspective on their masters' love intrigues with a practical, down-to-earth assessment of the milkmaid whom Lance plans to marry.
1 **give us leave** A polite expression: 'excuse us, leave us alone'.
2 **confer about** discuss
  Exit Thurio His entry and immediate dis-

missal has been called 'purposeless' (Sanders), evidence of cutting, or an example of the young Shakespeare's dramatic incompetence. But at the height of his powers, at *1 Henry IV* 3.2.1–3, Shakespeare brings on the King with lords whom he immediately dismisses, and for the same reason: 'the Prince of Wales and I | Must have some private conference'. In both cases, the device emphasizes the privacy, even secrecy, of the subsequent conversation.
4–50 This exchange between the Duke and Proteus is interestingly handled in the BBC television version, where the Duke scarcely reacts, facially, to the revelations of a very nervous Proteus: he is sizing up Proteus and sees through his protestations of duty to himself, especially Proteus' claim that Silvia's flight would press the Duke to his 'timeless grave' (Paul Daneman's Duke is clearly in the prime of life). He accepts Proteus' information, but regards him as a treacherous creep to betray his friend.
4 **discover** reveal

The law of friendship bids me to conceal.   5
But when I call to mind your gracious favours
Done to me, undeserving as I am,
My duty pricks me on to utter that
Which else no worldly good should draw from me.
Know, worthy prince, Sir Valentine my friend   10
This night intends to steal away your daughter;
Myself am one made privy to the plot.
I know you have determined to bestow her
On Thurio, whom your gentle daughter hates,
And should she thus be stol'n away from you   15
It would be much vexation to your age.
Thus, for my duty's sake, I rather chose
To cross my friend in his intended drift
Than by concealing it heap on your head
A pack of sorrows which would press you down,   20
Being unprevented, to your timeless grave.

DUKE

Proteus, I thank thee for thine honest care,
Which to requite, command me while I live.
This love of theirs myself have often seen,
Haply when they have judged me fast asleep,   25
And oftentimes have purposed to forbid
Sir Valentine her company and my court.
But fearing lest my jealous aim might err,
And so unworthily disgrace the man—
A rashness that I ever yet have shunned—   30
I gave him gentle looks, thereby to find
That which thyself hast now disclosed to me.
And that thou mayst perceive my fear of this,
Knowing that tender youth is soon suggested,
I nightly lodge her in an upper tower,   35

---

8 **pricks me on** spurs, urges (as with Falstaff at 1 *Henry IV* 5.1.129–30: 'honour pricks me on')

12 **made privy to** let in on the secret of

18 **drift** scheme (as at 2.6.43)

21 **timeless** untimely, premature (perhaps a recollection of the biblical 'bring my gray head with sorrow unto the grave' (Genesis 42: 38, cited by Shaheen, p. 84)).

23 **command** ask anything of
   while I live Several Dukes have made this an ironic reply to Proteus' allusion to the Duke's 'timeless grave' at l. 21.

26 **purposed** planned

28 **jealous aim** suspicious conjecture

34 **suggested** tempted

The key whereof myself have ever kept;
And thence she cannot be conveyed away.

PROTEUS

Know, noble lord, they have devised a mean
How he her chamber-window will ascend,
And with a corded ladder fetch her down,   40
For which the youthful lover now is gone,
And this way comes he with it presently,
Where, if it please you, you may intercept him.
But, good my lord, do it so cunningly
That my discovery be not aimèd at;   45
For love of you, not hate unto my friend,
Hath made me publisher of this pretence.

DUKE

Upon mine honour, he shall never know
That I had any light from thee of this.

PROTEUS

Adieu, my lord. Sir Valentine is coming.   *Exit*   50
        Enter Valentine

DUKE

Sir Valentine, whither away so fast?

VALENTINE

Please it your grace, there is a messenger
That stays to bear my letters to my friends,
And I am going to deliver them.

DUKE Be they of much import?   55

VALENTINE

The tenor of them doth but signify
My health and happy being at your court.

DUKE

Nay then, no matter; stay with me awhile.
I am to break with thee of some affairs

---

50 *Exit] not in* F   50.1 *Enter Valentine] not in* F

36 **ever** always
37 **conveyed** stolen
38 **mean** means
45 **discovery** revelation
   aimèd guessed
47 **publisher** one who makes public
   pretence plan
49 **light** illumination, i.e. information

52 **Please it** if it please (a polite phrase)
53 **stays** is waiting
55 **import** significance (stressed on the second syllable)
56 **tenor** general drift
57 **being** life
59 **break . . . of** disclose to you

That touch me near, wherein thou must be secret.   60
'Tis not unknown to thee that I have sought
To match my friend Sir Thurio to my daughter.
VALENTINE
I know it well, my lord; and sure the match
Were rich and honourable. Besides, the gentleman
Is full of virtue, bounty, worth, and qualities   65
Beseeming such a wife as your fair daughter.
Cannot your grace win her to fancy him?
DUKE
No, trust me. She is peevish, sullen, froward,
Proud, disobedient, stubborn, lacking duty,
Neither regarding that she is my child   70
Nor fearing me as if I were her father.
And may I say to thee, this pride of hers
Upon advice hath drawn my love from her,
And where I thought the remnant of mine age
Should have been cherished by her child-like duty,   75
I now am full resolved to take a wife,
And turn her out to who will take her in.
Then let her beauty be her wedding dower,
For me and my possessions she esteems not.
VALENTINE
What would your grace have me to do in this?   80

---

60 **touch me near** concern me intimately
64 **Were** would be
66 **Beseeming** befitting
67 **Cannot . . . him** A nicely feline jibe at Thurio from one who knows that he himself is Silvia's beloved.
win persuade
fancy love (but with something of the modern sense of *fancy*—be immediately attracted to)
68–79 anticipate the opening scene of *King Lear* (see subsequent notes).
68 **trust** believe
peevish wayward
froward perverse; rebellious (a somewhat stronger version of modern 'forward')

70 **regarding** considering
71 **fearing . . . father** respecting me as a father should be respected (Norton)
73 **advice** consideration
74 **where** whereas
75 **Should . . . duty** Compare *Tragedy of Lear* 1.1.123–4: 'I loved her most, and thought to set my rest | On her kind nursery.'
77 **turn . . . in** Compare Capulet's threat to turn Juliet out to 'starve, die in the streets' (*Romeo* 3.5.188–92).
who whoever
78 **let . . . dower** Closely echoed at *Tragedy of Lear* 1.1.108: 'Thy truth then be thy dower.'

DUKE

There is a lady of Verona here
Whom I affect, but she is nice, and coy,
And naught esteems my agèd eloquence.
Now therefore would I have thee to my tutor—
For long ago I have forgot to court;   85
Besides the fashion of the time is changed—
How and which way I may bestow myself
To be regarded in her sun-bright eye.

VALENTINE

Win her with gifts if she respect not words.
Dumb jewels often in their silent kind   90
More than quick words do move a woman's mind.

DUKE

But she did scorn a present that I sent her.

VALENTINE

A woman sometime scorns what best contents her.
Send her another; never give her o'er,
For scorn at first makes after-love the more.   95
If she do frown, 'tis not in hate of you,
But rather to beget more love in you.
If she do chide, 'tis not to have you gone,
Forwhy the fools are mad if left alone.
Take no repulse, whatever she doth say: 100
For 'Get you gone' she doth not mean 'Away'.
Flatter and praise, commend, extol their graces;

---

81 of] HALLIWELL; in F

81 **of Verona here** F reads 'in Verona'; they
are of course in Milan. This is probably
Shakespeare's own slip (see Introduction,
p. 22), easily remedied by substituting *of*.
82 **affect** love
nice fastidious, reserved
83 **naught esteems** does not value
84 **to** as
85 **ago** F reads 'agone', but *OED* makes no
distinction between the two forms.
forgot forgotten how to
86 **fashion of the time** modes of courtship
(Johnson)
87 **bestow** conduct

88 **regarded** esteemed
89 **respect not** disregards
90–105 As Valentine moves into the clichés
of wooing, ultimately derived from Ovid's
Ars Amatoria (*The Art of Love*), 2.275–8,
he slips into rhyme. See Introduction,
p. 43.
90 **kind** nature
91 **quick** lively
99 **Forwhy** because (*OED conj.* B¹)
fools women (often an endearment, as at
Tragedy of Lear 5.3.281, where Lear says
of Cordelia 'my poor fool is hanged')
101 **For** by

Though ne'er so black, say they have angels' faces.
That man that hath a tongue I say is no man
If with his tongue he cannot win a woman.   105
DUKE

But she I mean is promised by her friends
Unto a youthful gentleman of worth,
And kept severely from resort of men,
That no man hath access by day to her.
VALENTINE

Why then I would resort to her by night.   110
DUKE

Ay, but the doors be locked and keys kept safe,
That no man hath recourse to her by night.
VALENTINE

What lets but one may enter at her window?
DUKE

Her chamber is aloft, far from the ground,
And built so shelving that one cannot climb it   115
Without apparent hazard of his life.
VALENTINE

Why then, a ladder quaintly made of cords
To cast up, with a pair of anchoring hooks,
Would serve to scale another Hero's tower,
So bold Leander would adventure it.   120

---

103 **Though ne'er so** however
   black dark-complexioned (as opposed
   to the Elizabethan ideal of fair-skinned
   beauty: see second note to 2.6.26, and
   note to 5.2.9–10)
106 **friends** family
108 **severely** strictly
   resort access
109, 112, 129 **That** so that
109 **access** (stressed on second syllable,
   throughout the play)
113 **lets** hinders
115 **shelving** projecting
116 **apparent** obvious
117 **quaintly** ingeniously
118 **anchoring hooks** This very precise
   detail may have been suggested by
   Arthur Brooke's *Romeus and Juliet* ll.
   813–14: 'a corden ladder' secured with
   'crooked iron hooks'.

119–20 In neither Marlowe's *Hero and
   Leander* (see note to 1.1.22) nor Ovid's
   Heroides does Leander need to scale
   Hero's tower, because the door is open. I
   suspect that Shakespeare is conflating
   two adjacent passages from Ovid's *Ars
   Amatoria* where the advice to a lover 'if
   the door be held by a fastened bolt, yet
   slip down headlong through an opening
   in the roof; or let a high window afford a
   secret path' is followed by a reference to
   Leander swimming the Hellespont
   (2.244–50). This is the likelier as another
   passage from *Ars Amatoria* twenty lines
   later is echoed at ll. 90–105 (see the
   note).
120 **So** provided that
   adventure risk

DUKE

  Now as thou art a gentleman of blood,

  Advise me where I may have such a ladder.

VALENTINE

  When would you use it? Pray sir, tell me that.

DUKE

  This very night; for love is like a child

  That longs for everything that he can come by.   125

VALENTINE

  By seven a clock I'll get you such a ladder.

DUKE

  But hark thee: I will go to her alone.

  How shall I best convey the ladder thither?

VALENTINE

  It will be light, my lord, that you may bear it

  Under a cloak that is of any length.   130

DUKE

  A cloak as long as thine will serve the turn?

VALENTINE

  Ay, my good lord.

DUKE   Then let me see thy cloak,

  I'll get me one of such another length.

VALENTINE

  Why, any cloak will serve the turn, my lord.

DUKE

  How shall I fashion me to wear a cloak?   135

  I pray thee let me feel thy cloak upon me.

      He removes Valentine's cloak and finds a letter and a

      rope-ladder

  What letter is this same? What's here? 'To Silvia'?

  And here an engine fit for my proceeding.

  I'll be so bold to break the seal for once.

136.1–2 *He . . . ladder*] *not in* F

---

121 **of blood** (a) of good parentage; (b) passionate, spirited

122 **Advise** inform

130 **any length** i.e. any considerable length

131, 134 **serve the turn** suffice, fit the occasion

133 **such another** a similar

135 **fashion . . . wear** get used to wearing

138 **engine** apparatus, instrument
proceeding course of action

139 **be so bold** (because the letter is addressed to someone else)

(Reads)
'My thoughts do harbour with my Silvia nightly,   140
   And slaves they are to me, that send them flying.
O, could their master come and go as lightly,
   Himself would lodge where, senseless, they are lying.
My herald thoughts in thy pure bosom rest them,
   While I, their king, that thither them importune,   145
Do curse the grace that with such grace hath blessed
      them,
   Because myself do want my servants' fortune.
I curse myself for they are sent by me,
That they should harbour where their lord should be.'
What's here?   150
'Silvia, this night I will enfranchise thee.'
'Tis so, and here's the ladder for the purpose.
Why, Phaëton—for thou art Merops' son—
Wilt thou aspire to guide the heavenly car,
And with thy daring folly burn the world?   155

---

140 *Reads*] not in F

140–9 Valentine's poem uses the first two quatrains and the final couplet of a Shakespearian sonnet.

140–1 **My thoughts . . . flying** Compare Sonnet 27.5–6: 'my thoughts, from far where I abide, | Intend a zealous pilgrimage to thee'.

140, 149 **harbour** dwell

142 **lightly** easily

143 **senseless** incapable of feeling

144 **herald thoughts** His *thoughts* are *heralds* because they precede him and deliver his message.
   bosom breast (covering the heart); if there is a secondary reference to the letter, *bosom* may also refer to the pocket on women's gowns described in the note to 1.2.115–16.

145 **importune** impel (*OED* v. 2; this line predates *OED*'s earliest example, which is from *Measure* 1.1.56). This sense of *importune* is unusual in Shakespeare, but the pronunciation is the same as the more usual examples, stressed on the second syllable.

146 **grace . . . grace** fortune . . . favour

147 **want** lack

151 **enfranchise** liberate. There may be a hint of poetic affectation in Valentine's choice of this word. In *Love's Labour's Lost* the fantastical Spaniard Don Armado uses it, and when he is misunderstood, reels off a series of explanations: 'setting thee at liberty, enfreedoming thy person, . . . set thee from durance' (3.1.117–25).

153–5 **Why, Phaëton . . . world** Phaëton was the illegitimate son of the sun-god Phoebus. His mother was married to Merops. He begged Phoebus to let him drive the chariot of the sun, but it ran out of control and burnt up much of the earth, so that Jupiter had to kill him with a thunderbolt (Ovid, *Metamorphoses* 2.1–328). He became famous as a figure of reckless aspiration, so the Duke calls Valentine *Phaëton*; but in the parenthesis that follows, he modifies that by contemptuously calling him *Merops'* son— i.e. he is the son of the mortal, not of the god. This matches his extremely insulting description of Valentine as a *base intruder* and an *over-weening slave* at l. 157.

154 **car** chariot

Wilt thou reach stars because they shine on thee?
Go, base intruder, over-weening slave,
Bestow thy fawning smiles on equal mates,
And think my patience, more than thy desert,
Is privilege for thy departure hence.   160
Thank me for this more than for all the favours
Which, all too much, I have bestowed on thee.
But if thou linger in my territories
Longer than swiftest expedition
Will give thee time to leave our royal court,   165
By heaven, my wrath shall far exceed the love
I ever bore my daughter or thyself.
Be gone, I will not hear thy vain excuse,
But as thou lov'st thy life, make speed from hence.   *Exit*

VALENTINE

And why not death, rather than living torment?   170
To die is to be banished from myself,
And Silvia is my self. Banished from her
Is self from self, a deadly banishment.
What light is light, if Silvia be not seen?
What joy is joy, if Silvia be not by,   175
Unless it be to think that she is by,

---

169 *Exit*] *not in* F

---

156 **Wilt . . . thee** Proverbial: 'One may look at a star but not reach at it' (Dent S825). Compare Lyly's *Campaspe* 3.5.41–2: 'stars are to be looked at, not reached at'. **reach** grasp at
157 **over-weening** presumptuous
158 **equal mates** social equals
160 **privilege for** grants the privilege of **departure** safe departure
163–7 **But . . . thyself** Compare Henry VI's banishment of Suffolk in *Contention* (2 *Henry VI*) 3.2.299–301: 'If after three days' space thou here beest found | On any ground that I am ruler of, | The world shall not be ransom for thy life.' There are several other such banishments in later Shakespeare, but, as Bond says, 'the formula must necessarily be more or less the same'.
164 **expedition** haste

170–87 Valentine's speech anticipates Romeo's when banishment separates him from Juliet: 'Hence banishèd is banished from the world, | And world's exile is death. . . . Heaven is here | Where Juliet lives' (*Romeo* 3.3.19–30); and Suffolk's when banishment separates him from Queen Margaret: 'where thou art, there is the world itself . . . And where thou art not, desolation. . . . If I depart from thee, I cannot live' (*Contention* (2 *Henry VI*) 3.2.366–92).
171–3 These lines echo, and contrast with, Proteus' 'If I keep them [i.e. Julia and Valentine] I needs must lose myself' (2.6.20).
172–3 **Silvia . . . from self** Compare Sonnet 109.3–4: 'As easy might I from myself depart' as from his friend.

And feed upon the shadow of perfection?
Except I be by Silvia in the night
There is no music in the nightingale.
Unless I look on Silvia in the day   180
There is no day for me to look upon.
She is my essence, and I leave to be
If I be not by her fair influence
Fostered, illumined, cherished, kept alive.
I fly not death to fly his deadly doom.   185
Tarry I here, I but attend on death,
But fly I hence, I fly away from life.
     Enter Proteus and Lance

PROTEUS Run, boy, run, run, and seek him out.
LANCE So-ho, so-ho!
PROTEUS What seest thou?   190
LANCE Him we go to find. There's not a hair on's head
   but 'tis a Valentine.
PROTEUS Valentine?
VALENTINE No.
PROTEUS Who then, his spirit?   195
VALENTINE Neither.
PROTEUS What then?
VALENTINE Nothing.

187.1 *Enter . . . Lance*] *not in* F

177 **shadow** image (i.e. not the substance). This contrast is frequent in Shakespeare, particularly in the Sonnets, e.g. 53.1–2: 'What is your substance, whereof are you made, | That millions of strange shadows on you tend?' And Julia uses it at 4.4.194–8.
178 **Except** unless
182 **essence** very being
  leave to be cease to live
185 **I fly . . . doom** I cannot escape death by fleeing the Duke's sentence (or perhaps Death's own sentence)
186 **Tarry** I if I linger
  but only
  attend on await
187.1 It has sometimes been suggested that there has been a cut here (or even that there is a missing scene) because there is so little time for the events described by Proteus at ll. 221–35; but the action is

obviously continuous, and this is surely an example of Shakespeare's use of 'stage time', condensing real time for dramatic purposes.
189 **So-ho** A huntsman's cry to the dogs when a hare has been sighted (*OED int.* and *sb.*[1] 1, which cites Turberville's *Noble Art of Venery* (1576), 177: 'So-ho sayeth one, as soon as he [the hare] spies'). In Guarini's *Il Pastor Fido* (1590), Silvio uses it in calling to his dog (who is on stage) at l. 1432, at least in Fanshawe's translation (1647). The cry leads Lance to pun on 'hair' at l. 191.
191–2 **There's . . . 'tis** every hair on his head proclaims that he is
192 **a Valentine** a lover (*OED sb.* 2)
198 **Nothing** (without Silvia: compare Innogen at *Cymbeline* 4.2.369, when she thinks her husband dead: 'I am nothing')

LANCE Can nothing speak?
>   *He threatens Valentine*
> Master, shall I strike?   200
PROTEUS Who wouldst thou strike?
LANCE Nothing.
PROTEUS Villain, forbear.
LANCE Why, sir, I'll strike nothing. I pray you—
PROTEUS
> Sirrah, I say forbear. Friend Valentine, a word.   205
VALENTINE
> My ears are stopped, and cannot hear good news,
> So much of bad already hath possessed them.
PROTEUS
> Then in dumb silence will I bury mine,
> For they are harsh, untuneable, and bad.
VALENTINE
> Is Silvia dead?
PROTEUS   No, Valentine.   210
VALENTINE
> No Valentine indeed, for sacred Silvia.
> Hath she forsworn me?
PROTEUS   No, Valentine.
VALENTINE
> No Valentine, if Silvia have forsworn me.
> What is your news?
LANCE Sir, there is a proclamation that you are vanished.   215
PROTEUS
> That thou art banishèd. O that's the news,
> From hence, from Silvia, and from me thy friend.
VALENTINE
> O, I have fed upon this woe already,

199.1 *He threatens Valentine*] not in F   204 you—] THEOBALD; you. F   216 banishèd]
BOND; banish'd F

---

201 **Who** F2 corrects *Who* to 'Whom', but
Shakespeare uses the forms indifferently
(Abbott 274).
203, 205 **forbear** stop it
209 **untuneable** out of tune, discordant
211, 213 **No Valentine** (a) 'no longer
myself'; (b) 'no true lover'

215 **vanished** Lance's malapropism for
'banished'.
218–19 **fed . . . excess . . . surfeit** This
strongly anticipates Orsino's opening
speech in *Twelfth Night*: 'If music be the
food of love, play on, | Give me excess of
it, that surfeiting, | The appetite may
sicken and so die' (1.1.1–3).

And now excess of it will make me surfeit.
Doth Silvia know that I am banishèd?   220

PROTEUS

Ay, ay; and she hath offered to the doom,
Which unreversed stands in effectual force,
A sea of melting pearl, which some call tears;
Those at her father's churlish feet she tendered,
With them, upon her knees, her humble self,   225
Wringing her hands, whose whiteness so became them
As if but now they waxèd pale for woe.
But neither bended knees, pure hands held up,
Sad sighs, deep groans, nor silver-shedding tears
Could penetrate her uncompassionate sire,   230
But Valentine, if he be ta'en, must die.
Besides, her intercession chafed him so
When she for thy repeal was suppliant,
That to close prison he commanded her,
With many bitter threats of biding there.   235

VALENTINE

No more, unless the next word that thou speak'st
Have some malignant power upon my life.
If so I pray thee breathe it in mine ear,
As ending anthem of my endless dolour.

PROTEUS

Cease to lament for that thou canst not help,   240
And study help for that which thou lament'st.

220 banishèd] BOND; banish'd F

219 **surfeit** sicken from over-indulgence
220–35 Compare Capulet's brutal treatment
of Juliet at *Romeo* 3.5.141–95.
221 **doom** sentence
222 **unreserved . . . force** is unrevoked and
so is binding
223 **A . . . tears** Compare Sonnet 34.13:
'those tears are pearl which thy love
sheds'.
224 **churlish** brutal (Onions)
tendered offered up
227 **waxèd** became
229 **silver-shedding tears** tears that flow
like silver streams (Norton)

232 **chafed** angered
233 **repeal** recall
234 **close** enclosed, strictly guarded (though
in her subsequent appearances she is
obviously not in prison)
235 **biding** staying
238 **breathe** speak, whisper
239 **ending anthem** requiem (as at *The
Phoenix and Turtle* l. 21: 'Here the anthem
doth commence'; the next line is also
relevant to the play: 'Love and constancy
is dead')
dolour grief
240 **that** what

Time is the nurse and breeder of all good.
Here if thou stay thou canst not see thy love;
Besides, thy staying will abridge thy life.
Hope is a lover's staff, walk hence with that,   245
And manage it against despairing thoughts.
Thy letters may be here, though thou art hence,
Which, being writ to me, shall be delivered
Even in the milk-white bosom of thy love.
The time now serves not to expostulate.   250
Come, I'll convey thee through the city gate,
And ere I part with thee confer at large
Of all that may concern thy love affairs.
As thou lov'st Silvia, though not for thyself,
Regard thy danger, and along with me.   255

VALENTINE

I pray thee, Lance, an if thou seest my boy
Bid him make haste, and meet me at the North Gate.

PROTEUS

Go, sirrah, find him out. Come, Valentine.

VALENTINE

O my dear Silvia! Hapless Valentine.

Exeunt Proteus and Valentine

LANCE I am but a fool, look you, and yet I have the wit to   260
think my master is a kind of a knave. But that's all one,

259.1 *Exeunt . . . Valentine*] not in F

---

244 **abridge** shorten
246 **manage** wield, make use of (*OED v.* 2a)
250 **expostulate** talk at length
251 **convey** escort
252 **confer at large** discuss in more detail
254 **thyself** your own sake
255 **Regard** pay attention to
　along go along
256 **boy** servant, i.e. Speed
259 **Hapless** unhappy, unfortunate
260–1 **I am . . . knave** Commentators have worried about Lance's suspicion of Proteus here, since he cannot know about Proteus' betrayal of Valentine. But perhaps Shakespeare is drawing upon the popular belief that fools or even madmen have an instinctive awareness of what

is denied to the intelligent or the sane. For an ingenious theatrical solution to the problem, see Introduction, p. 14.
fool . . . knave The distinction between a fool and a knave is proverbial: 'Knaves and fools divide the world' (Tilley K144).
260, 262 **but** only
261–2 **But . . . knave** Lance takes the common phrase *that's all one* ('all there is to it, no matter') and shifts the sense to mean 'it doesn't matter so long as he is only a single knave', not a double one, like Iago in *Othello*, who deals in 'double knavery' (1.3.386). Compare Richard Edwards's *Damon and Pithias* 1.109: 'You lose money by him if you sell him for one knave, for he serves for twain.'

if he be but one knave. He lives not now that knows
me to be in love, yet I am in love, but a team of horse
shall not pluck that from me, nor who 'tis I love; and
yet 'tis a woman, but what woman I will not tell myself;   265
and yet 'tis a milkmaid; yet 'tis not a maid, for she
hath had gossips; yet 'tis a maid, for she is her
master's maid, and serves for wages. She hath more
qualities than a water-spaniel, which is much in a bare
Christian.   270

He takes out a paper

Here is the catalogue of her conditions. '*Imprimis*, she
can fetch and carry'—why, a horse can do no more;

270.1 *He . . . paper*] *not in* F   271 catalogue] DOVER WILSON; Cate-log F   conditions]
F4; Condition F1; *Imprimis*] F4; *Inprimis* F1

---

262 **He ... that** i.e. no one
263 **yet I am in love** The extended discussion of Lance's belovèd that follows provides an ironic perspective on his betters,
perhaps particularly on Valentine's
soliloquy earlier in this scene, and Silvia's
use of 'and yet' at 2.1.108–9.
263–4 **a team . . . from me** This alludes to
the execution of criminals by tying them
to four horses, which were then driven in
opposite directions, tearing the victim
apart.
263 **horse** The singular for the plural was in
general use down to the seventeenth century (*OED sb.* 1b), especially for words
ending in a sibilant.
265 **myself** even myself. For the secrecy, see
the note to 2.5.34.
266 **maid** virgin
267 **gossips** Literally 'godparents', but
extended to mean 'tattling women who
attend confinements' (Steevens, cited by
Bond). There is a brilliant scene of *gossips*
attending a birth in Middleton's *A Chaste
Maid in Cheapside* (*c.*1613), 3.2. The point
here is that since Lance's milkmaid has
had such *gossips*, she has also had a child,
and cannot be a virgin.
267–8 **for she . . . wages** As well as the
obvious sense (she is a servant), Williams (p. 207) detects a lewd one: taking
milk as 'causing ejaculation', she *serves*
her master sexually. See ll. 274–5 and
note.

269 **water-spaniel** A dog used to retrieve
ducks from rivers or ponds, hence *water*.
Water-spaniels and a duck are brought on
stage in Middleton and Dekker's *The
Roaring Girl* (*c.*1611), 2.1.398.3.
269 **bare** mere
271 **catalogue** Bond retains F's 'Cate-log' as
'a pun on the girl's name ("Kate-log", a
record or account of Kate)'. He compares
the pun in the near-contemporaneous
Shrew 2.1.189: 'For dainties are all cates'
(i.e. delicacies and 'Kates'). It is true that
Kate was clearly a favourite name with
Shakespeare, who changed the historical
name of Hotspur's wife, Elizabeth, to
Kate in 1 *Henry IV*, but in *The Two Gentlemen* 'the girl is not . . . named, and "log"
in this sense is not recorded till 1679'
(*TC*, p. 167). *OED* says that it is simply
an 'obsolete form of *catalogue*', to which
it is accordingly modernized here. The
catalogue closely resembles Dromio of
Syracuse's account of the fat kitchen-
maid who pursues him (*Errors* 3.2.96–
152) and Lyly's *Midas* 1.2.1–89. See
Introduction, p. 20.
conditions qualities, abilities. F1's 'condition' is probably a slip: 'all the citations
for "catalogue of" in *OED* are followed by
a plural' (*TC* p. 167).
Imprimis firstly (the normal Latin opening of an official document including a
list of items)

nay, a horse cannot fetch, but only carry, therefore is
she better than a jade. '*Item*, she can milk.' Look you, a
sweet virtue in a maid with clean hands.   275
    Enter Speed

SPEED How now, Signor Lance, what news with your
    mastership?

LANCE With my master's ship? Why, it is at sea.

SPEED Well, your old vice still, mistake the word. What
    news then in your paper?   280

LANCE The blackest news that ever thou heard'st.

SPEED Why, man, how 'black'?

LANCE Why, as black as ink.

SPEED Let me read them.

LANCE Fie on thee, jolt-head, thou canst not read.   285

SPEED Thou liest; I can.

LANCE I will try thee. Tell me this: who begot thee?

SPEED Marry, the son of my grandfather.

LANCE O illiterate loiterer, it was the son of thy grand-
    mother. This proves that thou canst not read.   290

SPEED Come, fool, come. Try me in thy paper.

LANCE (*giving Speed the paper*) There: and Saint Nicholas
    be thy speed.

275.1 *Enter Speed*] not in F   291 Try F (*corrected state*); thy (*uncorrected*)   292 *giving . . .
paper*] not in F

273 **fetch** 'To *fetch* can also be an erotic
    activity (i.e. to draw forth, bring to
    ejaculation) which his *milkmaid* can
    accomplish but his *horse* cannot', as
    Carroll nicely puts it.

274 **jade** (a) tired horse; (b) 'over-used
    whore' (Williams)
    Item likewise (Latin, used to introduce
    each new article in an official document).
    Compare *Contention* (*2 Henry VI*) 1.1.48,
    and Olivia's mocking list of her own
    beauties at *Twelfth Night* 1.5.234–7.

274–5 **milk . . . hands** See note to ll. 267–8;
    Williams adds that the 'concluding detail
    suggests masturbation' (p. 207).

278 **at sea** The ship is 'afloat', the master is
    'confused'.

279 **mistake the word** indulge in word-

play. This is as much Speed's vice as
Lance's, as at 1.1.72–138.

283 **as . . . ink** Proverbial (Dent I73).

285 **jolt-head** blockhead, as at *Shrew*
    4.1.152: 'heedless jolt-heads and
    unmannered slaves'.

287, 291 **try** test

287–90 **Tell . . . read** This presumably
    alludes to the proverb 'It is a wise child
    that knows his own father' (Dent C309).

289 **loiterer** idler; but perhaps Lance specif-
    ically means one who has not worked
    hard and learnt to read.

292 **Saint Nicholas** (patron saint of
    scholars)

293 **be thy speed** assist you (perhaps with a
    pun on Speed's name)

SPEED 'Imprimis, she can milk.'

LANCE Ay, that she can.   295

SPEED 'Item, she brews good ale.'

LANCE And thereof comes the proverb 'Blessing of your
heart, you brew good ale'.

SPEED 'Item, she can sew.'

LANCE That's as much as to say 'Can she so?'   300

SPEED 'Item, she can knit.'

LANCE What need a man care for a stock with a wench
when she can knit him a stock?

SPEED 'Item, she can wash and scour.'

LANCE A special virtue, for then she need not be washed   305
and scoured.

SPEED 'Item, she can spin.'

LANCE Then may I set the world on wheels, when she can
spin for her living.

SPEED 'Item, she hath many nameless virtues.'   310

LANCE That's as much as to say 'bastard virtues', that
indeed know not their fathers, and therefore have no
names.

SPEED Here follow her vices.

LANCE Close at the heels of her virtues.   315

SPEED 'Item, she is not to be broken with fasting, in
respect of her breath.'

---

314 follow] F (*corrected state*); followes (*uncorrected*)   316 be broken with] OXFORD; be F; be
kissed ROWE

---

295 **can** (with a probable pun on 'milk-can')
297 **the proverb** (Dent B450)
302 **stock** dowry
303 **stock** stocking. Perhaps *knit him a stock*
has the secondary (sexual) meaning
'provide him with a stupid heir' (*OED,
knit, v.* 5d, *ppl. a.* 3).
305–6 **washed and scoured** i.e. knocked
down and beaten (Dover Wilson)
308 **set . . . wheels** take life easily (proverbial: Dent W893)
309 **spin** Literally 'spin flax on a distaff' but
also 'earn her living by prostitution'.
Compare *Twelfth Night* 1.3.98–100,
where Sir Toby says of Sir Andrew's hair:
'I hope to see a housewife take thee
between her legs and spin it off.'

310 **nameless** (a) inexpressible; (b) 'too
small to be worth detailed description'
(Sanders)
314 **follow** This edition follows the corrected state of this page, though the
uncorrected 'follows' is also acceptable.
Singular verbs preceding plural subjects
are common in Shakespeare (Abbott
335).
316 **broken with** Gary Taylor's reading in
Oxford, meaning 'be tamed with',
'moving into "be intimately conferred
with"' (*OED, break, v.* 22a and b), sup-
poses a pun on "breakfast"' (*TC*, p. 167).
Compare l. 59.
316–17 **in respect of** on account of

LANCE Well, that fault may be mended with a breakfast.
  Read on.

SPEED '*Item*, she hath a sweet mouth.'   320

LANCE That makes amends for her sour breath.

SPEED '*Item*, she doth talk in her sleep.'

LANCE It's no matter for that, so she sleep not in her talk.

SPEED '*Item*, she is slow in words.'

LANCE O villain, that set this down among her vices! To be   325
  slow in words is a woman's only virtue. I pray thee out
  with't, and place it for her chief virtue.

SPEED '*Item*, she is proud.'

LANCE Out with that, too. It was Eve's legacy, and cannot
  be ta'en from her.   330

SPEED '*Item*, she hath no teeth.'

LANCE I care not for that neither, because I love crusts.

SPEED '*Item*, she is curst.'

LANCE Well, the best is, she hath no teeth to bite.

SPEED '*Item*, she will often praise her liquor.'   335

LANCE If her liquor be good, she shall. If she will not, I
  will; for good things should be praised.

SPEED '*Item*, she is too liberal.'

LANCE Of her tongue she cannot, for that's writ down she
  is slow of. Of her purse she shall not, for that I'll keep 340
  shut. Now of another thing she may, and that cannot I
  help. Well, proceed.

323 talk] F (*corrected state*); take (*uncorrected*)   325 villain] F (*corrected state*); villanie
(*uncorrected*)   332 love] F (*corrected state*); lone (*uncorrected*)

320 **sweet mouth** (a) likes sweets, as in
  modern 'sweet tooth'; (b) wanton nature
  —or perhaps it just means 'kissable'
323 **so** provided that
  she . . . talk is not slow or stupid in her
  speech (Sanders). There is a quibble on
  sleep and 'slip' like the 'sheep/ship' one at
  1.1.72–3; Lance almost certainly means
  'she is not careless, idle (or even doesn't
  fall asleep) during intercourse' (*OED*,
  sleep, *v.* 5), and see Williams, 'conversation', p. 81.
328 **proud** (a) arrogant; (b) lascivious, as at
  Lucrece 712: 'The flesh being proud,
  desire doth fight with grace'.
329 **Eve's legacy** Pride was the original

deadly sin; Eve tempted Adam to eat
from the Tree of Knowledge, and so
aspire above his, and her, station (Genesis
3: 1–7).
332 **I love crusts**—and so won't have to
share them with her
333 **curst**   shrewish.   Compare   *Shrew*
1.2.127–8: 'Katherine the curst—| A
title for a maid of all titles the worst.'
335 **praise** appraise, test (which Lance
twists into 'applaud' at l. 337)
338 **liberal**   generous   (and   perhaps
'licentious',   as   with   the   'liberal
shepherds' at *Hamlet* 4.7.142, leading
into the 'another thing' of which she is
liberal at l. 341)

SPEED '*Item*, she hath more hair than wit, and more faults
 than hairs, and more wealth than faults.'

LANCE Stop there. I'll have her. She was mine and not 345
 mine twice or thrice in that last article. Rehearse that
 once more.

SPEED '*Item*, she hath more hair than wit.'

LANCE 'More hair than wit.' It may be I'll prove it: the
 cover of the salt hides the salt, and therefore it is more 350
 than the salt; the hair that covers the wit is more than
 the wit, for the greater hides the less. What's next?

SPEED 'And more faults than hairs.'

LANCE That's monstrous. O that that were out!

SPEED 'And more wealth than faults.' 355

LANCE Why, that word makes the faults gracious. Well, I'll
 have her, and if it be a match—as nothing is impossible—

SPEED What then?

LANCE Why then will I tell thee that thy master stays for 360
 thee at the North Gate.

SPEED For me?

LANCE For thee? Ay, who art thou? He hath stayed for a
 better man than thee.

SPEED And must I go to him? 365

LANCE Thou must run to him, for thou hast stayed so long
 that going will scarce serve the turn.

---

343 hair] F (*corrected state*); haires (*uncorrected*) 346 last] F (*corrected state*); *not in*
uncorrected 349 be I'll] F; be. I'll THEOBALD (*subs.*)

343–56 she hath . . . gracious These lines
 build (twice) through various faults to
 the item that compensates for all the
 faults—that she is wealthy.
343 more hair than wit Proverbial (Dent
 B736), also used at *Errors* 2.2.83–4:
 'there's many a man hath more hair than
 wit'.
345–6 mine and not mine Lance's hesitation is developed into something more
 romantically mysterious at *Dream*
 4.1.190–1: 'And I have found Demetrius
 like a jewel, | Mine own and not mine
 own.'
346 article item
 Rehearse repeat

349 prove demonstrate
349–50 the cover . . . hides the salt 'The
 lid of the salt-cellar conceals the salt.
 The quibble is on *salt* meaning "wit"'
 [*OED sb.*[1] 3c] (Sanders). From there, the
 punning develops into *salt* meaning
 'licentious' (*OED a.*[2] b) and *the hair that
 covers the wit* meaning 'pubic hair'.
352 the greater . . . less Proverbial (Dent
 G437), also used at *Lucrece* l. 663: 'The
 lesser thing should not the greater hide.'
356 gracious agreeable, acceptable
357–8 nothing is impossible Proverbial
 (Dent N298.1).
367 going walking

SPEED Why didst not tell me sooner? Pox of your love
　　letters!   *Exit*
LANCE Now will he be swinged for reading my letter. An   370
　　unmannerly slave, that will thrust himself into secrets.
　　I'll after, to rejoice in the boy's correction.   *Exit*

3.2 *Enter the Duke and Thurio*

DUKE

Sir Thurio, fear not but that she will love you
Now Valentine is banished from her sight.

THURIO

Since his exile she hath despised me most,
Forsworn my company and railed at me,
That I am desperate of obtaining her.   5

DUKE

This weak impress of love is as a figure
Trenchèd in ice, which with an hour's heat
Dissolves to water and doth lose his form.
A little time will melt her frozen thoughts,
And worthless Valentine shall be forgot.   10

　　Enter Proteus

How now, Sir Proteus, is your countryman,
According to our proclamation, gone?

PROTEUS Gone, my good lord.

368 Pox] ROWE; 'pox F　369 *Exit*] *not in* F　372 *Exit*] *Exeunt.* F
　3.2.0.1 *Enter . . . Thurio*] *Enter Duke, Thurio, Protheus.* F　10.1 *Enter Proteus*] *not in* F
13 PROTEUS] F (*corrected state*); *not in uncorrected*

368 **Pox of** a curse upon (a common phrase;
　　pox literally means 'venereal disease', or
　　smallpox)
370 **swinged** beaten
371 **unmannerly** rude (perhaps with a pun
　　on 'unmanly')
372 **after** follow
　　correction punishment
3.2.1 **but that she will** that she will not
3–5 This implies quite an interval of time
　　since the previous scene, whereas ll. 11–
　　12 suggest that it follows soon. As at
　　3.1.187.1, Shakespeare is using 'stage
　　time': see the note.
3 **exile** (stressed on the second syllable)
5 **That** so that

5 **desperate** without hope
6–8 **This . . . form** This comparison of love
　　to an image quickly melted by heat recalls
　　that used by Proteus at 2.4.198–200.
　　There, it was a wax image; here it is cut
　　in ice.
6 **impress** impression on the mind
　　(stressed on the second syllable)
7 **Trenchèd** cut or carved
8 **his** its. *His* was the common form of the
　　possessive pronoun; the first occurrence
　　of *its* recorded by *OED* is from 1598 (*poss.
　　pron.* A).
　　form shape
9 **frozen thoughts** i.e. coldness towards
　　Thurio

DUKE

My daughter takes his going grievously.

PROTEUS

A little time, my lord, will kill that grief.   15

DUKE

So I believe, but Thurio thinks not so.

Proteus, the good conceit I hold of thee—

For thou hast shown some sign of good desert—

Makes me the better to confer with thee.

PROTEUS

Longer than I prove loyal to your grace   20

Let me not live to look upon your grace.

DUKE

Thou know'st how willingly I would effect

The match between Sir Thurio and my daughter?

PROTEUS I do, my lord.

DUKE

And also, I think, thou art not ignorant   25

How she opposes her against my will?

PROTEUS

She did, my lord, when Valentine was here.

DUKE

Ay, and perversely she persevers so.

What might we do to make the girl forget

The love of Valentine, and love Sir Thurio?   30

PROTEUS

The best way is to slander Valentine

With falsehood, cowardice, and poor descent,

Three things that women highly hold in hate.

---

14 grievously] F (*corrected state*); heauily (*uncorrected*)

---

14 **grievously** An uncorrected state of this page in F has 'heavily'. Both make sense; both mean 'sorrowfully'. But *grief* in Proteus' reply picks up from *grievously*. In both F versions this is a question by the Duke, but that must be a slip: he, not Proteus, is in a position to know about Silvia's feelings.

15 **A . . . grief** Proverbial: 'Time tames the strongest grief' (Dent T322).

17 **conceit** opinion, conception

18 **desert** deserving

19 **better** readier
    confer discuss (as at 3.1.2, 252; all three lines suggest confidential conversations)

26 **her** herself

28 **persevers** perseveres (stressed on the second syllable, as always in Shakespeare)

DUKE

Ay, but she'll think that it is spoke in hate.

PROTEUS

Ay, if his enemy deliver it.   35

Therefore it must with circumstance be spoken

By one whom she esteemeth as his friend.

DUKE

Then you must undertake to slander him.

PROTEUS

And that, my lord, I shall be loath to do.

'Tis an ill office for a gentleman,   40

Especially against his very friend.

DUKE

Where your good word cannot advantage him

Your slander never can endamage him.

Therefore the office is indifferent,

Being entreated to it by your friend.   45

PROTEUS

You have prevailed, my lord. If I can do it

By aught that I can speak in his dispraise

She shall not long continue love to him.

But say this weed her love from Valentine,

It follows not that she will love Sir Thurio.   50

THURIO

Therefore, as you unwind her love from him,

Lest it should ravel and be good to none

---

49 weed] F; wean ROWE; wind KEIGHTLEY; woo SISSON

34 **spoke** spoken. The '-en' inflection was often dropped for past participles in Elizabethan English (Abbott 343).

35 **deliver** report

36 **circumstance** supporting detail, evidence (and perhaps 'circumlocution', as at 1.1.36)

40, 44 **office** task

41 **very** special, faithful

43 **endamage** harm, discredit (*OED v.* 1, 2)

44 **indifferent** neutral, neither good nor bad (as at *Hamlet* 2.2.229: 'the indifferent children of the earth')

45 **your friend** i.e. myself, your friend

46 **You have prevailed** The speed with which Proteus agrees to slander Valentine often draws laughter in performance.

49 **weed** uproot. Some editors have found this unsatisfactory, arguing, amongst other suggestions (see Collation) for *wind*, anticipating *unwind* at l. 51. But *weed* makes perfect sense; compare *Measure* 3.1.526: 'weed my vice, and let his grow'.

51–3 **as you unwind . . . on me** The image is of unwinding a ball of thread. Instead of becoming tangled, it must be wound on to a *bottom*, which was like a modern 'bobbin' or cotton-reel.

52 **ravel** tangle

You must provide to bottom it on me;
Which must be done by praising me as much
As you in worth dispraise Sir Valentine.   55

DUKE

And Proteus, we dare trust you in this kind
Because we know, on Valentine's report,
You are already love's firm votary,
And cannot soon revolt, and change your mind.
Upon this warrant shall you have access   60
Where you with Silvia may confer at large.
For she is lumpish, heavy, melancholy,
And for your friend's sake will be glad of you;
Where you may temper her, by your persuasion,
To hate young Valentine and love my friend.   65

PROTEUS

As much as I can do, I will effect.
But you, Sir Thurio, are not sharp enough.
You must lay lime to tangle her desires
By wailful sonnets, whose composèd rhymes
Should be full-fraught with serviceable vows.   70

---

53 **provide** take care
bottom wind on to a *bottom* (see note to ll. 51–3). Another example of Shakespeare characteristically using one part of speech for another (here a noun as a verb).
56 **this kind** an affair of this kind
58 **firm votary** loyal disciple. This echoes 1.1.52; the religious overtone there (see note) now becomes ironical.
60 **warrant** guarantee (as at 2.4.100)
61 **confer at large** discuss in detail (the second echo in this scene of 3.1.2, 252)
62 **lumpish** dejected, 'down in the mouth' (unique in Shakespeare; but for the tone, see next note)
heavy serious, sad. Compare Adriana's description of her husband at *Errors* 5.1.45: 'This week he hath been heavy, sour, sad'.
64 **temper** mould, influence
66 **effect** carry out
67 **sharp** keen, ardent (with the implication that Thurio is dull)

68 **lime** Birds were caught by smearing bird-lime (a white sticky paste that dries very slowly) on branches. It is a favourite Shakespearian metaphor of entrapment, especially erotic entrapment, as when Malvolio says of Olivia: 'I have limed her' (*Twelfth Night* 3.4.72).
tangle ensnare
69 **wailful** sorrowful
sonnets short poems, not necessarily in sonnet form
composèd well-crafted
70 **full-fraught** weighted (freighted)
serviceable expressing readiness to serve. In view of the increasing mood of treacherous manoeuvre in this scene (see next note), this may have a sinister overtone; compare Edgar's description of Goneril's servant Oswald as 'a serviceable villain' (*Tragedy of Lear* 4.5.250)—i.e. one who will carry out dishonourable tasks.

DUKE

Ay, much is the force of heaven-bred poesy.

PROTEUS

Say that upon the altar of her beauty
You sacrifice your tears, your sighs, your heart.
Write till your ink be dry, and with your tears
Moist it again; and frame some feeling line   75
That may discover such integrity;
For Orpheus' lute was strung with poets' sinews,
Whose golden touch could soften steel and stones,
Make tigers tame, and huge leviathans
Forsake unsounded deeps to dance on sands.   80
After your dire-lamenting elegies,
Visit by night your lady's chamber-window
With some sweet consort; to their instruments
Tune a deploring dump. The night's dead silence

71–86 The Duke's praise of poetry, in this context, has an ironical ring; and Proteus goes on to provide a lesson in courtship, expressed in the lyrical language characteristic of this play—but for deceptive purposes. Shakespeare was to develop this idea in Viola's 'willow cabin' speech (*Twelfth Night* 1.5.257–65), and this speech may have been suggested by one of the sources of *Twelfth Night*, Barnaby Riche's *Farewell to Military Profession*, which describes 'the manner of wooers: besides fair words, sorrowful sighs, and piteous countenances, there must be sending of loving letters [to] become a scholar in love's school' (Bullough, ii. 351).

71 **heaven-bred** For the divine inspiration of poetry, Shakespeare could have turned to his favourite Ovid, *Ars Amatoria* 3.550: 'From celestial places comes our inspiration'; but it was a commonplace.

72–3 **altar . . . sacrifice** Once again, as in *votary* at l. 58 and elsewhere, the language of religion is employed in the service of love—and for dishonest purposes.

75 **Moist** moisten
frame compose
feeling heartfelt

76 **discover** reveal
integrity sincere devotion

77 **Orpheus . . . sinews** Orpheus was a hero of Greek myth who was able to enchant all nature with the beauty of his music (e.g. Ovid, *Metamorphoses* 11.1–2). As Jonathan Bate says, Orpheus is 'always a figure of the poet', adding that 'Orpheus only gets strings for his lute if sinews are torn from the poet's body. Shakespeare was fascinated by the extremes of harmony and violence in the Orpheus story' (*Shakespeare and Ovid* (Oxford, 1993), p. 110): Orpheus was eventually torn in pieces.
sinews Animal sinews were used to string musical instruments.

79–80 **leviathans . . . sands** The image of whales (*leviathans*) being lured out of the depths of the ocean to dance on the beach might have been grotesque; but it is surely delightful, and characteristic of the style of *The Two Gentlemen* at its most successful.

81 **elegies** love poems

82 **Visit** 'come to (a person) with some accompaniment' (*OED v.* 11)

83 **consort** band of musicians

84 **Tune** sing
deploring dump sad melody. Compare Munday, *Fedele and Fortunio* (see Introduction, p. 17): 'The third act being done, the consort sounds a solemn dump.'

Will well become such sweet-complaining grievance.   85
This, or else nothing, will inherit her.

DUKE

This discipline shows thou hast been in love.

THURIO

And thy advice this night I'll put in practice.
Therefore, sweet Proteus, my direction-giver,
Let us into the city presently   90
To sort some gentlemen well skilled in music.
I have a sonnet that will serve the turn
To give the onset to thy good advice.

DUKE About it, gentlemen.

PROTEUS

We'll wait upon your grace till after supper,   95
And afterward determine our proceedings.

DUKE

Even now about it, I will pardon you.

Exeunt Thurio and Proteus at one door,
and the Duke at another

4.1 *Enter certain Outlaws*

FIRST OUTLAW

Fellows, stand fast. I see a passenger.

SECOND OUTLAW

If there be ten, shrink not, but down with 'em.

Enter Valentine and Speed

THIRD OUTLAW

Stand, sir, and throw us that you have about ye.
If not, we'll make you sit, and rifle you.

97.1–2 *Exeunt . . . another*] *Exeunt.* F
   4.1.0.1 *Enter certain Outlaws*] *Enter Valentine, Speed, and certaine Out-lawes.* F   2.1 *Enter
. . . Speed*] *not in* F

85 **sweet-complaining** sweetly lamenting
   grievance grief
86 **inherit** win
87 **discipline** knowledge, learning
89 **direction-giver** counsellor (Schmidt)
91 **sort** select
93 **give the onset** make a beginning (*OED,
   onset, sb.*[1] 2a, derived from the military
   sense 'begin the attack' (*OED v. Obs.*))
97 **pardon** excuse (you from attending
   upon me)

4.1.0.1 *certain Outlaws* These outlaws
   present special problems of interpretation
   and theatrical presentation. See Introduction, pp. 27–9.
1 **passenger** traveller
2 **shrink** cower
3 **that** what
4 **sit** (set against 'Stand' in the previous
   line)
   rifle search thoroughly (and rob)

SPEED *(to Valentine)*
  Sir, we are undone; these are the villains 5
  That all the travellers do fear so much.
VALENTINE *(to the Outlaws)* My friends.
FIRST OUTLAW
  That's not so, sir; we are your enemies.
SECOND OUTLAW Peace, we'll hear him.
THIRD OUTLAW Ay, by my beard will we; for he is a proper 10
  man.
VALENTINE
  Then know that I have little wealth to lose.
  A man I am, crossed with adversity.
  My riches are these poor habiliments,
  Of which if you should here disfurnish me 15
  You take the sum and substance that I have.
SECOND OUTLAW Whither travel you?
VALENTINE To Verona.
FIRST OUTLAW Whence came you?
VALENTINE From Milan. 20
THIRD OUTLAW Have you long sojourned there?
VALENTINE
  Some sixteen months, and longer might have stayed
  If crookèd fortune had not thwarted me.
FIRST OUTLAW
  What, were you banished thence?
VALENTINE   I was.
SECOND OUTLAW   For what offence?
VALENTINE
  For that which now torments me to rehearse: 25
  I killed a man, whose death I much repent,

---

5 **undone** come to grief (Sanders)
10 **by my beard** A common, mild oath.
    proper handsome
13 **crossed with** thwarted by. With the
    phrase (and the rhythm of) *crossed with*
    adversity, compare Adriana's description
    of herself at *Errors* 2.1.34: 'A wretched
    soul, bruised with adversity'.
14 **habiliments** clothes (as at *Shrew*
    4.3.168: 'honest, mean habiliments')
15 **disfurnish** deprive, divest

16 **sum and substance** i.e. everything
21 **sojourned** dwelt
23 **crookèd** malignant
25 **rehearse** relate
26 **I killed a man** Valentine's false claim
    here is the same as Lucentio's at *Shrew*
    1.1.229–30: 'For in a quarrel since I came
    ashore | I killed a man'. Perhaps Valen-
    tine is trying to impress the outlaws, in
    which case he seems to have succeeded
    since they make him their captain.

But yet I slew him manfully, in fight,
Without false vantage or base treachery.

FIRST OUTLAW

Why, ne'er repent it, if it were done so.
But were you banished for so small a fault? 30

VALENTINE

I was, and held me glad of such a doom.

SECOND OUTLAW Have you the tongues?

VALENTINE

My youthful travel therein made me happy,
Or else I had been often miserable.

THIRD OUTLAW

By the bare scalp of Robin Hood's fat friar, 35
This fellow were a king for our wild faction.

FIRST OUTLAW

We'll have him. Sirs, a word.
          The Outlaws confer

SPEED (*to Valentine*)   Master, be one of them.
It's an honourable kind of thievery.

VALENTINE Peace, villain.

SECOND OUTLAW

Tell us this: have you anything to take to? 40

VALENTINE Nothing but my fortune.

THIRD OUTLAW

Know, then, that some of us are gentlemen
Such as the fury of ungoverned youth

---

34 had been often] COLLIER; often had beene often F   37 *The Outlaws confer*] not in F

28 **false vantage** unfair advantage
30 **so small a fault** See Introduction, p. 27.
31 **held . . . doom** considered myself lucky to be given such a [light] sentence. Contrast Romeo's reaction to his banishment at *Romeo* 3.3.12: 'banishment? Be merciful, say "death"'.
32 **Have you the tongues** do you speak foreign languages
33 **travel** F's 'trauaile' could mean 'travel' or 'work hard'. Either would make sense, but languages are often picked up in the course of travelling.
happy fortunate

34 **I had been often** F reads 'I often had been often'. 'Editors usually follow F2 in omitting the second "often", but Collier's version scans better' (*TC*, p. 167).
35 **Robin Hood's fat friar** Friar Tuck, a well-known character in the Robin Hood legends. Perhaps this allusion suggests how we are to interpret these outlaws. See ll. 69–71 and note.
36 **were** would be
faction band
39 **villain** rascal, 'often used goodhumouredly' (Leech)
40 **anything to take to** any means of subsistence

Thrust from the company of aweful men.
Myself was from Verona banishèd   45
For practising to steal away a lady,
An heir, and near allied unto the Duke.

SECOND OUTLAW

And I from Mantua, for a gentleman
Who, in my mood, I stabbed unto the heart.

FIRST OUTLAW

And I, for suchlike petty crimes as these.   50
But to the purpose, for we cite our faults
That they may hold excused our lawless lives;
And partly seeing you are beautified
With goodly shape, and by your own report
A linguist, and a man of such perfection   55
As we do in our quality much want.

SECOND OUTLAW

Indeed because you are a banished man,
Therefore above the rest we parley to you.
Are you content to be our general,
To make a virtue of necessity   60
And live as we do in this wilderness?

THIRD OUTLAW

What sayst thou? Wilt thou be of our consort?
Say 'Ay', and be the captain of us all.
We'll do thee homage, and be ruled by thee,
Love thee as our commander and our king.   65

---

47 An heir, and near] THEOBALD; And heire and Neece F

---

44 **aweful**   law-abiding,   commanding
  respect (Sanders)
45–7 This outlaw's crime precisely parallels
  Valentine's.
46 **practising** plotting
47 **allied** (stressed on the second syllable)
49 **mood** anger, angry mood
50 **petty crimes** For this understatement,
  see Introduction, p. 27.
52 **That** so that
53 **beautified** Although Polonius criticizes
  beautified as 'a vile phrase' at *Hamlet*
  2.2.111, 'beautify' does not seem to be
  used for critical effect elsewhere in the
  Shakespeare canon, though, since most

of its occurrences are in earlier plays, it
may have seemed old-fashioned by the
time of *Hamlet* (*c*.1600).
55 **perfection** completeness
56 **quality** profession
58 **above the rest** i.e. more than for any
  other reason
  parley to negotiate with (as one army
  does with its opponent)
60 **make . . . necessity** Proverbial (Dent
  V73).
62 **thou** The outlaws shift to the familiar
  thou as they attempt to recruit Valentine.
  consort band (stressed on second
  syllable)

FIRST OUTLAW

  But if thou scorn our courtesy, thou diest.

SECOND OUTLAW

  Thou shalt not live to brag what we have offered.

VALENTINE

  I take your offer and will live with you,
  Provided that you do no outrages
  On silly women or poor passengers.   70

THIRD OUTLAW

  No, we detest such vile, base practices.
  Come, go with us. We'll bring thee to our crews
  And show thee all the treasure we have got,
  Which, with ourselves, all rest at thy dispose.   *Exeunt*

4.2 *Enter Proteus*

PROTEUS

  Already have I been false to Valentine,
  And now I must be as unjust to Thurio.
  Under the colour of commending him
  I have access my own love to prefer.
  But Silvia is too fair, too true, too holy,   5
  To be corrupted with my worthless gifts.
  When I protest true loyalty to her
  She twits me with my falsehood to my friend.
  When to her beauty I commend my vows
  She bids me think how I have been forsworn   10
  In breaking faith with Julia, whom I loved;

4.2.0.1 *Enter Proteus*] *Enter Protheus, Thurio, Iulia, Host, Musitian, Siluia.* F

69–71 **Provided . . . practices** This is the
'Robin Hood code' in folklore: see Introduction, p. 28.

70 **silly** simple, hence defenceless

72 **crews** bands. Sometimes emended to
'caves' (compare 5.3.11) since there is a
crew of outlaws on stage already; but the
more outlaws that can be mustered for
the final scenes, the more plausible.

74 **dispose** disposal, use

4.2 For a discussion of the theatrical per-
spectives in this scene, see Introduction,
pp. 44–5.

3 **colour** pretext

4 **prefer** advance, recommend

5 **holy** The language of religion is once
more used to express love, as it is in the
words of the song (l. 40).

7 **protest** declare, affirm

8 **twits** reproaches (a stronger term than
in modern usage, as at *Contention* (*2
Henry VI*) 3.1.178–9: 'Hath he not twit
our sovereign lady here | With ignomini-
ous words')

9 **commend** deliver, entrust

And notwithstanding all her sudden quips,
The least whereof would quell a lover's hope,
Yet, spaniel-like, the more she spurns my love,
The more it grows and fawneth on her still.   15
But here comes Thurio; now must we to her window,
And give some evening music to her ear.
  Enter Thurio with Musicians

THURIO
How now, Sir Proteus, are you crept before us?
PROTEUS
Ay, gentle Thurio, for you know that love
Will creep in service where it cannot go.   20
THURIO
Ay, but I hope, sir, that you love not here.
PROTEUS
Sir, but I do, or else I would be hence.
THURIO
Who, Silvia?
PROTEUS   Ay, Silvia—for your sake.
THURIO
I thank you for your own. Now, gentlemen,
Let's tune, and to it lustily awhile.   25
  Enter the Host, and Julia dressed as a page.
  They talk apart
HOST Now, my young guest, methinks you're allycholly.
  I pray you, why is it?
JULIA Marry, mine host, because I cannot be merry.

17.1 *Enter . . . Musicians*] not in F   25.1–2 *Enter . . . apart*] not in F

12 **sudden   quips**   sharp   (perhaps
unexpected) retorts. This may be a
standard phrase, since Thomas Wilson's
Art of Rhetoric (1553) has 'make him at
his wit's end through the sudden quip'
(Malone). Lyly's *Campaspe* defines a *quip*
as 'a short saying of a sharp wit with a
bitter sense in a sweet word' (3.2.30–2).
Silvia is giving Proteus a hard time.
14–15 **spaniel-like   .   .   .   fawneth** The
fawning of the spaniel was proverbial
(Dent S704). Compare Helena at *Dream*
2.1.203–4: 'I am your spaniel, and, |
Demetrius, | The more you beat me I will
fawn on you.'
18 **crept** moved stealthily. There is a hint of

suspicion in Thurio's choice of this word,
which Proteus parries in his reply.
19–20 **love . . . go** The antithesis between
creep (crawl) and *go* (walk) is proverbial:
'Love will creep where it cannot go' (Dent
K49).
24 **your own** i.e. your own sake
25 **lustily** vigorously (*OED adv.* 2)
26 **allycholly** The Host's slip for 'melancholy' anticipates the more extensive
verbal eccentricities of mine Host of
the Garter in *Merry Wives*, in which play
'allicholly' appears, used by Mistress
Quickly at 1.4.148.
28 **because . . . merry** Proverbial: 'I am sad
because I cannot be glad' (Dent S14).

HOST Come, we'll have you merry. I'll bring you where
   you shall hear music, and see the gentleman that you   30
   asked for.
JULIA But shall I hear him speak?
HOST Ay, that you shall.
JULIA That will be music.
HOST Hark, hark.   35
JULIA Is he among these?
HOST Ay, but peace, let's hear 'em.

                    Song

        Who is Silvia? What is she,
           That all our swains commend her?
        Holy, fair, and wise is she.   40
           The heaven such grace did lend her
        That she might admirèd be.

        Is she kind as she is fair?
           For beauty lives with kindness.
        Love doth to her eyes repair   45
           To help him of his blindness,
        And, being helped, inhabits there.

        Then to Silvia let us sing,
           That Silvia is excelling.
        She excels each mortal thing   50
           Upon the dull earth dwelling.
        To her let us garlands bring.

HOST How now, are you sadder than you were before? How
   do you, man? The music likes you not.

---

35 **Hark, hark** listen. The Host draws
attention either to the musicians tuning
or, more likely, playing an introduction
to the song.

38–52 See Appendix A.

39 **swains** country youths, applied to lovers
in pastoral poetry

41 **the heaven** Schmidt gives several
examples of 'the heaven' (rather than
'heaven' or 'the heavens', as might have
been expected here; Johnson emended to
'heav'ns'), e.g. Sonnet 28.10: 'do'st him
grace when clouds do blot the heaven'.

42 **That** so that
   admirèd wondered at. *Admirèd* was a
stronger term then than now (as at

Cymbeline 1.6.39: 'What makes your
admiration?'), but here merged with the
modern sense.

44 **beauty . . . kindness** beauty flourishes in
the doing of generous actions (Sanders)

45 **Love** Cupid, the blind god of love
   repair resort (perhaps, in view of what
follows, with a play on 'mend, cure')

46 **help . . . blindness** Compare Sonnet
152.9–11: 'I . . . to enlighten thee gave
eyes to blindness'.
   help cure

47 **inhabits** dwells

53 **How now** See first note to 1.2.16.

54, 55 **likes** pleases. In l. 55, it takes on the
additional meaning 'does not love me'.

JULIA You mistake: the musician likes me not. 55

HOST Why, my pretty youth?

JULIA He plays false, father.

HOST How, out of tune on the strings?

JULIA Not so, but yet so false that he grieves my very heart-
strings. 60

HOST You have a quick ear.

JULIA Ay, I would I were deaf. It makes me have a slow
heart.

HOST I perceive you delight not in music.

JULIA Not a whit when it jars so. 65

HOST Hark what fine change is in the music.

JULIA Ay, that 'change' is the spite.

HOST You would have them always play but one thing?

JULIA I would always have one play but one thing. But
host, doth this Sir Proteus that we talk on often resort 70
unto this gentlewoman?

HOST I tell you what Lance his man told me, he loved her
out of all nick.

JULIA Where is Lance?

HOST Gone to seek his dog, which tomorrow, by his 75
master's command, he must carry for a present to his
lady.

JULIA Peace, stand aside, the company parts.

PROTEUS

Sir Thurio, fear not you, I will so plead

That you shall say my cunning drift excels. 80

---

57 **plays false** (a) is out of tune; (b) is
unfaithful
father (a respectful reference to an older
man)
61 **quick** perceptive
62 **deaf** (quibbling on *quick* meaning 'alive',
as opposed to a 'dead' or 'deaf' ear
(Sanders))
slow heavy
65 **a whit** at all
jars is discordant
66–7 **change** The Host reacts to a musical
modulation; in her reply, Julia comments
on Proteus' inconstancy. Compare
Sonnet 76.1–2: 'Why is my verse . . . So
far from variation or quick change?'
67 **spite** injury
69 **I . . . thing** i.e. she wishes that Proteus

would be constant to her. Editors say,
correctly, that *play* and *thing* had bawdy
connotations; but I find these unhelpful
in expressing Julia's heartbreak—unless
her affair with Proteus had gone much
further than the text appears to suggest
(see Introduction, p. 9).
70 **on** of
70–1 **resort unto** frequent
73 **out of all nick** beyond all reckoning
(from the keeping of an account by nicks
or notches on a stick or tally (Bond))
75–7 **by . . . lady** The misleading information here is clarified at 4.4.44–56: Shakespeare is thinking ahead, to confusing
effect.
78 **parts** departs
80 **drift** scheme

THURIO

Where meet we?

PROTEUS   At Saint Gregory's well.

THURIO   Farewell.

                     Exeunt Thurio and the Musicians

     Enter Silvia, above

PROTEUS

Madam, good even to your ladyship.

SILVIA

I thank you for your music, gentlemen.

Who is that that spake?

PROTEUS

One, lady, if you knew his pure heart's truth   85

You would quickly learn to know him by his voice.

SILVIA Sir Proteus, as I take it.

PROTEUS

Sir Proteus, gentle lady, and your servant.

SILVIA

What's your will?

PROTEUS   That I may compass yours.

SILVIA

You have your wish: my will is even this,   90

That presently you hie you home to bed.

Thou subtle, perjured, false, disloyal man,

Think'st thou I am so shallow, so conceitless

To be seducèd by thy flattery,

That hast deceived so many with thy vows?   95

Return, return, and make thy love amends.

For me—by this pale queen of night I swear—

81.1–2 *Exeunt . . . above*] *not in* F

81 **Saint Gregory's well** An actual well near Milan: more travellers' tales? See note to 1.1.54.

81.2 *above* There are no stage directions in F, but this is a natural deduction from the reference to Silvia's 'window' at l. 16; she presumably appeared on the upper level of the Elizabethan theatre.

89 **will** wish, desire
compass achieve, obtain (playing on *will* as both 'good will' and 'sexual desire'; Silvia picks up both in her reply)

91 **presently** at once
hie hasten

92 **Thou** In her anger, Silvia adopts the contemptuous *thou* (though she controls herself and reverts to the polite 'you' at l. 125).
subtle cunning

93 **conceitless** witless, unintelligent

97 **pale queen of night** Diana, goddess of the moon and of chastity

I am so far from granting thy request
That I despise thee for thy wrongful suit,
And by and by intend to chide myself   100
Even for this time I spend in talking to thee.

PROTEUS

I grant, sweet love, that I did love a lady,
But she is dead.

JULIA (*aside*)   'Twere false if I should speak it,
For I am sure she is not burièd.

SILVIA

Say that she be, yet Valentine, thy friend,   105
Survives, to whom, thyself art witness,
I am betrothed; and art thou not ashamed
To wrong him with thy importunacy?

PROTEUS

I likewise hear that Valentine is dead.

SILVIA

And so suppose am I, for in his grave,   110
Assure thyself, my love is burièd.

PROTEUS

Sweet lady, let me rake it from the earth.

SILVIA

Go to thy lady's grave and call hers thence,
Or at the least, in hers sepulchre thine.

JULIA (*aside*) He heard not that.   115

PROTEUS

Madam, if your heart be so obdurate,
Vouchsafe me yet your picture for my love,
The picture that is hanging in your chamber.
To that I'll speak, to that I'll sigh and weep;
For since the substance of your perfect self   120

110 his] F2; her F1

108 **importunacy** importuning, urging
112 **rake . . . earth** This striking phrase may derive from one in Lyly's *Euphues* about desires: 'yet will I rake them up' (Bullough, p. 222).
114 **sepulchre** bury (stressed on the second syllable)
115 **He . . . that** he will deliberately ignore that (Sanders)

116 **obdurate** hard, stubborn (accented on the second syllable)
117 **Vouchsafe** allow
120–1 **substance . . . shadow** This begins the very Shakespearian contrast which is developed in the following lines and at 4.4.194–8.
120 **perfect** complete

Is else devoted, I am but a shadow,
And to your shadow will I make true love.

JULIA (*aside*)

If 'twere a substance, you would sure deceive it
And make it but a shadow, as I am.

SILVIA

I am very loath to be your idol, sir,   125
But since your falsehood shall become you well
To worship shadows and adore false shapes,
Send to me in the morning, and I'll send it.
And so, good rest.   *Exit*

PROTEUS   As wretches have o'ernight,
That wait for execution in the morn.   *Exit*   130

JULIA   Host, will you go?

HOST   By my halidom, I was fast asleep.

JULIA   Pray you, where lies Sir Proteus?

HOST   Marry, at my house. Trust me, I think 'tis almost
day.   135

JULIA

Not so; but it hath been the longest night
That e'er I watched, and the most heaviest.   *Exeunt*

4.3   *Enter Eglamour*

EGLAMOUR

This is the hour that Madam Silvia
Entreated me to call, and know her mind.

---

129 *Exit*] *not in* F   130 *Exit*] *not in* F   137 *Exeunt*] *not in* F
4.3.0.1 *Enter Eglamour*] *Enter Eglamore, Siluia.* F

---

121 **else devoted** given to someone else
(Valentine)
122 **shadow** image
124 **shadow** Perhaps with the sense 'actor'
(*OED sb.* 6b), as at *Dream* 5.1.210: 'The
best in this kind are but shadows', and
Robin's epilogue: 'If we shadows have
offended'.
125 **idol** This picks up the religious imagery
of 3.2.58 and 4.2.40–1.
132 **By my halidom** A common (mild)
oath, sworn by our 'holy dame', our Lady
(the Virgin Mary).
133 **lies** lodges

134 **house** inn
136–7 **longest . . . heaviest** This echoes an
earlier stage in Montemayor's story,
when Felismena (Julia) is deciding
whether to accept Felix/Proteus' suit or
not: it was 'the longest and most painful
night that ever I passed' (Bullough, p.
231).
137 **watched** remained awake through
most heaviest saddest. The double
superlative is typical Elizabethan grammar, used for emphasis (Abbott 11).
4.3.0.1 *Eglamour* See note to 1.2.9.

There's some great matter she'd employ me in.
Madam, madam!

Enter Silvia ⌈above⌉

SILVIA   Who calls?

EGLAMOUR   Your servant, and your friend.
One that attends your ladyship's command.   5

SILVIA

Sir Eglamour, a thousand times good morrow!

EGLAMOUR

As many, worthy lady, to yourself.
According to your ladyship's impose
I am thus early come, to know what service
It is your pleasure to command me in.   10

SILVIA

O Eglamour, thou art a gentleman—
Think not I flatter, for I swear I do not—
Valiant, wise, remorseful, well accomplished.
Thou art not ignorant what dear good will
I bear unto the banished Valentine,   15
Nor how my father would enforce me marry
Vain Thurio, whom my very soul abhors.
Thyself hast loved, and I have heard thee say
No grief did ever come so near thy heart
As when thy lady and thy true love died,   20
Upon whose grave thou vowed'st pure chastity.
Sir Eglamour, I would to Valentine,
To Mantua, where I hear he makes abode;

4 *Enter Silvia ⌈above⌉] not in* F   17 abhors] HANMER; abhor'd F

3 **There's . . . in** Eglamour is a chivalric knight errant, ready to be employed in *some great matter*, awaiting Silvia's *command* (l. 5) and one who, when his *lady* died, *vowed pure chastity* on her grave (ll. 20–1).

4 *above* 'The direction seems consistent with Silvia's entry in the previous scene and with the knight's calling to her, though the action could take place on the level' (*TC*, p. 167).

8 **impose** command imposed

13 **remorseful** compassionate (*OED*'s earliest example in this sense: *a.* 2)
well accomplished This graceful

compliment is also used by Catherine to describe Dumaine at *Love's Labour's Lost* 2.1.56.

14 **dear** fond, loving

17 **abhors** F has 'abhor'd'. 'Leech defends F, but the error is an easy one and the probable omission referred to in the . . . note [to ll. 37–8] suggests a compositor prone to error' (*TC*, p. 167).

22 **would** wish to go

23 **Mantua** Romeo, too, like his namesake in Brooke's *Romeus*, was banished to Mantua.
makes abode is living

And for the ways are dangerous to pass
I do desire thy worthy company,   25
Upon whose faith and honour I repose.
Urge not my father's anger, Eglamour,
But think upon my grief, a lady's grief,
And on the justice of my flying hence
To keep me from a most unholy match,   30
Which heaven and fortune still rewards with plagues.
I do desire thee, even from a heart
As full of sorrows as the sea of sands,
To bear me company and go with me;
If not, to hide what I have said to thee   35
That I may venture to depart alone.

EGLAMOUR
Madam, I pity much your grievances,
Which, since I know they virtuously are placed,
I give consent to go along with you,
Recking as little what betideth me   40
As much I wish all good befortune you.
When will you go?

SILVIA   This evening coming.

EGLAMOUR
Where shall I meet you?

SILVIA   At Friar Patrick's cell,
Where I intend holy confession.

EGLAMOUR
I will not fail your ladyship.   45
Good morrow, gentle lady.

---

24 **for** because
26 **repose** (my trust), rely
27 **Urge not** do not argue (against my plan)
30 **unholy** (because enforced (l. 16))
31 **still** always
   plagues i.e. with a bad end
33 **as the sea of sands** Proverbial: 'as many as the sands of the sea' (Dent S90.1.).
37–8 **grievances, | Which** 'The use of *which* is warranted as a connective particle without antecedent; see note in Taylor's Oxford *Henry V* to 3.2.46 . . . The construction has caused difficulty: Keightley suggested a missing line "And sympathize with your affections"' (*TC*,

p. 167). This suggestion certainly makes better sense than the rather forced leap in sense from *grievances* (sufferings) to Silvia's *virtue* (her love for Valentine) that has led to them. Johnson glossed *grievances* as 'sorrowful affections', which makes the transition easier.
40 **Recking** caring
   betideth happens to
41 **befortune** befall (the earlier of only two recorded instances in *OED*)
43–4 **At . . . confession** In Brooke's *Romeus*, and in Shakespeare's play, Juliet uses the excuse of going to confession at a friar's cell to meet (and marry) her lover.

SILVIA

Good morrow, kind Sir Eglamour.   *Exeunt*

4.4 *Enter Lance and his dog Crab*

LANCE (*To the audience*) When a man's servant shall play
the cur with him, look you, it goes hard. One that I
brought up of a puppy, one that I saved from drowning
when three or four of his blind brothers and sisters went
to it. I have taught him, even as one would say precisely,   5
'Thus I would teach a dog'. I was sent to deliver him as a
present to Mistress Silvia from my master, and I came
no sooner into the dining-chamber but he steps me to
her trencher and steals her capon's leg. O, 'tis a foul thing
when a cur cannot keep himself in all companies. I would   10
have, as one should say, one that takes upon him to be
a dog indeed, to be, as it were, a dog at all things. If I had
not had more wit than he, to take a fault upon me that
he did, I think verily he had been hanged for't. Sure as I
live, he had suffered for't. You shall judge. He thrusts me   15
himself into the company of three or four gentleman-
like dogs under the Duke's table. He had not been
there—bless the mark—a pissing-while but all the
chamber smelt him. 'Out with the dog', says one. 'What

4.4.0.1 *Enter . . . Crab*] *Enter Launce, Protheus, Iulia, Siluia.* F

4.4.1–38 For a discussion of this, the second
of Lance's great comic monologues, see
Introduction, p. 52.
2 **cur** Lance plays on the senses 'dog' and
'worthless person', as at 2.3.9.
goes hard fares badly (with a man)
3 **of** from
4 **blind** i.e. so young that they had not yet
opened their eyes
5 **to it** to drowning, death
precisely exactly (a nicely pedantic
touch to lead into *Thus would I teach a dog*)
6–7 **I was . . . master** Lance modifies this
statement at ll. 44–56.
8, 15, 23 **me** Examples of the so-called 'ethic
dative', used for emphasis: see note to
2.7.61, 67.
9 **trencher** wooden plate
capon's chicken's
10 **keep** restrain (or more generally
'behave')

12 **a dog at** good at. The proverbial expression was 'be old dog at it' (Dent D506),
used by Sir Andrew Aguecheek at *Twelfth
Night* 2.3.59–60. Lance varies the phrase
to '*a* dog at all things' in order to apply it
to the real dog standing beside him.
14 **verily** truly
Sure as I live A proverbial phrase (Dent
L374), used for emphasis.
18 **bless the mark** An exclamatory
phrase, probably originally used to avert
an evil omen, and hence used by way of
apology when something indecent is
mentioned (*OED, mark, sb.*[1] 18). The full
phrase is 'God bless the mark', used by
Lancelot Gobbo at *Merchant* 2.2.22, so
the version here may reflect censorship;
see Introduction, p. 61.
18 **a pissing-while** Proverbial for 'a very
short time' (Dent P355), but also literal in
this case.

cur is that?' says another. 'Whip him out', says the   20
third. 'Hang him up', says the Duke. I, having been
acquainted with the smell before, knew it was Crab, and
goes me to the fellow that whips the dogs. 'Friend',
quoth I, 'you mean to whip the dog.' 'Ay, marry do I',
quoth he. 'You do him the more wrong', quoth I, ''twas   25
I did the thing you wot of.' He makes me no more
ado, but whips me out of the chamber. How many
masters would do this for his servant? Nay, I'll be
sworn I have sat in the stocks for puddings he hath
stolen, otherwise he had been executed. I have stood   30
on the pillory for geese he hath killed, otherwise he
had suffered for't. (*To Crab*) Thou think'st not of this
now. Nay, I remember the trick you served me when
I took my leave of Madam Silvia. Did not I bid thee still
mark me, and do as I do? When didst thou see me   35
heave up my leg and make water against a gentlewoman's farthingale? Didst thou ever see me do such
a trick?

    Enter Proteus, with Julia dressed as a page
PROTEUS (*to Julia*)
  Sebastian is thy name? I like thee well,

38.1 *Enter . . . page] not in* F

---

23 **the fellow . . . dogs** 'An official
    formerly employed to whip dogs out of a
    church or chapel' (*OED*, *dog-whipper*, 1).
26 **wot** know. Richard Proudfoot, in
    Carroll, calls the phrase *the thing you wot*
    of 'an evasive euphemism for something
    unmentionable'. Compare *Measure*
    2.1.107–8: 'past cure of the thing you
    wot of'—i.e. venereal disease.
27–8 **How many . . . servant** This antici-
    pates Julia's 'How many women would
    do such a message' (l. 88): Lance's loyalty
    to Crab is a comic counterpart of Julia's
    to Proteus.
28–9 **I'll be sworn** Literally 'I'll take my oath
    upon it', it is simply used for emphasis.
29, 31 **stocks . . . pillory** Wooden struc-
    tures in which prisoners were exposed
    to public humiliation: the *stocks* held the
    feet, the *pillory* the head and hands.
29 **puddings** Savoury mixture cooked in
    animal intestines, as in modern black
    pudding.

33 **Nay** As at the opening of Lance's
    previous monologue (2.3.1), this is not a
    negative, but used for emphasis, as he
    turns from the audience to Crab to rebuke
    him directly for his misdemeanours.
    served played on
34–5 **still mark** always pay attention to
36 **heave up my leg** The modern colloquial-
    ism is 'cock the leg'.
37 **farthingale** The hooped support for a
    lady's dress also mentioned at 2.7.51,
    though here just a synonym for 'skirt'.
39 **Sebastian** The name of Viola's twin
    brother in *Twelfth Night*, another of the
    many links between the two plays.
    I like thee well Proteus' instant attrac-
    tion to 'Sebastian' (see also ll. 65–8)
    is a nice touch: he is unconsciously
    responding to Julia, and in a way reviving
    his earlier affection for her. This helps to
    prepare for their ultimate reunion.

And will employ thee in some service presently.   40

JULIA

In what you please, I'll do what I can.

PROTEUS

I hope thou wilt.—How now, you whoreson peasant,
Where have you been these two days loitering?

LANCE Marry, sir, I carried Mistress Silvia the dog you
bade me.   45

PROTEUS And what says she to my little jewel?

LANCE Marry, she says your dog was a cur, and tells you
currish thanks is good enough for such a present.

PROTEUS But she received my dog?

LANCE No indeed did she not. Here have I brought him   50
back again.

PROTEUS What, didst thou offer her this from me?

LANCE Ay, sir. The other squirrel was stolen from me by
the hangman boys in the market place, and then I
offered her mine own, who is a dog as big as ten of yours,   55
and therefore the gift the greater.

PROTEUS

Go, get thee hence, and find my dog again,

---

54 hangman] SINGER; Hangmans F

40, 69 **presently** right away
41 **I'll do** F2's 'I'll do, sir' regularizes the
metre; but perhaps F1's irregularity
suggests some hesitation in Julia's part.
42 **whoreson** See note to 2.5.41.
46 **jewel** An expression of affection (which
Valentine uses of Silvia at 2.4.167) rather
than the name of the dog, as the capital-
ization of the word in F led some editors
(e.g. Dover Wilson) to believe.
47–8 **cur . . . currish thanks** bad-tempered
dog, and so ill-tempered thanks. The
word-play recurs at *Shrew* 5.2.54–6:
'Lucentio slipped me like his greyhound
. . . | A good swift simile, but something
currish.'
52 Actors make the most of Proteus' contempt for Crab in this line, as in Ian Richardson's outraged emphasis 'didst thou
offer her *this* from me?' at Stratford-upon-
Avon in 1970.
53 **squirrel** Again, as with *jewel* at l. 46,
this is probably not the dog's name, but a
reference to his size. Bond points out that

squirrels were carried by ladies as pets,
citing Lyly's *Endymion* 2.2.147–9: 'What
is that the gentlewoman carrieth in a
chain? | Why, it is a squirrel.'
54 **hangman boys** F has 'Hangmans
boyes', which could be right: 'the servants of the public hangman' (and
dogs were sometimes hanged in the
Elizabethan period). But *hangman*, a
derogatory expression ('rough-necks',
says Sanders), is likelier.
55 **as big . . . yours** This implies that Crab
is a large dog, although if Proteus' dog
was merely the size of a squirrel (red at
that time, smaller than the modern grey),
it wouldn't be difficult for Crab to be bigger. In performance, Crabs have ranged
from a small white Sealyham (see fig. 2),
via mongrels of all sorts, to lurchers and
wolfhounds.
57–9 **Go . . . here** So Lance is fired, to be
replaced by Julia/Sebastian. He does not
reappear. See Introduction, pp. 52–3, for
a discussion of this.

Or ne'er return again into my sight.
Away, I say. Stay'st thou to vex me here?

                       Exit Lance with Crab

A slave, that still on end turns me to shame.   60
Sebastian, I have entertainèd thee
Partly that I have need of such a youth
That can with some discretion do my business,
For 'tis no trusting to yon foolish lout,
But chiefly for thy face and thy behaviour,   65
Which, if my augury deceive me not,
Witness good bringing up, fortune, and truth.
Therefore know thou, for this I entertain thee.
Go presently, and take this ring with thee.
Deliver it to Madam Silvia.   70
She loved me well delivered it to me.

JULIA

It seems you loved not her, to leave her token.
She is dead belike?

PROTEUS   Not so. I think she lives.

JULIA

Alas.

PROTEUS Why dost thou cry 'Alas'?

JULIA

I cannot choose but pity her.   75

PROTEUS

Wherefore shouldst thou pity her?

JULIA

Because methinks that she loved you as well
As you do love your lady Silvia.

---

59 *Exit . . . Crab*] *not in* F   60 on end] F (an end)   68 thou] F2; thee FI   72 to] F2; not FI

60 **still on end** continuously
  turns . . . shame brings shame upon me
61 **entertainèd** employed
65 **behaviour** manner
66 **augury** prediction (derived from the classical augurers who used omens to predict the future)
69–70 **Go . . . Silvia** Compare *Twelfth Night* 2.4.123–4: 'Give her this jewel. Say | My love can give no place, bide no denay.' From this point, the triangular relationship between Proteus, Julia/Sebastian, and Silvia, closely resembles that between Orsino, Viola/Cesario, and Olivia in *Twelfth Night*, but with significant differences. For a discussion, see Introduction, p. 37.
71 **delivered** (who) gave. Relative pronouns were frequently omitted in the period (Abbott 244).
72 **leave** part with
73 **belike** perhaps
76 **Wherefore** why
77 **methinks** it seems to me

She dreams on him that has forgot her love;
You dote on her that cares not for your love.   80
'Tis pity love should be so contrary,
And thinking on it makes me cry 'Alas'.

PROTEUS

Well, give her that ring, and therewithal
This letter. That's her chamber. Tell my lady
I claim the promise for her heavenly picture.   85
Your message done, hie home unto my chamber,
Where thou shalt find me sad and solitary.   *Exit*

JULIA

How many women would do such a message?
Alas, poor Proteus, thou hast entertained
A fox to be the shepherd of thy lambs.   90
Alas, poor fool, why do I pity him
That with his very heart despiseth me?
Because he loves her, he despiseth me;
Because I love him, I must pity him.
This ring I gave him when he parted from me,   95
To bind him to remember my good will;
And now am I, unhappy messenger,
To plead for that which I would not obtain;
To carry that which I would have refused;
To praise his faith, which I would have dispraised.   100
I am my master's true-confirmèd love,
But cannot be true servant to my master
Unless I prove false traitor to myself.

87 *Exit*] *not in* F

79–80, 93–4 More balanced antitheses, typical of the play's style.
79, 82 **on** of
81 **contrary** perverse (stressed on the first syllable, unlike modern usage in this sense)
83 **Well** This is all that Proteus can say to Julia's heartfelt lines, a point usually brought out in performance. The situation is becoming emotionally charged (compare, again, *Twelfth Night* 2.4), and Proteus brings the dialogue back to practicalities. (In *Twelfth Night*, it is Viola herself who does so: 'Sir, shall I to this lady?' (2.4.122).)

83 **therewithal** along with it
84 **That's her chamber** On the unlocalized Elizabethan stage, all Proteus has to do is to indicate one of the doors set in the back wall for the action to move to Silvia's chamber.
86 **hie** hasten
88 See note to ll. 27–8.
90 **A fox . . . lambs** Proverbial: 'Give not the wolf (fox) the wether (sheep) to keep' (Dent W602). Compare *Contention* (*2 Henry VI*) 3.1.252–3: 'were't not madness then | To make the fox surveyor of the fold'.

Yet will I woo for him, but yet so coldly
As, heaven it knows, I would not have him speed.   105
    Enter Silvia
Gentlewoman, good day. I pray you be my mean
To bring me where to speak with Madam Silvia.
SILVIA
What would you with her, if that I be she?
JULIA
If you be she, I do entreat your patience
To hear me speak the message I am sent on.   110
SILVIA From whom?
JULIA
From my master, Sir Proteus, madam.
SILVIA O, he sends you for a picture?
JULIA Ay, madam.
SILVIA Ursula, bring my picture there.   115
    ⌈*An attendant brings a picture*⌉
Go, give your master this. Tell him from me
One Julia, that his changing thoughts forget,
Would better fit his chamber than this shadow.
JULIA
Madam, please you peruse this letter.
    She gives Silvia a letter
Pardon me, madam, I have unadvised   120
Delivered you a paper that I should not.
    She takes back the letter and gives Silvia another
This is the letter to your ladyship.
SILVIA
I pray thee, let me look on that again.

105.1 *Enter Silvia*] *not in* F   115.1 *An . . . picture*] *not in* F   119.1 *She . . . letter*] *not in* F   121.1 *She . . . another*] *not in* F

---

104 **Yet . . . but** yet Julia here picks up, in a more serious vein, Silvia's equivocating repetitions of Valentine's 'And yet' at 2.1.108–9, a nice example of the way in which Shakespeare develops, and transforms, the language of the play as he goes along.

105 **heaven it knows** heaven knows (a common Elizabethan construction)
speed succeed

106 **mean** means

107 **where to** where I may

120 **unadvised** inadvertently

121 **Delivered . . . should not** Julia obviously produces a letter from Proteus to herself; Silvia recognizes the handwriting, which is why she is keen to read it (l. 123). Whether Julia genuinely confuses the letters, or does so deliberately, is discussed in the Introduction, p. 48.

JULIA
It may not be. Good madam, pardon me.

SILVIA
There, hold. I will not look upon your master's lines. 125
I know they are stuffed with protestations,
And full of new-found oaths, which he will break
As easily as I do tear his paper.
She tears the letter

JULIA
Madam, he sends your ladyship this ring.
She offers Silvia a ring

SILVIA
The more shame for him, that he sends it me; 130
For I have heard him say a thousand times
His Julia gave it him at his departure.
Though his false finger have profaned the ring,
Mine shall not do his Julia so much wrong.

JULIA She thanks you. 135

SILVIA What sayst thou?

JULIA
I thank you, madam, that you tender her.
Poor gentlewoman, my master wrongs her much.

SILVIA Dost thou know her?

JULIA
Almost as well as I do know myself. 140
To think upon her woes I do protest
That I have wept a hundred several times.

SILVIA
Belike she thinks that Proteus hath forsook her?

128.1 *She . . . letter*] *not in* F   129.1 *She . . . ring*] *not in* F

125 **hold** Either 'stop' or 'take back (the letter)'.
126 **protestations** declarations (of love)
127 **new-found** newly-created. Perhaps she means oaths that were once vowed to Julia, now re-routed to her; or perhaps 'new-fangled', as at Sonnet 76.4: 'new-found methods and . . . compounds strange'.
128 **I do tear his paper** This parallels

Julia's tearing of Proteus' letter at 1.2, and perhaps lends support to Harold Brooks's conjecture, in Leech, that that was the letter which Julia gave mistakenly to Silvia at l. 121.
133 **profaned** desecrated
137 **tender** show concern for
141 **protest** declare
142 **several** separate
143 **Belike** perhaps

JULIA

  I think she doth; and that's her cause of sorrow.

SILVIA Is she not passing fair?   145

JULIA

  She hath been fairer, madam, than she is.

  When she did think my master loved her well

  She, in my judgement, was as fair as you.

  But since she did neglect her looking-glass,

  And threw her sun-expelling mask away,   150

  The air hath starved the roses in her cheeks

  And pinched the lily tincture of her face,

  That now she is become as black as I.

SILVIA How tall was she?

JULIA

  About my stature; for at Pentecost,   155

  When all our pageants of delight were played,

  Our youth got me to play the woman's part,

  And I was trimmed in Madam Julia's gown,

  Which servèd me as fit, by all men's judgements,

  As if the garment had been made for me;   160

  Therefore I know she is about my height.

  And at that time I made her weep agood,

  For I did play a lamentable part.

  Madam, 'twas Ariadne, passioning

  For Theseus' perjury and unjust flight;   165

---

145 **passing** surpassingly

150 **sun-expelling mask** Fashionable ladies in Elizabethan England used masks to protect their skin from the sun.

151 **starved** withered

152–3 **pinched . . . black** Compare *Antony* 1.5.28, where Cleopatra says that she is with Phoebus' (the sun-god's) 'amorous pinches black'. Julia may have dirtied her face as part of her disguise, as Celia plans to do at *As You Like It* 1.3.111: 'with a kind of umber smirch my face.'

152 **tincture** colouring

153 **That** so that

155 **Pentecost** Whitsunday (the seventh Sunday after Easter) was, until the late twentieth century, celebrated as a major Christian festival.

156 **pageants of delight** enjoyable performances. *Pageants* were originally the carts upon which medieval mystery plays were acted (usually on the feast of Corpus Christi, shortly after Pentecost).

157 **woman's part** Compare Orsino's response to Viola in her male disguise: 'all is semblative a woman's part' (1.4.34).

158 **trimmed** dressed

159 **fit** well

162 **agood** in earnest

163 **lamentable** sorrowful (stressed on the first syllable)

164–5 **Ariadne . . . flight** Ariadne helped Theseus kill the monster, the Minotaur; he abandoned her on the island of Naxos (Ovid, *Heroides* 10; *Metamorphoses* 8.169–82). She is, therefore, an apt parallel for the abandoned Julia.

164 **passioning** sorrowing

Which I so lively acted with my tears
That my poor mistress, movèd therewithal,
Wept bitterly; and would I might be dead
If I in thought felt not her very sorrow.

SILVIA
She is beholden to thee, gentle youth.   170
Alas, poor lady, desolate and left.
I weep myself to think upon thy words.
Here, youth; there is my purse; I give thee this
For thy sweet mistress' sake, because thou lov'st her.
Farewell.   *Exit*   175

JULIA
And she shall thank you for't, if e'er you know her.—
A virtuous gentlewoman, mild, and beautiful.
I hope my master's suit will be but cold,
Since she respects my mistress' love so much.
Alas, how love can trifle with itself.   180
Here is her picture: let me see, I think
If I had such a tire, this face of mine
Were full as lovely as is this of hers;
And yet the painter flattered her a little,
Unless I flatter with myself too much.   185
Her hair is auburn, mine is perfect yellow.
If that be all the difference in his love,
I'll get me such a coloured periwig.
Her eyes are grey as glass, and so are mine.
Ay, but her forehead's low, and mine's as high.   190

---

170 beholden] F (beholding)   175 *Exit*] *not in* F

---

167 **therewithal** at it
170 **beholden** F's 'beholding' is '"an ancient error . . . now obsolete" (Fowler, *Modern English Usage*), and with no independent significance' (*TC*, p. 167).
173 **there is my purse** Compare Olivia at *Twelfth Night* 1.5.273: 'Spend this for me', though the motives are different: Olivia is falling in love with Viola/Cesario, Silvia sympathizing with Julia/Sebastian 'For thy sweet mistress' sake' (l. 174).
178 **but cold** unsuccessful
179 **my mistress'** i.e. her own
182 **tire** headdress

185 **flatter with** The phrase recurs at *Twelfth Night* 1.5.293.
186 **auburn** Originally 'of a yellowish or brownish-white colour; now, of a golden-brown' (*OED a.*); the distinction seems to be between yellow-brown and *perfect yellow* in the next phrase.
188 **such . . . periwig** a wig of that colour
189 **grey as glass** *Grey* may mean 'grey-blue': 'Elizabethan glass had a light blue tint' (Leech).
190 **high** High foreheads were regarded as beautiful, as Mercutio mockingly makes plain at *Romeo* 2.1.18.

What should it be that he respects in her
But I can make respective in myself,
If this fond love were not a blinded god?
Come, shadow, come, and take this shadow up,
For 'tis thy rival.
          She picks up the portrait
                              O thou senseless form,   195
Thou shalt be worshipped, kissed, loved, and adored;
And were there sense in his idolatry
My substance should be statue in thy stead.
I'll use thee kindly, for thy mistress' sake,
That used me so; or else, by Jove I vow,   200
I should have scratched out your unseeing eyes,
To make my master out of love with thee.   *Exit*

5.1 *Enter Eglamour*

EGLAMOUR

The sun begins to gild the western sky,
And now it is about the very hour
That Silvia at Friar Patrick's cell should meet me.
She will not fail; for lovers break not hours,
Unless it be to come before their time,   5
So much they spur their expedition.

195 *She . . . portrait*] *not in* F   202 *Exit*] *Exeunt.* F
5.1.0.1 *Enter Eglamour*] *Enter Eglamoure, Siluia.* F

191 **respects** esteems
192 **But I can** that I cannot
    respective worthy of respect
193 **fond** foolishly doting
194 **shadow . . . shadow** The first means
    'actor' (Julia playing Sebastian), the
    second 'image, portrait'.
    take . . . up (a) pick up, carry; (b) accept
    a challenge (from a rival)
195, 197 **senseless . . . sense** (playing on
    'insensible' and 'reason')
197 **idolatry** The language of religion
    again: see 4.2.125 and note.
198 **My substance . . . stead** 'Julia is
    setting herself as a substantial image
    against the *shadow*—the two-
    dimensional image of the painting'
    (Sanders).

199 **use** treat
201, 202 **your . . . thee** 'Julia expresses her
    animus strongly' in l. 201, with the
    switch to the formal *your*, 'but is quieter
    and friendlier in the following line', with
    the more familiar *thee* (Leech).
5.1.1 **gild** turn to gold. This antedates
    OED's earliest reference in this sense
    (*v.*[1] 4), to *Titus* 2.1.6: 'having gilt the
    ocean with his beams'. Compare *Dream*
    3.2.394: 'Turns into yellow gold his salt
    green streams'.
2 **very** exact
4 **hours** appointments
6 **spur their expedition** hasten their
    progress (proverbial: 'He that has love
    in his breast has spurs in his sides' (Dent
    L481))

Enter Silvia

See where she comes. Lady, a happy evening!

SILVIA

Amen, amen. Go on, good Eglamour,

Out at the postern by the abbey wall.

I fear I am attended by some spies.   10

EGLAMOUR

Fear not; the forest is not three leagues off,

If we recover that, we are sure enough.   *Exeunt*

5.2 *Enter Thurio, Proteus, and Julia dressed as a page*

THURIO

Sir Proteus, what says Silvia to my suit?

PROTEUS

O sir, I find her milder than she was,

And yet she takes exceptions at your person.

THURIO

What? That my leg is too long?

PROTEUS

No, that it is too little.   5

THURIO

I'll wear a boot, to make it somewhat rounder.

JULIA *(aside)*

But love will not be spurred to what it loathes.

THURIO

What says she to my face?

6.1 *Enter Silvia*] *not in* F   5.2.0.1 *Enter . . . page*] *Enter Thurio, Protheus, Iulia, Duke.* F
7 JULIA] COLLIER (*conj.* Boswell); *Pro.* F

8 **Amen** The standard answer to a prayer, here used by Silvia to hurry Eglamour along: 'let's get on with it'.
9 **postern** small gate set into a wall
10 **attended** watched
11 **leagues** A *league* is approximately three modern English miles.
12 **recover** reach
sure safe
5.2.1–29 During this conversation between Proteus and Thurio, Julia-as-Sebastian keeps up a witty running commentary. Sometimes these are asides to the audience, sometimes played to Proteus, though of course unheard by Thurio. F gives l. 7 to Proteus, ll. 13–14 to Thurio, which must be slips, since this would spoil the shape of the scene. The scribe Ralph Crane's habit of writing the text first and adding the speech-prefixes later might explain the slips.
3 **takes exceptions at** finds fault with
5 **little** thin
7 **spurred** (quibbling with *boot* in the previous line)

PROTEUS

  She says it is a fair one.

THURIO

  Nay then, the wanton lies; my face is black.   10

PROTEUS

  But pearls are fair; and the old saying is,

  'Black men are pearls in beauteous ladies' eyes'.

JULIA (*aside*)

  'Tis true, such pearls as put out ladies' eyes,

  For I had rather wink than look on them.

THURIO

  How likes she my discourse?   15

PROTEUS

  Ill, when you talk of war.

THURIO

  But well when I discourse of love and peace.

JULIA (*aside*)

  But better indeed when you hold your peace.

THURIO

  What says she to my valour?

PROTEUS

  O sir, she makes no doubt of that.   20

JULIA (*aside*)

  She needs not, when she knows it cowardice.

THURIO

  What says she to my birth?

PROTEUS

  That you are well derived.

---

13 JULIA] ROWE; *Thu.* F   18 your] F3; you F1

9–10 **fair . . . black** A *fair*, pale, complexion was considered beautiful in Elizabethan England; a *black* one (i.e. swarthy or simply tanned) was not; compare Sonnet 127.1: 'In the old age black was not counted fair'. The Elizabethans did not share modern fashions: for them, a tanned complexion was the mark of one who laboured all day in the sun.

12 **Black . . . eyes** A version of the proverb 'A black man is a pearl (jewel) in a fair woman's eye' (Dent M79), widely used in the writing of the period, as when Aaron the Moor in *Titus* is called 'the pearl that pleased your Empress' eye' (5.1.42).

13 **such . . . eyes** Julia plays on another sense of *pearls*: the Elizabethan doctor, Thomas Vicary (cited by Bond), calls cataracts 'the pearl on the eye', which thus *put out*, blind, *ladies'* eyes.

14 **wink** close my eyes

    them i.e. the swarthy men of the proverb

18 **hold your peace** keep quiet

20 **makes no doubt of** does not question

23 **derived** descended (in birth); Julia in the next line takes it to mean a decline.

JULIA (*aside*)
  True: from a gentleman to a fool.
THURIO
  Considers she my possessions? 25
PROTEUS
  O ay, and pities them.
THURIO Wherefore?
JULIA (*aside*)
  That such an ass should owe them.
PROTEUS
  That they are out by lease.
JULIA   Here comes the Duke.
      Enter the Duke
DUKE
  How now, Sir Proteus, how now, Thurio. 30
  Which of you saw Eglamour of late?
THURIO
  Not I.
PROTEUS Nor I.
DUKE   Saw you my daughter?
PROTEUS   Neither.
DUKE
  Why then, she's fled unto that peasant Valentine,
  And Eglamour is in her company.
  'Tis true, for Friar Laurence met them both 35
  As he in penance wandered through the forest.
  Him he knew well, and guessed that it was she,
  But being masked, he was not sure of it.
  Besides, she did intend confession
  At Patrick's cell this even, and there she was not. 40
  These likelihoods confirm her flight from hence;
  Therefore I pray you stand not to discourse,

29.1 *Enter the Duke*] *not in* F   31 saw] F1; saw Sir F2

28 **owe** own
29 **out by lease** rented out
30 **How now . . . how now** Usually, as at
  1.2.16, an expression of surprise or irrita-
  tion, but surely here a brusque greeting.
33 **peasant** low-born fellow. In his fury, the
  Duke insults Valentine even more than he
  does at 3.1.156–8.

35 **Friar Laurence** The name of the
  Friar in Brooke's *Romeus*, and hence in
  Romeo.
38 **being** she being
40 **even** evening
41 **likelihoods** indications, signs
42 **stand** delay

But mount you presently, and meet with me
Upon the rising of the mountain foot
That leads toward Mantua, whither they are fled.   45
Dispatch, sweet gentlemen, and follow me.   *Exit*
THURIO
Why, this it is to be a peevish girl,
That flies her fortune when it follows her.
I'll after, more to be revenged on Eglamour
Than for the love of reckless Silvia.   ⌈*Exit*⌉   50
PROTEUS
And I will follow, more for Silvia's love
Than hate of Eglamour that goes with her.   ⌈*Exit*⌉
JULIA
And I will follow, more to cross that love
Than hate for Silvia, that is gone for love.   ⌈*Exit*⌉

5.3 *Enter the Outlaws with Silvia captive*
FIRST OUTLAW
Come, come, be patient. We must bring you to our captain.
SILVIA
A thousand more mischances than this one
Have learned me how to brook this patiently.
SECOND OUTLAW Come, bring her away.
FIRST OUTLAW
Where is the gentleman that was with her?   5

---

46 *Exit*] *not in* F   50 *Exit*] *not in* F   52 *Exit*] *not in* F   54 *Exit*] *Exeunt.* F
5.3.0.1 *Enter . . . captive*] *Siluia, Out-lawes.* F

---

43 **mount you** mount your horses
presently immediately (emphasizing the
increasing haste of the scene)
44 **mountain foot** foothills
46 **Dispatch** make haste
47 **peevish** perverse
48 **flies . . . follows her** Thurio alludes to
the proverb 'Woman, like a shadow, flies
one following' (Dent L518) to suggest
how perverse Silvia is to run away from
her good luck (*fortune*) in being wooed by
him.
50 **reckless** having no care or consideration
50, 52, 54 *Exit* F merely gives one *Exeunt* at

the end of the scene; but these individual
exits, with the parting lines addressed to
the audience, are surely justified by the
accelerating pace of the scene. They were
first introduced by Capell in his edition.
53 **cross** thwart, hinder
5.3.3 **learned** taught
brook endure
5–6 Eglamour's behaviour comes as a
surprise after his chivalric image earlier.
Some productions minimize the inconsistency by increasing the number of
outlaws, so that he is outnumbered. See
Introduction, pp. 28–9.

THIRD OUTLAW

Being nimble-footed he hath outrun us;
But Moses and Valerius follow him.
Go thou with her to the west end of the wood,
There is our captain. We'll follow him that's fled.
The thicket is beset, he cannot scape.   10
                    Exeunt the Second and Third Outlaws

FIRST OUTLAW (*to Silvia*)

Come, I must bring you to our captain's cave.
Fear not; he bears an honourable mind,
And will not use a woman lawlessly.

SILVIA

O Valentine! This I endure for thee.   *Exeunt*

5.4 *Enter Valentine*

VALENTINE

How use doth breed a habit in a man!
This shadowy desert, unfrequented woods
I better brook than flourishing peopled towns.
Here can I sit alone, unseen of any,
And to the nightingale's complaining notes   5

10.1 *Exeunt . . . Outlaws*] *not in* F
   5.4.0.1 *Enter Valentine*] *Enter Valentine, Protheus, Siluia, Iulia, Duke, Thurio, Out-lawes.* F

---

7 **Valerius** This is the name that Felismena
   adopts for her male disguise in Montemayor's *Diana*.
10 **beset** surrounded. This certainly
   suggests a large number of outlaws: see
   note to ll. 5–6.
   cannot scape cannot escape—though
   he clearly does, since he doesn't appear in
   the final scene
13 **use** treat
5.4.1–3 **How use . . . towns** Valentine's
   soliloquy anticipates the Banished Duke's
   opening speech at *As You Like It* 2.1.1–17,
   especially 'Hath not old custom made this
   life more sweet | Than that of painted
   pomp?'
 1 **use** custom. Compare the speech quoted
   in the previous note.
   a habit familiarity
 2 **desert** 'any wild, uninhabited region,
   including forest-land' (*OED sb.*[2] 1b), as
   at *As You Like It* 2.7.110, where Orlando
   calls the forest 'this desert inaccessible'.

3 **brook** put up with
5 **nightingale's complaining notes** In
   Ovid's *Metamorphoses* 6.424–674, Tereus
   rapes his sister-in-law Philomela and
   tears out her tongue to prevent her
   revealing it; she is subsequently turned
   into a nightingale, the sweetest-singing
   bird, as a compensation for losing her
   tongue. The myth was a favourite with
   Shakespeare. In *Titus*, for example, he
   constantly alludes to it as a parallel to
   that play's events, and at 2.1.115–17
   Aaron says that the forest's
   'unfrequented plots' are 'Fitted . . . for
   rape', an interesting link with this play.
   Valentine's reference to the nightingale's
   complaining (lamenting) *notes* unconsciously prepares for the rape that is
   to be attempted. For a staging that linked
   Titus and *The Two Gentlemen*, see Introduction, pp. 28–9.

Tune my distresses and record my woes.
O thou that dost inhabit in my breast,
Leave not the mansion so long tenantless
Lest, growing ruinous, the building fall
And leave no memory of what it was.   10
Repair me with thy presence, Silvia.
Thou gentle nymph, cherish thy forlorn swain.
    Shouts within
What hallooing and what stir is this today?
These are my mates, that make their wills their law,
Have some unhappy passenger in chase.   15
They love me well, yet I have much to do
To keep them from uncivil outrages.
Withdraw thee, Valentine. Who's this comes here?
    He stands aside.
    Enter Proteus, Silvia, and Julia dressed as a page
PROTEUS

Madam, this service I have done for you—
Though you respect not aught your servant doth—   20

12.1 *Shouts within*] *not in* F   18.1–2 *He . . . page*] *not in* F

---

6 **record** sing of (picking up from *Tune* earlier in the line). Compare *Pericles* Sc. 15.26–7, where the nightingale 'still records with moan'.
7 **thou** i.e. Silvia
  inhabit live
8–9 **the mansion . . . fall** The comparison of the body in which love dwells (in the heart) to a building (sometimes ruined) is frequent in Shakespeare. Compare *Cymbeline* 3.4.68: 'The innocent mansion of my love, my heart'; *Errors* 3.2.4: 'Shall love, in building, grow so ruinous?'; *Romeo* 3.2.26–7: 'O, I have bought the mansion of a love | But not possessed it'.
11–12 **Repair . . . swain** It is interesting that Valentine uses words also used by Proteus in the song with which *he* addresses Silvia (4.2.39, 45, and notes).
11 **Repair** restore, renovate
12 **nymph** Like the *swain* that follows, this is the language of pastoral poetry.
  cherish comfort
  forlorn ruined, doomed (stronger than in modern usage; stressed on the first syllable)

13 **hallooing** shouting (literally cries of hunters, but often transferred to other contexts, as here and at *Twelfth Night* 1.5.261: 'Halloo your name to the reverberate hills')
  stir commotion
15 **Have** i.e. who have
17 **uncivil** uncivilized, barbarous
  outrages excesses, violence. For the wobbling presentation of the outlaws, see Introduction, pp. 27–9; but also see next note.
19–22 Proteus claims to have rescued Silvia from a rape attempt (*forced*, l. 22) by the First Outlaw, but given that character's gentlemanly disclaimer at 5.3.12–13, Proteus is surely projecting his own sexual intentions on to someone else.
19–20 **service . . . servant** Proteus continues to use the language of chivalry, or courtly love, as he prepares to rape her.
20 **respect** regard, value
  aught anything

To hazard life, and rescue you from him
That would have forced your honour and your love.
Vouchsafe me for my meed but one fair look.
A smaller boon than this I cannot beg,
And less than this I am sure you cannot give.   25

VALENTINE (*aside*)
How like a dream is this I see and hear!
Love lend me patience to forbear awhile.

SILVIA
O miserable, unhappy that I am!

PROTEUS
Unhappy were you, madam, ere I came.
But by my coming I have made you happy.   30

SILVIA
By thy approach thou mak'st me most unhappy.

JULIA (*aside*)
And me, when he approacheth to your presence.

SILVIA
Had I been seizèd by a hungry lion
I would have been a breakfast to the beast
Rather than have false Proteus rescue me.   35
O heaven be judge how I love Valentine,
Whose life's as tender to me as my soul.
And full as much, for more there cannot be,
I do detest false perjured Proteus.
Therefore be gone, solicit me no more.   40

PROTEUS
What dangerous action, stood it next to death,
Would I not undergo for one calm look!
O 'tis the curse in love, and still approved,
When women cannot love where they're beloved.

SILVIA
When Proteus cannot love where he's beloved.   45
Read over Julia's heart, thy first, best love,

21 **hazard** risk
23 **meed** reward
24 **boon** favour
27 **Love** may love
29 **ere** before
31 **approach** (playing on the sense 'amorous advance')
37 **tender** precious
40 **solicit** woo
41 **stood . . . death** however dangerous it was
42 **calm** gentle
43 **still approved** always confirmed

For whose dear sake thou didst then rend thy faith
Into a thousand oaths, and all those oaths
Descended into perjury to love me.
Thou hast no faith left now, unless thou'dst two,   50
And that's far worse than none. Better have none
Than plural faith, which is too much by one,
Thou counterfeit to thy true friend.

PROTEUS   In love
Who respects friend?

SILVIA   All men but Proteus.

PROTEUS

Nay, if the gentle spirit of moving words   55
Can no way change you to a milder form
I'll woo you like a soldier, at arm's end,
And love you 'gainst the nature of love: force ye.

SILVIA

O heaven!

PROTEUS   I'll force thee yield to my desire.

VALENTINE

Ruffian, let go that rude uncivil touch,   60
Thou friend of an ill fashion.

PROTEUS   Valentine!

VALENTINE

Thou common friend, that's without faith or love,
For such is a friend now. Treacherous man,
Thou hast beguiled my hopes. Naught but mine eye

---

50 **thou'dst two** i.e. could be faithful to
Julia and me at the same time

53 **counterfeit** to deceiver of

53–4 **In love . . . friend** This may draw on
the proverbial expression 'When love puts
in, friendship is gone' (Dent L549), and
on Lyly's *Endymion* 3.4.116: 'Love
knoweth neither friendship nor kindred.'
Compare also the jealous Claudio in *Much
Ado* when he suspects (wrongly) that Don
Pedro has betrayed him: 'Friendship is
constant in all other things | Save in the
office and affairs of love' (2.1.165–6). See
Introduction, pp. 53–9.

57 **arm's end** sword-point

58 **force ye** rape you

59 **thee** Proteus slips from the formal 'you'

to the intimate, or abusive, *thee* as he
attempts to rape Silvia.

60 **uncivil** barbarous (as at l. 17—though
Proteus' behaviour is surely worse than
anything shown by the outlaws)
touch grasp, embrace. *OED sb.* 1a says
that this is a unique use.

61 **ill** evil
fashion sort, kind

62 **common** ordinary, commonplace (i.e.
not the special friend I thought you
were). For the force of *common* here,
compare the sense of deep disappointment in a friend expressed at Sonnet
69.14: 'The soil is this: that thou dost
common grow.'

63 **now** i.e. now that you have betrayed me

Could have persuaded me. Now I dare not say   65
I have one friend alive; thou wouldst disprove me.
Who should be trusted, when one's own right hand
Is perjured to the bosom? Proteus,
I am sorry I must never trust thee more,
But count the world a stranger for thy sake.   70
The private wound is deepest. O time most accursed,
'Mongst all foes that a friend should be the worst!

PROTEUS

My shame and guilt confounds me.
Forgive me, Valentine. If hearty sorrow
Be a sufficient ransom for offence,   75
I tender't here. I do as truly suffer
As e'er I did commit.

VALENTINE   Then I am paid,
And once again I do receive thee honest.
Who by repentance is not satisfied
Is nor of heaven nor earth, for these are pleased;   80
By penitence th'Eternal's wrath's appeased.
And that my love may appear plain and free,
All that was mine in Silvia I give thee.

JULIA

O me unhappy!
    She faints

PROTEUS   Look to the boy.

VALENTINE   Why, boy!

---

67 own] JOHNSON; *not in* F   84 *She faints*] *not in* F

67–8 **one's . . . bosom** one's closest friend is
false to the core (Moore, who cites *OED*,
right hand, 1c: an 'indispensable helper
or aid', and 1b: 'a symbol of friendship or
alliance', and compares the proverbial
'He is at his right hand' (Dent H73))

67 **one's own** F has 'ones', which leaves the
line a syllable short. F2 reads 'Trusted
now' to emend it; but Johnson's addition
'own' is admirable, catching the intensity
of Valentine's sense of betrayal.

68 **perjured to the bosom** false to the heart

70 **count . . . sake** 'cut myself off from the
world (in disillusionment) because of
your treachery' (Norton)
count account

71 **private** personal

73 **confounds** ruins

74–6 **If . . . here** For a discussion of the
important parallel with Sonnet 34, see
Introduction, p. 31.

76 **tender** offer

77 **commit** sin
paid satisfied

78 **receive thee** accept that you are
honest honourable

79 **Who** whoever

81 **th'Eternal** God

82–3 For the exact meaning (or possible
meanings) of these crucial lines, see
Introduction, pp. 55–6.

85 **wag** A term of endearment: 'boy'.

Why wag, how now? What's the matter? Look   85
  up; speak.
JULIA O good sir, my master charged me to deliver a ring to
  Madam Silvia, which out of my neglect was never done.
PROTEUS Where is that ring, boy?
JULIA Here 'tis; this is it.   90
        She gives Proteus a ring
PROTEUS How, let me see.
  Why, this is the ring I gave to Julia.
JULIA
  O cry you mercy, sir, I have mistook.
        She offers Proteus another ring
  This is the ring you sent to Silvia.
PROTEUS
  But how cam'st thou by this ring? At my depart   95
  I gave this unto Julia.
JULIA
  And Julia herself did give it me,
  And Julia herself hath brought it hither.
PROTEUS How? Julia?
JULIA (*revealing herself*)
  Behold her that gave aim to all thy oaths   100
  And entertained 'em deeply in her heart.
  How oft hast thou with perjury cleft the root?
  O Proteus, let this habit make thee blush.
  Be thou ashamed that I have took upon me
  Such an immodest raiment, if shame live   105
  In a disguise of love.
  It is the lesser blot, modesty finds,
  Women to change their shapes than men their minds.

90.1 *She . . . ring*] *not in* F   93.1 *She . . . ring*] *not in* F   100 *revealing herself*] *not in* F

93 **cry you mercy** I beg your pardon
mistook mistaken. See note to 3.2.34.
95 **depart** departure
100 **gave aim to** was the object of (probably
   the language of archery: see note to
   l. 102)
101 **entertained** received
102 **cleft the root** cleaved the pin (the peg
   at the centre of the archer's target, i.e.
   her heart), as at *Romeo* 2.3.14–15, where
   Mercutio says of Romeo that 'the very

pin of his heart [is] cleft with the blind
   bow-boy's [Cupid's] butt-shaft'.
103 **habit** (her boy's clothes)
104 **took** taken. See note to 3.2.34.
105 **immodest raiment** It is harder to
   make this work in a modern-dress production than in Renaissance costume,
   with its stricter gender distinctions.
105–6 **if . . . love** if there is any shame in a
   disguise assumed for the sake of love
108 **shapes** (a) appearances; (b) stage
   costumes

PROTEUS

    Than men their minds! 'Tis true. O heaven, were man

    But constant, he were perfect. That one error   110

    Fills him with faults, makes him run through all th' sins;

    Inconstancy falls off ere it begins.

    What is in Silvia's face but I may spy

    More fresh in Julia's, with a constant eye?

VALENTINE Come, come, a hand from either.   115

    Let me be blessed to make this happy close.

    'Twere pity two such friends should be long foes.

        Julia and Proteus join hands

PROTEUS

    Bear witness, heaven, I have my wish for ever.

JULIA

    And I mine.

        Enter the Outlaws with the Duke and Thurio as captives

OUTLAWS A prize, a prize, a prize!

VALENTINE

    Forbear, forbear, I say. It is my lord the Duke.   120

        The Outlaws release the Duke and Thurio

    (*To the Duke*) Your grace is welcome to a man disgraced,

    Banishèd Valentine.

DUKE   Sir Valentine!

THURIO

    Yonder is Silvia, and Silvia's mine.

VALENTINE

    Thurio, give back, or else embrace thy death.

    Come not within the measure of my wrath.   125

    Do not name Silvia thine; if once again,

117.1 *Julia . . . hands*] *not in* F   119 *Enter . . . captives*] *not in* F   120.1 *The . . . Thurio*] *not in* F

---

110 **constant** faithful. For the importance of 'constant' and 'constancy' in the play, see Introduction, p. 34.

111 **run through** pass through, experience

112 **Inconstancy . . . begins** 'The inconstant man is unfaithful before he even begins to love' (Sanders).

116 **close** union

120 **Forbear** stop

121 **grace . . . disgraced** Valentine plays on the courtesy title of the Duke and on his own disgrace.

124 **give back** back off

124–5 **or else . . . wrath** Valentine surely takes out on Thurio the pent-up rage he hasn't been able fully to release on Proteus. Compare *Tragedy of Lear* 1.1.122: 'Come not between the dragon and his wrath.'

125 **measure** reach

Verona shall not hold thee. Here she stands.
Take but possession of her with a touch—
I dare thee but to breathe upon my love.

THURIO

Sir Valentine, I care not for her, I.   130
I hold him but a fool that will endanger
His body for a girl that loves him not.
I claim her not, and therefore she is thine.

DUKE

The more degenerate and base art thou
To make such means for her as thou hast done,   135
And leave her on such slight conditions.
Now by the honour of my ancestry
I do applaud thy spirit, Valentine,
And think thee worthy of an empress' love.
Know then I here forget all former griefs,   140
Cancel all grudge, repeal thee home again,
Plead a new state in thy unrivalled merit,
To which I thus subscribe: Sir Valentine,
Thou art a gentleman and well derived.
Take thou thy Silvia, for thou hast deserved her.   145

VALENTINE

I thank your grace, the gift hath made me happy.
I now beseech you, for your daughter's sake,
To grant one boon that I shall ask of you.

DUKE

I grant it for thine own, whate'er it be.

---

127 **Verona** Perhaps another Shakespearian
geographical slip. *TC* suggests that 'This
Milan' or 'Our Milan' might be substi-
tuted (p. 168); but perhaps Valentine in
incoherent fury naturally refers to his
own home town.
hold thee keep you safe
128 **Take . . . touch** if you even *touch* her
135 **make such means** make such efforts,
take such pains
136 **slight conditions** easy terms
139 **an empress' love** This echoes 2.4.74–
5; see note.
140 **griefs** grievances

141 **repeal** recall
142 **Plead . . . merit** take up a new position
about your unequalled merit
143 **subscribe** bear witness
144 **derived** descended (as at 5.2.23). The
Duke is withdrawing his insults at
3.1.156–8 and 5.2.33, whether at pistol-
point (as at the Old Vic in 1957) or
otherwise.
147, 149 **for your daughter's sake . . . for
thine own** For such distinctions, compare
Measure 5.1.489–90: 'for his sake', 'for
your lovely sake'.

VALENTINE

These banished men that I have kept withal   150

Are men endowed with worthy qualities.

Forgive them what they have committed here,

And let them be recalled from their exile.

They are reformèd, civil, full of good,

And fit for great employment, worthy lord.   155

DUKE

Thou hast prevailed, I pardon them and thee.

Dispose of them as thou know'st their deserts.

Come, let us go, we will conclude all jars

With triumphs, mirth, and rare solemnity.

VALENTINE

And as we walk along I dare be bold   160

With our discourse to make your grace to smile.

What think you of this page, my lord?

DUKE

I think the boy hath grace in him, he blushes.

VALENTINE

I warrant you, my lord, more grace than boy.

DUKE What mean you by that saying?   165

VALENTINE

Please you, I'll tell you as we pass along,

---

151 endowed] F (endu'd)   158 conclude] HANMER; include F

150 **kept withal** lived with

151–5 **men . . . employment** A likely story, in view of Valentine's own comments at ll. 16–17. Productions have taken advantage of Shakespeare's varying presentation of the outlaws, as at the Old Vic in 1957, when 'evil-looking brigands surrounded the Duke', influencing his decision (Mary Clarke, *Shakespeare at the Old Vic* (1957)).

157 **Dispose of** employ

158 **conclude** F reads 'include', which *OED v.* 4, citing this line as its only example, glosses 'conclude'; so this edition adopts Hanmer's reading, since this is what it means, and F's 'include' is probably an error.
jars discord

159 **With . . . solemnity** Compare Theseus' resolve to celebrate his wedding 'With pomp, with triumph, and with revelling' (*Dream* 1.1.19).
triumphs pageants (including tournaments; compare *Pericles* Sc. 6.1: 'Are the knights ready to begin the triumph?')
solemnity festivity

163–4 **grace** personal radiance, beauty (as at *Antony* 5.2.341–2, where Octavius Caesar says of Cleopatra 'she would catch another Antony | In her strong toil of grace', or at Sonnet 78.12: 'arts with thy sweet graces gracèd be')

163 **the boy . . . blushes** Proverbial: 'Blushing is a sign of grace' (Dent B480).

164 **more grace than boy** i.e. more (feminine?) radiance than boyishness

That you will wonder what hath fortunèd.
Come, Proteus, 'tis your penance but to hear
The story of your loves discoverèd.
That done, our day of marriage shall be yours,   170
One feast, one house, one mutual happiness.   *Exeunt*

167 **That** so that   168 **but** only
   wonder marvel at   169 **discoverèd** revealed
   fortunèd happened

THE MUSIC

ALTHOUGH music can be introduced at various points during the play, as David Thacker's production in 1991 demonstrated so successfully (see Introduction, p. 9), Shakespeare specifically asks for it only once, in the serenade scene, 4.2, where it has an important dramatic function: it simultaneously marks a stage in Proteus' wooing of Silvia, and demonstrates his betrayal of Julia, who is listening in her page's disguise. The song 'Who is Silvia?' is probably intended to be sung by Proteus himself, though no speech-prefix is given in the Folio. The musicians probably tune during the first conversation between Julia and the Host (4.2.26–37), accompany the song, and then play an instrumental postlude, which underpins the second Host/Julia dialogue (4.2.53–77).

No contemporary setting of the song survives. The earliest (1727) is thought to be by Richard Leveridge; the most famous is Schubert's (1826). The present setting has been specially prepared for this edition by Guy Woolfenden, former Head of Music at the RSC. It adapts a setting of a poem attributed to Sir Walter Raleigh, 'Now what is love', by Robert Jones (flourished 1597–1615) from his *Second Book of Songs and Airs* (published 1601). Originally for voice, lute, and bass viol, this arrangement is for voice and keyboard. Robert Jones's song 'Farewell dear heart' was parodied as a comic duet for Sir Toby and Feste at *Twelfth Night* 2.3.98–108; and his setting of 'Now what is love' fits 'Who is Silvia?' remarkably well.

Who is Silvia?

4.2. 38-52

Robert Jones (1601)
arranged Guy Woolfenden

ALTERATIONS TO LINEATION

1.1.110–11 You . . . 'Ay'] CAPELL; *verse in* F, *divided after first* 'nod'

117–18 Marry . . . pains] CAPELL; *verse in* F, *divided after* 'orderly'

129–33 Sir . . . steel] CAPELL; *five lines of verse in* F, *divided after* 'her', 'letter', 'mind', 'mind'

135–8 No . . . master] CAPELL; *four lines of verse in* F, *divided after* 'pains', 'me', 'letters yourself'

1.2.88 Let's . . . minion] HANMER; *two lines in* F, *divided after* 'song'

2.1.50–1 I . . . infinite] CAPELL; *verse in* F, *divided after* 'exquisite'

62–3 I have . . . beautiful] CAPELL; *verse in* F, *divided after* 'saw her'

73–4 Belike . . . shoes] ROWE; *verse in* F, *divided after* 'morning'

80–1 Last . . . loves] POPE; *verse in* F, *divided after* 'me'

85–6 No . . . comes] CAMBRIDGE; *verse in* F, *divided after* 'them'

87–8 O . . . her] THEOBALD; *verse in* F, *divided after* 'puppet'

112 What . . . it] POPE; *two lines in* F, *divided after* 'ladyship'

130 That . . . letter] POPE; *two lines in* F, *divided after* 'scribe'

131–2 How . . . yourself] POPE; *two lines in* F, *divided after* 'sir'

141–2 What . . . jest] CAPELL; *three lines of verse in* F, *divided after* 'need she', 'yourself'

144–5 No . . . earnest] POPE; *verse in* F, *divided after* 'sir'

156–7 All . . . dinner-time] DYCE; *verse in* F, *divided after* 'it'

2.2.6 Why . . . this] POPE; *two lines in* F, *divided after* 'exchange'

2.4.36–8 Yourself . . . company] POPE; *three lines of verse in* F, *divided after* 'fire', 'looks'

41–4 I . . . words] POPE; *four lines of verse in* F, *divided after* 'words', 'followers', 'liveries'

45–6 No . . . father] POPE; *verse in* F, *divided after second* 'more'

3.1.150–1 What's . . . thee] CAPELL; *one line in* F

191–2 Him . . . Valentine] CAPELL; *verse in* F, *divided after* 'find'

302–3 What . . . stock] POPE; *verse in* F, *divided after* 'wench'

325–7 O . . . virtue] POPE; *three lines of verse in* F, *divided after* 'vices', 'only virtue'

329–30 Out . . . her] POPE; *verse in* F, *divided after* 'too'

356–8 Why . . . impossible] POPE; *two lines in* F, *divided after* 'gracious'

4.2.59–60 Not . . . heart-strings] POPE; *verse in* F, *divided after* 'yet'

69–73 I . . . nick] POPE; *five lines of verse in* F, *divided after* 'thing', 'on', 'gentlewoman', 'me'

134–5 Marry . . . day] POPE; *verse in* F, *divided after* 'house'

4.4.42	I . . . peasant] POPE; *two lines in* F, *divided after* 'wilt'
50–1	No . . . again] POPE; *verse in* F, *divided after* 'not'
53–6	Ay . . . greater] POPE; *four lines of verse in* F, *divided after* 'me', 'place', 'dog'
125	There . . . lines] OXFORD; *two lines in* F, *divided after* 'hold'
174–5	For . . . Farewell] F2; *one line in* F
5.2.33	Why . . . Valentine] CAPELL; *two lines in* F, *divided after* 'then'
5.3.1	Come . . . captain] POPE; *two lines in* F, *divided after* 'patient'

INDEX

This is a selective guide to the Commentary and Introduction, though it does not duplicate the section headings of the latter. Characters in the play are only listed if their names are discussed. Asterisks identify entries which supplement the information given in *OED*.

Travel Writing 1700–1830

Women's Writing 1778–1838

WILLIAM BECKFORD   **Vathek**

JAMES BOSWELL   **Life of Johnson**

FRANCES BURNEY   **Camilla**
                      Cecilia
                      Evelina
                      The Wanderer

LORD CHESTERFIELD   **Lord Chesterfield's Letters**

JOHN CLELAND   **Memoirs of a Woman of Pleasure**

DANIEL DEFOE   **A Journal of the Plague Year**
                      Moll Flanders
                      Robinson Crusoe
                      Roxana

HENRY FIELDING   **Jonathan Wild**
                      Joseph Andrews and **Shamela**
                      Tom Jones

WILLIAM GODWIN   **Caleb Williams**

OLIVER GOLDSMITH   **The Vicar of Wakefield**

MARY HAYS   **Memoirs of Emma Courtney**

ELIZABETH INCHBALD   **A Simple Story**

SAMUEL JOHNSON   **The History of Rasselas**
                      The Major Works

CHARLOTTE LENNOX   **The Female Quixote**

MATTHEW LEWIS   **Journal of a West India Proprietor**
                      The Monk

HENRY MACKENZIE   **The Man of Feeling**

ALEXANDER POPE	**Selected Poetry**
ANN RADCLIFFE	**The Italian**
	The Mysteries of Udolpho
	The Romance of the Forest
	A Sicilian Romance
CLARA REEVE	**The Old English Baron**
SAMUEL RICHARDSON	**Pamela**
RICHARD BRINSLEY SHERIDAN	**The School for Scandal and Other Plays**
TOBIAS SMOLLETT	**The Adventures of Roderick Random**
	The Expedition of Humphry Clinker
LAURENCE STERNE	**The Life and Opinions of Tristram Shandy, Gentleman**
	A Sentimental Journey
JONATHAN SWIFT	**Gulliver's Travels**
	Major Works
	A Tale of a Tub and Other Works
JOHN VANBRUGH	**The Relapse and Other Plays**
HORACE WALPOLE	**The Castle of Otranto**
MARY WOLLSTONECRAFT	**Mary and The Wrongs of Woman**
	A Vindication of the Rights of Woman

CHARLES DICKENS	**A Tale of Two Cities**
GEORGE DU MAURIER	**Trilby**
MARIA EDGEWORTH	**Castle Rackrent**
GEORGE ELIOT	**Daniel Deronda**
	The Lifted Veil and Brother Jacob
	Middlemarch
	The Mill on the Floss
	Silas Marner
SUSAN FERRIER	**Marriage**
ELIZABETH GASKELL	**Cranford**
	The Life of Charlotte Brontë
	Mary Barton
	North and South
	Wives and Daughters
GEORGE GISSING	**New Grub Street**
	The Odd Women
EDMUND GOSSE	**Father and Son**
THOMAS HARDY	**Far from the Madding Crowd**
	Jude the Obscure
	The Mayor of Casterbridge
	The Return of the Native
	Tess of the d'Urbervilles
	The Woodlanders
WILLIAM HAZLITT	**Selected Writings**
JAMES HOGG	**The Private Memoirs and Confessions of a Justified Sinner**
JOHN KEATS	**The Major Works**
	Selected Letters
CHARLES MATURIN	**Melmoth the Wanderer**
JOHN RUSKIN	**Selected Writings**
WALTER SCOTT	**The Antiquary**
	Ivanhoe

HONORÉ DE BALZAC	**Père Goriot**
CHARLES BAUDELAIRE	**The Flowers of Evil**
DENIS DIDEROT	**Jacques the Fatalist** **The Nun**
ALEXANDRE DUMAS (PÈRE)	**The Count of Monte Cristo** **The Three Musketeers**
GUSTAVE FLAUBERT	**Madame Bovary**
VICTOR HUGO	**The Essential Victor Hugo** **Notre-Dame de Paris**
J.-K. HUYSMANS	**Against Nature**
PIERRE CHODERLOS DE LACLOS	**Les Liaisons dangereuses**
GUY DE MAUPASSANT	**Bel-Ami** **Pierre et Jean**
MOLIÈRE	**Don Juan and Other Plays** **The Misanthrope, Tartuffe, and Other** **Plays**
ABBÉ PRÉVOST	**Manon Lescaut**
ARTHUR RIMBAUD	**Collected Poems**
EDMOND ROSTAND	**Cyrano de Bergerac**
JEAN-JACQUES ROUSSEAU	**Confessions**
MARQUIS DE SADE	**The Crimes of Love**
STENDHAL	**The Red and the Black** **The Charterhouse of Parma**
PAUL VERLAINE	**Selected Poems**
VOLTAIRE	**Candide and Other Stories**
ÉMILE ZOLA	**L'Assommoir** **The Kill**